DIFFERENCE AND GIVENNESS

Topics in Historical Philosophy

General Editors David Kolb
John McCumber

Associate Editor Anthony J. Steinbock

DIFFERENCE AND GIVENNESS

Deleuze's Transcendental Empiricism and the Ontology of Immanence

Levi R. Bryant

Northwestern University Press
Evanston, Illinois

Northwestern University Press
www.nupress.northwestern.edu

Printed in the United States of America

10 9 8 7 6 5 4 3 2 1

Library of Congress Cataloging-in-Publication Data

Bryant, Levi R.
  Difference and givenness : Deleuze's transcendental empiricism and the ontology of immanence / Levi R. Bryant.
    p. cm. — (Topics in historical philosophy)
  Includes bibliographical references and index.
  ISBN-13: 978-0-8101-2452-3 (cloth : alk. paper)
  ISBN-10: 0-8101-2452-1 (cloth : alk. paper)
  ISBN-13: 978-0-8101-2454-7 (pbk. : alk. paper)
  ISBN-10: 0-8101-2454-8 (pbk. : alk. paper)
  1. Deleuze, Gilles, 1925–1995. 2. Empiricism. 3. Immanence (Philosophy)
I. Title. II. Title: Deleuze's transcendental empiricism and the ontology of imma-
nence. III. Series: Northwestern University topics in historical philosophy.
  B2430.D454B79 2008
  146'.44092—dc22

                                                                2007043985

Difference is not diversity. Diversity is given, but difference is that by which the given is given, that by which the given is given as diverse.
—Gilles Deleuze, *Difference and Repetition*

Contents

Preface

This is a book on Deleuze. In particular, it is a book on Deleuze's metaphysics which makes no reference to his ethics, politics, or aesthetics. It is not a book on Deleuze and Guattari. Nor is it a book on Hume, Spinoza, Nietzsche, or Bergson. I do not seek to demonstrate that Deleuze is really a Bergsonian vitalist in disguise. Nor do I seek to show how Deleuze is really a thinker of active and passive forces. I do not, above all, seek to make any comment on Deleuze's collaborative works with Guattari and how these might represent departures or continuations of his earlier work. In fact, in order to adequately engage in such a project it would first be necessary to do something similar to what I am attempting here. Rather, the present volume seeks to speak simply and in an informed way about what Deleuze means by "transcendental empiricism" in his two early masterpieces *Difference and Repetition* and *The Logic of Sense.*

In what follows I seek to demonstrate that Deleuze's transcendental empiricism attempts to overcome the opposition between concepts and intuitions, *noesis* and *aisthesis,* that has characterized most of the history of philosophy and which arises from the assumption of a finite subject whose receptivity is conceived of as passive. In executing this project I have also sought to determine how Deleuze is able to avoid falling into criticisms of being a speculative dogmatist and how the subject must be rethought in its relationship to being. Contrary, then, to the somewhat standard picture of Deleuze, which treats his ontology as an empiricism, I have sought to present a hyper-rationalist version of his thought, contextualizing it in terms of debates that surround classical rationalism but also German idealism as exemplified in the figures of Kant and Salomon Maïmon. This has not been out of a desire to present yet another "monstrous" version of Deleuze, but because the problematics surrounding German idealism and rationalism struck me as closest to those governing Deleuze's project of a transcendental empiricism and seemed to best explain his engagement with differential calculus that is so often ignored in treatments of Deleuze's thought. In short, if Deleuze is able to depart from the philosophy of representation characterized by the primacy of the concept, then this is because he discovers intelligibility in the aesthetic itself, in the very fabric of the given, in the form of the differentials of perception. Deleuze does not so much give us a way of mediating the relation between the universal and the particular, but dispenses with the problem altogether. In this connection, I am able to provide a justification of his project that need make no reference to a politics or ethics based on a preference for difference over identity. Deleuze's ethics and politics follow—rightly—from his ontology, not the reverse. Deleuze thinks of himself as having solved a very traditional and central problem in the history of philosophy and proceeds to draw the consequences of this solution. I leave it to my readers to decide whether emphasizing Deleuze's debt to thinkers such as Descartes, Leibniz, Kant, and Maïmon does not prove more illuminating to his text than a discussion of his thought that relies heavily on his debt to English empiricism.

It might seem strange to emphasize that this is a book on Deleuze when this can be clearly discerned from the very title of the book. However, given the standard image of Deleuze, it is imperative that I do so. Too often it is assumed that the names "Deleuze" and "Deleuze and Guattari" are identical and can be used interchangeably.[1] The question of whether or not significant transformations take place in the encounter of these two individuals is not even raised. This constitutes a betrayal of the singularity of Deleuze's thought as well as that of Deleuze *and* Guattari. Moreover, Deleuze insists that continuous multiplicities change in kind when divided. We might claim equally that they change in kind when new dimensions are added to them. To simply equate "Deleuze" with "Deleuze and Guattari" is to ignore this fundamental principle belonging to a logic of multiplicities. Unable to adequately deal with such complex issues in the space of a single essay, I thus opted to restrict myself to Deleuze's thought.

By contrast, as a rejoinder one might object to treating the name of Deleuze as a unity, pointing out that the various texts by him alone display very different styles and concerns. However, as I hope to show in the course of this book, this argument falls prey to what I will later call the empiricist fallacy in that it individuates that which belongs to Deleuze by the empirical texts marked by his name and not by what belongs to Deleuze's style. Deleuze himself was fond of pointing out that events are not individuated by the individuals that belong to them, but rather that individuals are individuated by the events that befall them. In this connection I am entirely in agreement with Badiou's claim that "Deleuze arrives at conceptual productions that I would unhesitatingly qualify as *monotonous,* composing a very particular regime of emphasis or almost infinite repetition of a limited repertoire of concepts, as well as a virtuosic variation of names, under which what is thought remains essentially identical."[2]

While Deleuze's language may change from text to text, one is nonetheless able to discern a distinct structure at work throughout his thought. Given this, I have not hesitated to emphasize some of his works to the detriment of others, for the very simple reason that it would be redundant and unnecessary to cite each instance in which a particular concept occurs. Thus, for instance, if I was able to find adequate textual support for a particular concept in *Difference and Repetition,* then I felt no obligation to discuss the concept as presented in *Nietzsche and Philosophy.* Since the aim of my project is philosophical and not historical, I do not feel my account of Deleuze's thought suffers from this strategy. Moreover, by emphasizing some texts of Deleuze's over others, I was able to suggest another picture of his project than the standard one that portrays him as a Nietzschean anarcho-desiring machine fighting reactive forces of *ressentiment* and bad conscience. Consequently, I attempt to read Deleuze as he himself read other thinkers. I ask what problems informed Deleuze's thought and seek to determine how these problems necessitated the construction of particular concepts.

There is also a tendency to attribute anything Deleuze had to say about another thinker or artist to his own position. While it is undeniable that Deleuze is deeply indebted to all the thinkers and artists he wrote on (including Kant), it is strange to assume that the works explicating his own philosophy consist of handy summations of what he had already written about other philosophers. Rather, we must be careful to determine whether what appears in one of Deleuze's studies of other philosophers repeats itself in the works articulating his own philosophy. We cannot assume that the contents of Deleuze's studies are identical to his independent philosophical works. As Deleuze says of his work in *Difference and Repetition:*

> There is a great difference between writing history of philosophy and writing philosophy. In the one case, we study the arrows or the tools of a great thinker, the trophies and the prey, the continents discovered. In the other case, we trim our own arrows, or gather those which seem to us the finest in order to try to send them in other directions, even if the distance covered is not astronomical but relatively small. We try to speak in our own name only to learn that a proper name designates no more than the outcome of a body of work—in other words, the concepts discovered, on the condition that we were able to express these and imbue them with life using all the possibilities of language.[3]

Discussions of Deleuze have not attended enough to the manner in which he trimmed his arrows. The idea of trimming one's arrows also suggests the idea of selection, of discernment between what one takes up and carries into the future and what is left behind. As brilliant and clear as Deleuze's discussion of Nietzsche's reactive forces may be, this does not merit us ascribing it to him if it does not appear in those works where Deleuze articulates his own philosophy. Similarly in the case of Bergson. I suspect that much of this practice has arisen due to the sheer obscurity and difficulty of Deleuze's own works, but this makes it no more justifiable.

To be sure, throughout this book I find ample opportunity to refer to Deleuze's works in the history of philosophy and aesthetics. However, in doing so I gave myself two simple rules. First, whenever reference is made to one of Deleuze's commentaries on an artist, art form, or another philosopher, then it must be possible to demonstrate in fact or in principle that Deleuze employs precisely these same terms and concepts in his own independent works. Second, whenever there is a divergence among concepts between Deleuze's own work and the conceptual work Deleuze attributes to another, then there must either be a tacit critique or divergence between Deleuze's project and that of the other thinker. In this way I have hoped to discover a singularity of Deleuze's own thought, marking his divergence from the history of philosophy that he grapples with and constructs for himself.

Abbreviations

Works by Gilles Deleuze are cited by the following abbreviations.

B	*Bergsonism*
"BCD"	"Bergson's Conception of Difference"
"CC"	"Coldness and Cruelty"
D	*Dialogues*
"DLS"	"Deleuze-Leibniz Seminar"
DR	*Difference and Repetition*
FLB	*The Fold: Leibniz and the Baroque*
"HRS"	"How Do We Recognize Structuralism?"
"IL"	"Immanence: A Life . . ."
KCP	*Kant's Critical Philosophy*
LS	*The Logic of Sense*
MI	*Cinema I: The Movement-Image*
N	*Negotiations*
NP	*Nietzsche and Philosophy*
PS	*Proust and Signs*
TI	*Cinema II: The Time-Image*

DIFFERENCE AND GIVENNESS

Introduction

The aim of this book is to determine what Deleuze understands when he describes his position as "transcendental empiricism." Deleuze's definition of transcendental empiricism is very simple: transcendental empiricism is that philosophical position which determines the conditions of real rather than possible experience. Consequently, to fully understand what Deleuze comprehends by "transcendental empiricism" we must determine how he understands the transcendental and the empirical, as well as the relationship between conditions of real experience as opposed to conditions of all possible experience. This proves difficult in that "transcendental empiricism" rings like an oxymoron to the philosophically trained ear. Kant, who first invented transcendental philosophy (or who, at the very least, first named it), certainly advocated a form of empiricism in that he held that experience necessarily requires both concepts *and* intuitions. As Heidegger puts it:

> In order to understand the *Critique of Pure Reason* this point must be hammered in, so to speak: knowing is primarily intuiting . . . All thinking is merely in service of intuition. Thinking is not simply alongside intuition, "also" at hand; but rather, according to its own inherent structure, it serves that to which intuition is primarily and constantly directed.[1]

However, Kant described his position as a "transcendental idealism" in that it demonstrated that objects conform to the mind rather than the mind to objects. Transcendental idealism is a position which holds that certain ideal and universal structures of mind must be at work in order for there to be something like experience at all. It seems that transcendental empiricism turns out to be something very different. Consequently, while the definition of "transcendental empiricism" may be simple, determining what it means and its implications turns out to be quite complex.

A fair amount has been written on Deleuze's transcendental empiricism in the secondary literature, which I will not rehearse here so that I might spare the reader. While some of these readings are much better than others—notably those of Ronald Bogue, Daniel Smith, Constantine Boundas, and Alain Badiou—it is my view that most of the work done on Deleuze has focused on the empirical to the detriment of the transcendental. For this reason, with the exception of the figures named above, this has led to a distorted picture of Deleuze that is unable to recognize the implications of his thought, the stakes in the name of which it is unfolded, and the substantial ontological claims that it is making. This is because these readings of Deleuze have not articulated his thought in terms of the problems to which he responds.

Throughout this book I have attempted to avoid writing an inventory of definitions of Deleuze's concepts as a way of neatly summing up his thought. There will be no set of chapters entitled "multiplicity," "virtuality," "univocity/immanence," "nomadism," "intensity," "singularity," and so on. Given the difficulty of Deleuze's prose and his potential fruitfulness in the domain of aesthetic analysis and political critique, it is understandable that so many texts have been written in this style; yet it is nonetheless the case that this approach has tended to distort and cover over what is at stake in transcendental empiricism. While all of the "key" Deleuzian terms shall appear below, they shall be mobilized in terms of the problems to which they respond rather than simply given as "tools" that one might opt to use or not to use.

This, then, is the methodology I have adopted . . . a methodology prescribed by Deleuze himself and employed in all of his readings of major philosophers. If Deleuze is to be understood, then his concepts, his thought, must be comprehended in terms of the problems to which it responds, and not solely in terms of the stated theses belonging to the philosophy. In seeking to state the Deleuzian problem, I have tried to avoid those tiresome clichés which posit Deleuze as being *against* representation, established morality, recognition, the State, and so on, ad nauseam. These points are true as far as they go, but the problem is that they do not go far enough. Moreover, positions such as these tend to cripple thought in that they invite one to adopt a certain stance, a certain praxis, without carefully grounding reasons as to why that position ought to be adopted. Although I do not develop this thesis in detail here, it is my position that Deleuze adopts these aims not as the motive factor of his ontology, but as a *consequence* of his ontology. One does not adopt the position of transcendental empiricism because it is *against* representation. Rather, one adopts the position because something is wrong with the philosophy of representation *and* transcendental empiricism is able to solve this problem. In short, these readings of Deleuze do not tell me why I should be against representation, the subject, established morality, recognition, the State, and so on; they only critique these things through a Deleuzian lens which amounts to begging the question. They begin from a normative standpoint and thereby fail to establish the necessity of what they argue. This strategy of commentary is epidemic in contemporary academic discourses surrounding Continental thought and does more damage to itself than to what it seeks to critique. These discourses give one the sense that perhaps Deleuze's thought amounts to a simple thought experiment that ultimately amounts to nothing more than a set of ideas that one might try out at one's leisure. What is worse, they seem to implicitly suggest a sort of romantic belief in the possibility of achieving an unmediated state of being in which identity and the State would no longer intervene in our desire or will to power.

What, then, is the problem to which Deleuze's transcendental empiricism responds? Deleuze's thought responds to a philosophical situation—in Badiou's sense of the term *situation*—characterized by the primacy of identity and representation as the common sense or historical a priori within which he finds himself. However, the problem *is not* identity nor is it representation. Contrary to what some of the more romantic Deleuzians might think, Deleuze is quite happy to say that representation, identity, and recognition are real phenomena of our experience. We recognize things. We identify things. We represent things. If we did not do these things, then there would be no problem of representation and identity. The problem, rather, is what emerges when representation and identity are taken as metaphysically or epistemically primitive terms upon which the questions of philosophy are posed. According to Deleuze, *when representation and identity are taken as metaphysically primitive, philosophy falls into insoluble problems.* Transcendental empiricism attempts to navigate a way through or beyond these insoluble problems.

If I attempted to state all of the problems that treating identity and representation as metaphysically primitive generate, I would likely satisfy no one. Consequently, I shall merely indicate some of the problems that readily come to mind. Hopefully, it is no exaggeration to claim that metaphysics is organized around four principal oppositions: the opposition between being and thinking, the one and the many, *noesis* and *aisthesis*, and the finite and the infinite. Under many different names and many different combinations, these terms seem to repeat throughout the history of philosophy wherever metaphysics occurs. Most often we take metaphysics to be a theoretical engagement that seeks to *think being* in terms of the relationships among the *one* and the *many*, the universal and the particular, the sensible and the conceptual, and essence and existence. Historically, this discourse has more often than not been unfolded in terms of the relationship between the divine and the worldly, the infinite and the finite, God and his creatures.

This is not meant as a rigorous definition of metaphysics, but hopefully it gives us some of the broad contours characterizing metaphysical speculation. On the basis of these four oppositions we can readily see a number of questions arising, as well as a number of possible characterizations of being. In particular, we can see that significant and vexing problems readily emerge with the most simple of judgments: S is P. Perhaps no form of judgment has been more vexing and troubling for philosophy than the simple judgment of predication. In making judgments of this form we simultaneously engage ourselves in questions about the nature of thought, being, and the relationship between thought and being, while also raising questions about *noesis, aisthesis,* and the relationship between *noesis* and *aisthesis.* What is the problem?

Suppose we take the following simple syllogism:

All humans are mortal.
Socrates is a human.
∴ Socrates is mortal.

On the surface, syllogisms such as this seem very straightforward and unproblematic, but closer inspection reveals that forms of reasoning such as this can be analyzed at a number of different levels.

In this case, we can analyze the syllogism at a syntactic, semantic, or existential level. Syntactically, I can examine the pure form of reasoning involved in the syllogism by abstracting from all the content belonging to the syllogism:

$(\forall x)(Cx \rightarrow Fx)$
Ct
∴ Ft

At the syntactical level, one can simply attend to the relations that hold among the terms and predicates without worrying about whether the syllogism existentially represents a true state of affairs or what meanings are involved in the terms. Similarly, one can focus on the contents of the terms and predicates, seeking to determine the basic meanings and how they relate to one another. Finally, one can seek to determine whether or not the judgment existentially represents a true state of affairs.

Problems emerge when we seek to determine the relations that hold among these three different approaches. Suppose that I take it as axiomatic—as I should—that questions of being pertain to questions involving the *is* or the verb *to be.* If I adopt this position, then the claim that being is existence and that existence is reality would be unduly restrictive, since I can use the verb *to be* in cases that involve no reality or existence, such as when I talk of unicorns. I can say what a unicorn *is,* even though I'm fairly certain that no unicorns exist. So far, so good. However, problems quickly begin to emerge as soon as I make judgments such as "Socrates is a human." Why does this form of judgment lead to problems? Well, we might ask ourselves whether being-a-human and Socrates are one and the same thing. The answer seems to be no. We can say what a human *is,* and we can also, in part, say what Socrates *is* independent of his "humanness." Consequently, there seems to be a way in which predicative judgments involve two different forms of being: namely, the being of the predicate and the being of the subject.

Perhaps this wouldn't be such a problem if we did not wish to relate the two elements of the judgment, if we were content to posit two realms of distinct forms of being independent of one another. However, it is precisely the relation between the elements of the judgment that gives rise to the problem. In short, the "thatness" of Socrates is different than the "whatness" of a human such that there seems to be a gap or chasm between the singular instance of the human and its essence. If these problems emerge at all, then it is by a tacit assumption of the primacy of finitude governing our experience. Heidegger has expressed this point with exceptional clarity in *Kant and the Problem of Metaphysics.* As he puts it:

> We can say negatively: finite knowledge is noncreative intuition. What has to be presented immediately in its particularity must already have been "at hand" in advance. Finite intuition sees that it is dependent upon the intuitable as a being which exists in its own right . . . Finite intuition of the being cannot give the object from out of itself. It must allow the object to be given. Not every intuition as such, but rather only the finite, is intuition that "takes things in stride." Hence, the character of the finitude of intuition is found in its receptivity . . . According to its essence, finite intuition must be solicited or affected by that which is intuitable in it.[2]

Consequently, part of the singularity of existence lies in the fact that I cannot create it myself, but that it has being independently of me such that I can only receive it passively in intuition. By contrast, concepts are characterized by spontaneity in that thought is not dependent upon receptivity for their creation, nor upon the actual experience of the thing in question in order for the concept to be put to use. For this reason, concepts have the curious ability to grasp the many under one in that they are able to think that which is absent as present.

> The determinative representing of what is intuitively represented indeed takes a look at the general, but only keeps it [the general] in view in or-

der to direct itself to the particular and thus to determine the particular from that viewpoint. This "general" representing, which as such is in service to the intuiting, makes what is represented in the intuition more representable in the sense that it grasps many under one, and on the basis of this comprehensive grasping it "applies to many" . . . Determinative representing, however, is in itself an assertion of something about something (predication).[3]

Concepts thus function as a sort of prosthesis or crutch for the subject in that they allow it to overcome the finitude of its receptivity so that it might grasp that which is absent in the presence of a unified concept. Where intuitions lack spontaneity in that one must await them so that they might become present, concepts are characterized by spontaneity in that we can think the concept of a thing in the absence of that thing. By contrast, from the perspective of an infinite intuition, this problem would not emerge at all insofar as thought would not require the intellect to supplement itself with the use of concepts to represent the many under one, but would entertain a direct relationship with things such that the very thinking of the thing would produce the thing.

It is precisely this dogma, this assumption of the non-productivity of intuition, of its lack of intelligibility as opposed to the rational structure of concepts, that Deleuze's transcendental empiricism is designed to overcome. As Deleuze states very clearly in *Difference and Repetition:*

> It is strange that aesthetics (as the science of the sensible) could be founded on what *can* be represented in the sensible. True, the inverse procedure is not much better, consisting of the attempt to withdraw the pure sensible from representation and to determine it as that which remains once representation is removed (a contradictory flux, for example, or a rhapsody of sensations). Empiricism truly becomes transcendental, and aesthetics an apodictic discipline, only when we apprehend directly in the sensible that which can only be sensed, the very being *of* the sensible: difference, potential difference and difference in intensity as the reason behind qualitative diversity. (*DR* 56–57)

Here Deleuze's statements are no mere comment on aesthetics or the nature of sensibility, but rather go straight to the heart of the central problems around which Western metaphysics has been organized. For to criticize aesthetics for founding itself on what *can* be represented— and by this Deleuze means not simply the branch of philosophy that studies art, but aesthetics as it characterizes the theory of sensibility from Plato to the present—is to criticize aesthetics for having reduced the given to passive receptivity rather than seeking, in the manner of a Leibniz or Maïmon, to give a genesis of the sensible itself. *Deleuze seeks to determine the conditions under which receptivity is itself possible.* This project is very different from determining the conditions under which *experience* is possible in that Deleuze rejects the Kantian claim that experience can only properly be said to occur when there is a synthesis of concepts *and* intuitions.

The consequences of Deleuze's project, should they hold up under scrutiny, are extreme and extend well beyond discussions surrounding aesthetics or the nature of sensibility. One could almost say that Deleuze, after the fashion of Quine, seeks to unfold his own critique of the two dogmas of empiricism. However, here the target of criticism is the standard thesis that (1) intuition is passive and merely receptive, and without productivity, and that (2) the givens of intuition are without intelligibility or *logos*. Here we are presented with yet another way of conceiving Deleuze's avowed anti-Platonism. To be an anti-Platonist is not simply to reject the forms as determinative of being and what counts as real, but also to reject the thesis that the field of sensible givens is a rhapsody of unintelligible and irrational appearances.

It is for this reason that Deleuze's transcendental empiricism is better conceived as a hyper-rationalism than as an empiricism. By emphasizing Deleuze's debt to empiricism, we risk maintaining the sensible or aesthetic as a passive given for receptivity and thereby miss Deleuze's central point that sensibility is itself the result of productive processes that actually create or produce the qualities of sensibility. Consequently, following the example of mathematics in which thought seems to actually create its mathematical objects of intuition by thinking them without needing the object to be present to one of the five senses, Deleuze seeks to comprehend sensibility in general as producing the objects of intuition rather than merely receiving them passively. Of course, the precise meaning of this thesis and its implications is something that can only be developed in the course of the present volume itself.

What is important is that Deleuze wishes to argue that all sensible givens and not simply mathematical intuitions are the result of a productive or creative intuition that produces the objects of sense. When Deleuze tells us that the aim of philosophy ought to be to determine the conditions under which something new can be created (*D* vii), we ought to understand that Deleuze is asking how it is possible for forms of intuition or sensibility to be produced. However, as we shall see, this production is not the work of a sovereign subject, but is a production that occurs at the level of being itself. Later in this book I shall attempt to show that we must be skeptical and conservative concerning our own powers of invention. Just as Nietzsche claimed that thoughts come to us, we don't originate thoughts, so too must we understand that we are not the creators but are the result of these invented intuitions. The *will* to create will most likely end up in trite imitations of what already belongs to the field of the recognized. We do not set the problems to be solved, but instead find ourselves in the midst of problems which function like imperatives to which we must respond. In this respect, Deleuze's position cannot be situated in terms of debates organized around realism and anti-realism, foundationalism and anti-foundationalism. Since we are not ourselves the creators, it would be wrong to call Deleuze's position an anti-realism or an anti-foundationalism. Anti-realism and anti-foundationalism only apply in discourses organized around the oppositions of subject and object, culture and nature. Thus, while Deleuze must advocate minimal skepticism in that not all of our intuitions have perfect clarity, this is not the skepticism found in a subjective idealism or a relativism, but arises from the very nature of being itself. This point will be developed in greater detail in the body of this book.

In this way Deleuze is able to undermine the distinction between the finite and the infinite, the universal and the particular, as well as that of being and thinking. With respect to the first distinction, the distinction between the infinite and the finite breaks down in that intuition which is apparently finite takes on creative characteristics normally reserved for infinite intuition. As Heidegger puts it:

> Absolute intuiting would not be absolute if it depended upon a being already at hand and if the intuitable first became accessible in its "taking the measure" of this being. Divine knowing is representing which, in intuiting, first creates the intuitable being as such. But because it immediately looks at the being as a whole, simply seeing through it in advance, it cannot require thinking.[4]

An infinite intuition that was required to experience the objects of its intuition would not be absolute but would be limited. However, if finite intuition proves capable of producing some objects of its intuition (as in the case of mathematics, as we shall see later), then the difference between finite intuition and infinite intuition becomes a difference in degree, not a difference in kind. Although the range of beings produced by thinking is relatively limited in the case of human beings, the fact that we are able to produce *any* objects of intuition allows us to claim that intuition, *in principle* (*quid juris*), is productive. Here, then, the relevant distinction is not that of the active intellect versus passive receptivity, but rather between those intuitions which are *clear* such as my intuition of a straight line and those that are *obscure* or *confused* such as the roar of the ocean mentioned by Leibniz. In both cases, according to Deleuze, the intuition is productive in that it creates the object of its intuition; however, they differ in that in the case of the straight line the rule for producing the straight line is present to consciousness, whereas in the case of the ocean the rule remains virtual or unconscious. It is in this latter respect that the vast majority of our experience can be described as confused or obscure, despite the fact that it results from productive processes.

Consequently, the aim of Deleuze's transcendental or superior empiricism would be to discover or uncover those differentials or rules out of which our intuition is produced (here it bears noting that these rules are not *representations* of the regularities we find in our intuition, but are, as Deleuze argues, the genetic factors that produce our intuition). For this reason, we can see why it is misleading to characterize Deleuze's position in terms of classical empiricism with respect to Locke and Hume. In the case of both Hume and Locke, their empiricism is based on the primacy of the given in sensible intuition as an irreducible feature of experience and ground of all subsequent knowledge. In short, both Locke and Hume continue to maintain the primacy of the subject or mind to which givens are given in sensibility. The given is given and is not itself to be explained but rather explains. Nothing could be further from Deleuze's own position. For Deleuze the given is that which must be accounted for or produced such that it does not explain but must be explained. The given is the result of a genesis or production and is thus not an origin but that which must be originated. As we shall see later in this book, the qualitative givens of experience are the result of differentials (in the sense of calculus). Insofar as differentials function as the productive rules for the qualitative givens of being, Deleuze's position is best thought of as a hyper-rationalism rather than an empiricism. In this way Deleuze undermines the opposition between the universal and the particular, concepts and intuitions, the sensible and the intelligible, or *noesis* and *aisthesis* by discovering intelligibility in the givens of experience itself. *The opposition between the sensible and the intelligible is not even operative in Deleuze's ontology.* As such, there can be no question or problem of the schematism for Deleuze insofar as there are not two terms requiring the mediation of a third term.

The empiricism of Deleuze's position thus refers not to the thesis that intuition or sensibility functions as the *origin* of our knowledge—this would refer Deleuze back to the position that finitude differs from infinitude not in degree but in kind—but to the opposition between the *clear* and the *obscure* or *confused* as it functions in intuition. Given that very few of our intuitions have the deductive and constructive attributes that we find in mathematical intuition, thought finds itself most frequently dependent upon obscure and confused intuitions in its thinking. In other words, in most cases we are unconscious of the productive rules governing our intuitions and must thereby have recourse to receptive affectivity—which consists only of the effects of these rules—in order to arrive at a knowledge of being.

Finally, we can see how Deleuze's strategy functions to overcome the opposition between being and thinking in that thought is no longer conceived of as a representation of being but is instead productive of being itself. For Deleuze, thought produces its intuitions through the differentials or rules that function as productive principles. Deleuze will hold that all intuition is of this nature, though admittedly only a very limited zone of thought consciously takes this form. In this respect it is better to say that *it thinks* than *I think*. In what follows I devote considerable attention to this point, which might be taken to be Deleuze's own version of finitude. It is my view that the creative functions Deleuze attributes to thought in his attempt to undermine representation have given rise to a sort of dogmatic enthusiasm or *Schwärmerei* in some commentators on Deleuze, leading to the notion that we are the thinkers and creators. Being creates, we are part of that creation. Being is not, for Deleuze, our creation. This is why ethically Deleuze tends to advocate a sort of fatalistic stoicism that is highly tolerant and democratic. The thought involved in the production of intuition is *not the thought of a subject* but is thought that unfolds on the part of being itself. In this respect, Deleuze's ontology is not organized around the opposition of the subject and object. Consequently, Deleuze is free of accusations of being a subjective idealist. The consequence of this move is that Deleuze is under the obligation to account for how subjects such as ourselves are produced and how we are led to interpret being in terms of an opposition between subject and object. In what follows, I contend that this opposition that characterizes so much of our thought is not a simple accident of history, but is rather a sort of inevitable illusion produced from within being itself.

These, then, are the concerns that organize this book. In what follows, my aim is to show how Deleuze's transcendental empiricism is an attempt to formulate an *ontology*—not an epistemology or theory of knowledge—that locates intelligibility at the level of the aesthetic or sensible itself and to determine what consequences follow from this position. In the first chapter I discuss the shortcomings of classical empiricism and Deleuze's reasons for rejecting the primacy of the sensible. Here I develop Deleuze's conception of the "empiricist fallacy," which consists in mistaking external difference for internal and determining difference, and I unfold his conception of transcendental philosophy. This sets the stage for demonstrating how Deleuze conceives the project of determining the conditions under which the given is given. In the second chapter, I discuss Deleuze's relationship to Bergson and the manner in which he makes use of Bergsonian duration and intuition in order to arrive at an account of internal or determining difference which surmounts the problems surrounding external difference assumed by empiricism and transcendental philosophies alike.

However, if Deleuze's thought is to avoid the problems that emerge in relation to external difference, then he must find a way of overcoming the subject-object opposition that characterizes so much of the history of philosophy and which is itself based on an external difference. For this reason, in chapter 3, I develop Deleuze's "phenomenology" of the encounter as a way of blurring the distinction between subject and object and simultaneously allowing for a critique of models based on recognition and opening experience to fields of differential relations that go beyond our habitual cognition. Deleuze's concept of the encounter functions in a twofold way. On the one hand, the encounter functions like the *epoche* in Husserlian phenomenology or anxiety in Heidegger's *Being and Time* in that it suspends our habitual relations of recognition with being and allows us to call these structures into question. The encounter is authenticating in that it provides the *opportunity* to withdraw ourselves from customary interpretations that shackle being to the recognized and contingent. On the other hand, the encounter functions as a sign of the transcendental, announcing an internal difference within intuition whose structure and essence must be unfolded. In chapters 4 through 6 I develop the onto-epistemic structure of the encounter in terms of its three moments and show how this allows us to think a new notion of essence based on differentials in intuition, rather than on forms distinguished from matters. These essences are what Deleuze refers to as multiplicities or Ideas. I have retained the term *essence* for polemical reasons as an agitation against those who would attempt to reduce Deleuze's thought to a form of social constructivism or anti-realism. The Ideas uncovered in the encounter are real, independent of subjectivity, and their intelligibility has a universality proper to it that is every bit as binding as that found in Platonic forms. Here the essences discovered through the encounter are not beings of a subject's thought, but belong to being itself in such a way that the opposition between thought and being is undermined. Just as Spinoza distinguishes between *natura naturata* and *natura naturans* in thinking the difference between process and product in nature, the thinking of being consists in the unfolding of these essences through all of their possible variations. I develop this point in more detail in the body of this book.

In chapter 7, which is in many ways crucial, I show how Deleuze is able to overcome criticisms of speculative dogmatism by demonstrating that the subject is split by the form of time in such a way that its solipsistic interiority is overcome so that it is open to a field of immanence in which immanence is not immanence to a subject (Descartes, Kant, Husserl, perhaps early Heidegger), but rather immanence is immanence to itself (Spinozist substance). Here I show how Deleuze's thought undermines the distinction between speculative and critical philosophy by undermining the premises upon which this opposition is based. Finally, in chapter 8 I develop Deleuze's account of individuation and how the Image of thought as the origin of transcendental illusions is produced. This chapter will come as something of a surprise to many Deleuzians because the Image of thought or transcendental illusions is usually taken to be something which we must overcome, not something which needs to be grounded. While I agree that the Image of thought is to be overcome, I nonetheless insist that it is an illusion internal to being itself and not a contingent obstacle to being in which, once overcome, we would finally enjoy full and unmediated *jouissance* of being. In this way Deleuze is able to account for why experience seems to be characterized by the opposition between form and matter, universal and particulars, while maintaining the productive intelligibility of the differentials of intuition.

1

Empiricism and the Search for the Conditions of Real Experience

Two Critical Problems of Transcendental Empiricism

Two very specific *critical* questions animate Deleuze's thought. On the one hand, Deleuze endorses the Cartesian project of breaking with all presuppositions as the precondition of philosophy. So long as philosophy remains within the orbit of unspoken and unjustified presuppositions, it proves unable to ground itself or to explain why one position ought to be preferred over another. In such cases, philosophy remains within the space of public sentiment, common sense, and culturally relative sensibility. As Deleuze puts it:

> Where to begin in philosophy has always—rightly—been regarded as a very delicate problem, for beginning means eliminating all presuppositions. However, whereas in science one is confronted by objective presuppositions which axiomatic rigor can eliminate, presuppositions in philosophy are as much subjective as objective. (*DR* 129)

So long as these presuppositions remain, philosophy is unable to truly begin insofar as it remains within the constellation of unspoken assumptions and ungrounded presuppositions. As I will discuss in greater detail later, these presuppositions are the result of what Deleuze refers to as the "Other-structure" which, in part, presides over the individuation of human individuals. The Other-structure is the condition under which we are produced as social subjects. As a result,

> the conditions of a philosophy which would be without any kind of presuppositions appear all the more clearly: instead of being supported by the moral Image of thought, it would take as its point of departure a radical critique of this Image and the "postulates" it implies. It would find its difference or true beginning, not in an agreement with the *pre-philosophical* Image, but in a rigorous struggle against this Image, which it would denounce as *non-philosophical*. (*DR* 132)

If there is a problem with the pre-philosophical Image of thought, it is that it remains merely *conventional* while nonetheless *universalizing* its presuppositions. Such an Image of thought fails to recognize that it is itself a point of view and therefore contingent or non-universal. In other words, the Image of thought is a matter of prejudice and a blindness to prejudice. By "conventional" I do not mean here that the Image of thought is conservative and based on the status quo. While Deleuze will, of course, make this claim, such a criticism fails to get at what is fundamentally at stake so long as we are not given necessary and sufficient reasons for rejecting the adequacy of the conventional or at least calling it into question. There is no inherent or a priori reason why being unconventional should be preferred to being conventional. Rather, by "conventional" I mean a set of conventions, practices, or beliefs resulting from a history and arising within a particular culture such that they are themselves arbitrary. The pre-philosophical Image of thought makes a claim to knowledge, while nonetheless being unable to ground this claim to knowledge. It illegitimately universalizes its own contingent perspective without determining the *conditions* under which this perspective is possible and the *limits* to which it is subject. The problem here is not that we have conventions and live within a socialized and historicized space of experience. It is unlikely that it is possible to live outside of such conventions, nor, I think, would it be desirable to do so.

In this connection, there is a sort of bad faith or misrecognition at work in some formulations of multiculturalism as an ethical stance rather than as a factual state of affairs. Naive enunciations of multiculturalist politics assert that we *ought* to be tolerant of other cultural practices and avoid imposing our own views on them. While tolerance is certainly an admirable practice, the problem with this position is that it fails to recognize that the claim that we ought to be tolerant is itself a claim that transcends various cultural practices and which is asserted as normatively binding on *all* cultural practices. On the other hand, this universal ethical stance arises from a very specific cultural context, namely, the Western philosophical tradition. In this respect, it is impossible to consistently hold multiculturalist tolerance as a binding ethical ideal without simultaneously asserting a necessary form of cultural universalism and intolerance. Consequently, far from being a variant of cultural relativism, multiculturalism is in fact a form of universalism that is intolerant of cultures that would practice intolerance and which asserts the ethical imperialism of Western values of universalism. This is not a weakness of the multiculturalist position, but is instead something that should be asserted outright and defended against forms of cultural relativism that would defend intolerance and the right to oppress other groups and cultures. However, if we endorse this specific form of universalism that is intolerant of intolerance, then why stop there? Why not go on to assert the universalism of equal rights, of respect for persons, of freedom, and so on? It is clear that cultural relativism, in its normative formulation as a position based on tolerance as something we *ought* to practice, rather quickly becomes the exact opposite of relativism such that we would do better to honestly assert universalist ideals than falsely claim that it is contingent cultural practices that determine virtue and right.

It is not a question of setting up an opposition between contingent and arbitrary conventions and an ahistorical, atemporal domain of being in itself, unsullied by culturally relative reality. Rather, the problem is one of the manner in which these presuppositions tend to conceal themselves and become invisible, foreclosing the possibility of difference and the production of the new. For these reasons, Deleuze claims that philosophies which begin with the Image of thought are

> a hindrance to philosophy. The supposed three levels—a naturally upright thought, an in principle natural common sense, and a transcendental model of recognition—can constitute only an ideal orthodoxy. Philosophy is left without means to realise its project of breaking with *doxa*. (*DR* 134)

In other words, so long as philosophy assumes that thought has a natural affinity with the true (a naturally upright thought), a specific form of objectivity (natural common sense), and bases itself on the model of recognition, thought cannot help but become unconsciously trapped in its own implicit presuppositions which are culturally, historically, and socially contingent. As a result, thought is led to denounce difference and divergence as aberrant or perverted departures from what is recognizable, normal, and therefore true . . . It cannot help but denounce divergence and difference as the difference which departs from those "conventions that are not conventional." Beginning with the Image of thought thus leads to a sort of Ptolemaic philosophizing in which all other individuations are understood relative to our own individuation, so that it becomes impossible to affirm the other individuations in their difference as anything but aberrations. Deleuze thus begins with a critique of the transcendental subject as a structure consisting of invariant categories. Before determining whether or not such a subject is metaphysically primitive or the result of specific individuations, it will first be necessary to subject the Image of thought to a radical critique.

In this respect, Deleuze stands squarely within the critical tradition characterized by Plato, Descartes, Kant, and phenomenology. This is not to say that Deleuze shares the positions of these thinkers, but rather that he shares the critical project of rejecting all dogma and breaking with unfounded belief and superstition. One aspect of practicing philosophy is to eradicate the subjective presuppositions plaguing thought, which in turn allows thought to depart from the Image of thought. Of course, Deleuze will level substantial and far-reaching criticisms against thinkers like Plato, Descartes, and Kant which will significantly differentiate his position from their own positions; however, we must not assume that Deleuze rejects these positions out of any perverse desire to champion some form of subjective or postmodern relativism. Postmodern positions remain tied to the premise of the primacy of a subject or culture as foundational, both assumptions of which are foreign to Deleuze's metaphysics. Although Deleuze certainly acknowledges the being of culture as well as what he calls the "truth of relativity" (as opposed to the relativity of truth), he is not interested in demonstrating that everything is culturally relative, constituted, or produced through the subjective whim of a subject. If Deleuze critiques these positions it is not because he is rejecting the notion of critique, of having to ground one's claims, *but rather because these positions are not critical enough.* In short, there is a very real sense in which Deleuze's rejection of these positions is based on an avowal or defense of (metaphysical) truth.

This, then, leads to a first critical problem: *What are the conditions under which critique is possible? Under what conditions is it possible to break with the Image of thought?* Deleuze's solution to this problem will be part of what he calls "transcendental empiricism," which is (1) what we might call an "apprenticeship in signs" following his argument in the brilliant *Proust and Signs,* and which is (2) that which delivers us to the conditions of *real* rather than merely *possible* experience. In one respect, then, transcendental empiricism is not simply a metaphysics or ontology (as Bruce Baugh has suggested), but rather a methodology of "anti-methodology." Where methodology is subject to the criticism of assuming the nature of the being it investigates in advance—as, for instance, in physics where the variables are already determined in advance as "places"—transcendental empiricism proceeds under the force of a "sign that can only be sensed" which "engenders thinking within thought" and which in turn explicates a new domain of experience. On the other hand, with Bruce Baugh, we can say that transcendental empiricism is only comprehensible in terms of a particular sort of ontology which accounts for the genesis of thought within thinking or which sees being and thought as identical. I shall develop this latter point in detail later in this book. Here, what is important is that we seem to arrive at a paradox that will need to be resolved if Deleuze is able to advance his position: on the one hand, transcendental empiricism is an anti-methodological methodology which allows us to arrive at ontological understanding; and on the other hand, the anti-methodological methodology of transcendental empiricism can only be accounted for, grounded, or established on the basis of a particular sort of transcendental philosophy or ontology.

Deleuze's object of critique takes on a specific form which seems to have been overlooked in much of the secondary literature on his work. It is this critique which determines the second and properly critical problem of Deleuze's thought. Having entitled his position "transcendental empiricism," and sometimes simply referring to it as a "superior empiricism" or even just "empiricism" (*DR* xx–xxi; *LS* 20; *D* vii), it may come as a surprise to readers of Deleuze that the central fallacy of previous attempts at critical philosophy itself consists of *empiricism*. Here Deleuze is entirely democratic. Metaphysical philosophies, transcendental philosophies, and empiricist philosophies all fall prey to this error of empiricism.

There is an abundance of textual evidence supporting this claim. The most precise formulation of this critique can be found in *Difference and Repetition*. According to Deleuze, "the mistake of dogmatism is always to fill that which separates, [while] that of *empiricism* is to leave external what is separated" (*DR* 170; modified). In other words, dogmatism posits an extra-worldly realm of essences that falsely unify the diversity of the world, while empiricism falls prey to a nominalistic atomism which treats all beings in terms of an indifferent diversity. Consequently, contrasting difference with diversity, Deleuze claims that "difference is the state in which one can speak of determination *as such*" (*DR* 28). And he goes on to criticize empiricism insofar as "the difference 'between' two things is only empirical, and the corresponding determinations are only extrinsic" (*DR* 28). In other words, nominalistic empiricism fails to arrive at the real determinations or articulations of being, but remains at the level of extrinsic and contingent determinations. We can schematically represent the difference between transcendental and empirical thought as shown in table 1.

We must, therefore, inquire into the nature of internal difference and determination *as such*. Alternatively, we might ask what transcendental difference consists of or what difference in itself is in contrast to difference determined relative to something else.

The problem with mere empiricism based on sensible givens received in passive intuition is that insofar as it treats differences as be-

	Form of Difference	Type of Determination
Empiricism	External difference; difference *between* two terms	Determination of being relative to some other being
Transcendental Thought	Internal difference	Determination *as such;* that which determines the being in the being of its being

Table 1: Schematic representation of the difference between transcendental and empirical philosophies

ing external differences between terms, it is unable to give an internal determination of what makes a being what it is. In Bergsonian terms, we might say that empiricism selects differences in degree rather than differences in kind. As Deleuze puts it:

> If we consider all the definitions, descriptions and characters of duration in Bergson's work, we realise that difference of nature, in the end, is not *between* these two tendencies. Finally, difference of nature is itself *one* of these tendencies, and is opposed to the other. What in effect is duration? Everything that Bergson says about duration always comes back to this: duration *is what differs from itself.* Matter on the contrary is what does not differ from itself, what repeats. ("BCD" 47–48)

In Deleuze's account of Bergson's method of intuition we first begin with a composite mixture or phenomenon, and then divide it into the tendencies which compose it in order to arrive at an account of the differences or determinations which determine it. When we divide the composite into its tendencies, the difference we are after is not the difference between the two tendencies, nor is it the external relations such as the spatial and temporal location it shares with other entities, but rather difference as such contained within one of the tendencies characterizing the composite phenomenon. On the one hand, there is the tendency which differs from itself, or duration, and which hence differs in kind. On the other hand, there is the tendency that differs only in degree from other entities, which consists of matter or a spatialization of difference. For instance, given any two entities, these two entities will always resemble one another in that they both necessarily occupy a position at a particular point in time at a particular point in space. Consequently, while space and time might function as grounds for a principle of individuation in that no two objects can occupy the same position at the same point in time, they fail to individuate *what* the object is in the difference of its being from other beings. For instance, we can imagine two identical twins that are alike in all respects down to their most intimate thoughts, which differ only in being located in different spaces at the same time. The difference between these two would be an external difference pertaining to the medium of space and time conceived as containers, not an internal difference defining the being of their being or what it means to be specifically *that* being.

By choosing the tendency which differs from itself, or which contains all the differences in kind, we are able to arrive at the determination determining the composite in question; while if we restrict ourselves to the composite, we prove unable to properly distinguish phenomena. For instance, we can distinguish, as Bergson does, the tendencies of matter and memory in which matter contains the principle in which the repetition of the same occurs and memory contains qualitative and spiritual differences that all differ in kind. If we do not make this distinction, then we are unable to arrive at those internal differences individuating phenomena, and are left only with differences in degree. This is precisely what happens in empiricism. Thus, for instance, while all sense-data might be singular individuals in that they are events unfolding in the order of time, they nonetheless all resemble one another in that they are located in the medium of space and time as a container. Consequently, red_1 differs from red_2 in that they are both absolutely singular events in the order of being such that they are united by no common form of essence or universality that subsumes them both and which is capable of being in multiple places at multiple times; however, we see that this difference is already trivial in that the relation between the two isn't merely one of resemblance, but of sameness implying a common essence. Space and time, far from undermining the identity of the two terms, presents the medium for their comparison. As a result, all determination becomes merely contingent, arbitrary, and relative and we encounter a sort of "euthanasia" of philosophy. In other words, while the particular form reality takes may indeed be arbitrary (meaning we could equally well imagine other configurations of reality governed by different principles giving birth to incompossible worlds or different compossible worlds), the principle of sufficient reason serving as the condition for this or that particular configuration of reality must not itself be arbitrary.

Difference, Diversity, and Empiricism

Initially we might assume that Deleuze is here offering two distinct criticisms: one against dogmatic or transcendental philosophies, and the other against empiricist philosophies. We might assume that Deleuze is seeking to chart a course between the dogmatic essentialism of the former and the skepticism of the latter. However, textually this line of argument cannot be supported. For instance, we might expect Deleuze to criticize Kant for treating the concepts of the understanding as having a sort of quasi-transcendent status which illicitly fills in the diversity of experience without itself being affected by this diversity. Similarly, we might expect him to criticize Platonically inspired transcendental and metaphysical philosophies for attributing a similar status to forms or essences. These would be exactly the sorts of criticisms we would expect in terms of the anti-essentialist position generally attributed to Deleuze. Yet, strangely, this does not occur. Rather, Deleuze criticizes Kant for leaving concepts and intuitions external to one another (*DR* 173–74), just as he criticizes Plato and essentialism for leaving copies and simulacra external to each other (*DR* 59–60; *LS* 105–6). In other words, the fallacy that Kant, Plato, and essentialism are equally subject to is, for Deleuze, an empiricist fallacy. *Paradoxically, for Deleuze, these philosophies are not transcendental enough.*

However, while both standard empiricism and transcendental philosophies may be subject to the same fallacy, the ways in which this fallacy manifests itself are distinct. In the case of empiricism, the problem is one of diversity such that we are only able to provide nominalistic definitions of a type of being and a *negative* account of difference (the difference between two entities is determined as one *not* being the other), rather than an affirmative account of difference that would deliver us to a concept of determination *as such*.[1] Empiricism arrives at these problems by conceiving determining difference in terms of the material content of experience or sense-data, while transcendental philosophy encounters these problems because it confuses a difference that differs merely in degree (the difference between concepts and intuitions) with a difference that differs in kind. Hence, with respect to classical empiricism, in "Coldness and Cruelty" we find Deleuze criticizing empiricist approaches to sadism and masochism for failing to provide an essential account of what these entities consist in.

> It would seem that the contents of sadism and masochism are each intended to fulfill a form. Variations in the distribution of the pleasure-pain complex as well as variations in the content of the fantasy (whether the mother or the father is the determinant image) depend on the

specific requirements of the form. If we take the *material content* as our starting point, we solve everything and we arrive besides at the supposed unity of sadism and masochism, but at the price of total confusion. Any given formula for the association of pleasure and pain must take into account certain specific formal conditions (e.g., the form of waiting, the form of projection). *"Material" definitions of masochism based on the pleasure-pain complex are insufficient: as the logician would say, they are purely nominal, they do not indicate the possibility of what they define, they do not show that particular conditions must follow.* But worse still, they lack distinctive features, and open up the way to all sorts of confusions between sadism and masochism such as the possibility of their reversing into each other. ("CC" 74; italics mine)

Ultimately, material or empirical definitions find themselves unable to maintain the difference they strive to explain and are thus arbitrary and insufficient. More importantly, the reason they are unable to arrive at the being of the being they seek to comprehend is that they seek to locate this being in the material content (sense-data) of its manifestations. In the case of sadism and masochism, they take pleasure and pain as mere givens, as the defining or determining features of sadism and masochism, without determining the conditions under which this pain and pleasure in their particular manifestation are possible. As a result, such approaches are led to postulate a complementarity between sadism and masochism that betrays their reality. As Deleuze remarks elsewhere in "Coldness and Cruelty":

> The belief in this unity [of sadism and masochism] is to a large extent the result of misunderstanding and careless reasoning. It may seem obvious that the sadist and the masochist are destined to meet. The fact that the one enjoys inflicting while the other enjoys suffering pain seems to be such striking proof of their complementarity that it would be disappointing if the encounter did not take place. A popular joke tells of the meeting between a sadist and a masochist; the masochist says: "Hurt me." The sadist replies: "No." This is a particularly stupid joke, not only because it is unrealistic but because it foolishly claims competence to pass judgment on the world of perversions. It is unrealistic because a genuine sadist could never tolerate a masochist victim (one of the monks' victims in *Justine* explains: "They wish to be certain their crimes cost tears; they would send away any girl who was to come here voluntarily"). Neither would the masochist tolerate a truly sadistic torturer. He does of course require a special "nature" in the woman torturer, but he needs to mold this nature, to educate and persuade it in accordance with his secret project, which could never be fulfilled with a sadistic woman. ("CC" 40–41)

Empiricism begins with the diversity of the given and seeks to determine the phenomena given in terms of the properties (material content) which appear in its composite manifestations. In the case of sadism and masochism, the most obvious properties are those of pleasure and pain. From the empiricist perspective, it is the rule of pleasure and pain that distinguishes or determines the difference of sadism and masochism from other sexual behaviors. What empiricism overlooks here are the relations which give sadism and masochism their specific sense or being. For the empiricist, the masochist is one who enjoys pain while the sadist is one who enjoys inflicting pain. It is this that leads the empiricist to posit their complementarity. What the empiricist misses is the specific *organization*—what Deleuze will later call a multiplicity or an Idea—that gives pleasure and pain their specific value in sadism and masochism.[2]

In short, the empiricist begins with the diversity of sense-data and seeks to determine how they are grouped together in a composite. For this reason, Deleuze is quick to claim that "difference is not diversity. Diversity is given, but difference is that by which the given is given, that by which the given is given as diverse. Difference is not phenomenon but the noumenon closest to the phenomenon" (*DR* 222). The philosophical position of empiricism assumes nothing but diversity as given, but for this very reason it finds itself unable to provide determining differences for that which it seeks to account for. In other words, empiricism is unable to account for the internal unity or essence of a phenomenon . . . It is unable to account for the distinctive features or determinations making up phenomena. Here Hegel perhaps expresses matters best.

> Identity *falls apart* within itself into diversity because, as absolute difference, it posits itself as its own negative within itself, and these its moments, namely, itself and the negative of itself, are reflections-into-self, are self-identical; or, in other words, precisely because identity itself immediately sublates its negating and in its *determination is reflected into itself.* The distinguished terms *subsist* as indifferently different towards one another because each is self-identical, because identity constitutes its ground and element; in other words, the difference is what it is, only in its very opposite, in identity.[3]

Hegel's description of diversity here is the quintessential expression of the *metaphysics* assumed by empiricism.

Even in the case of empiricisms that modestly situate themselves in merely epistemological terms, one begins with the assumption that *there are* sensations. In other words, one begins with a claim about being. Moreover, such claims about the being of being are unavoidable, which should render us suspicious of Anglo-American tendencies to suggest that they endorse positions free of metaphysics and are just engaged in ordinary language analysis. The minute one makes claims about being one is engaged in metaphysics. These sensations are treated as theoretically primitive elements that explain without themselves having to be explained, and which all differ from one another. That which differs from one another is a diversity. Thus, epistemological agnosticism as to whether this diversity actually resembles being which exists independently of the mind still assumes a metaphysics. We are therefore unimpressed by claims that empiricism can be defined without reference to a certain positing of diversity. A mental diversity of sensations is no less a diversity of being than a materialist diversity of atoms.

On the one hand, empiricism, with its celebration or assumption of diversity, seems to be the perfect embodiment of a philosophy of difference. This is precisely what Hegel's description of diversity seems to express. The nominalistic empiricist treats every entity as different from every other, and, more fundamentally, as indifferent to all these others. Here each entity just is what it is. This is what Hegel means when he claims that diversity reflects difference into itself. Each entity just is what it is regardless of how it stands to other entities and therefore "contains" its difference in itself. But the more we think about this diversity, the more problematic it becomes. At what level do we locate these self-identical terms? Are they systems: biological, ecological, cosmological? Simple objects: chairs, balls? Qualities belonging to objects: red, sweet? Diversity attempts to preserve difference by granting each element its own self-identity, but it invariably ends up reducing the differences among terms to differences in degree on the basis of the level at which self-identity is located. In the case of the supposed sado-masochistic entity, the diversity in question is pleasure and pain, which are each treated as qualitatively self-identical qualities given in and of themselves. In short, it is assumed that pleasure is pleasure—that it is the same pleasure—regardless of whether the sadist or masochist experiences it as such. As a result, the empiricist position, which begins with a celebration of difference and a desire to determine types based on concrete reality, ends up being unable to locate the differences that count.

External Difference and Transcendental Philosophy

In the case of transcendental philosophies, the problem manifests itself differently. Where the philosophical position of empiricism encounters difficulty in proceeding from the instance to the principle, from the given to the difference it expresses, transcendental philosophies, on the contrary, encounter difficulty proceeding from the principle to the instance. In the case of Plato, Deleuze presents this difficulty in the form of how to select among rival claimants to the truth. Thus,

> we divide art into arts of production and arts of acquisition: but then why is fishing among the arts of acquisition? What is missing here is a mediation—that is, the identity of a concept capable of serving as the middle term . . . It is not a question of dividing a determinate genus into definite species, but of dividing a confused species into pure lines of descent, or of selecting a pure line from material which is not . . . The search for gold provides the model for this process of division. Difference is not between species, between two determinations of a genus, but entirely on one side, within the chosen line of descent: there are no longer contraries within a single genus, but pure and impure, good and bad, authentic and inauthentic, in a mixture which gives rise to a large species. Pure difference, the pure concept of difference, not difference mediated within the concept in general, in the genus and the species. The meaning and the goal of the method of division is selection among rivals, the testing of claimants. (*DR* 59–60)

Initially we might expect Deleuze to reject Plato for having asserted the primacy of the model over appearances. However, to our great surprise and astonishment, he does not reject Plato for establishing or assuming a hierarchy within being, but rather for establishing such a hierarchy on the basis of a myth:

> Our question is not yet that of knowing whether the selective difference is indeed between the true and the false claimants, as Plato says it is, but rather of knowing how Plato establishes the difference thanks to the method of division. To the reader's great surprise, he does so by introducing a "myth." It is as though division, once it abandons the mask of determining species and discloses its true goal, nevertheless renounces the realisation of this goal and is instead relayed by the simple "play" of a myth. (*DR* 60)

If Platonism fails, it is because it fails to provide us with the selective mechanism that would allow us to choose among rival claimants for the truth, that would allow us to choose between copies which participate in models and illicit simulacra. In other words, it fails to establish a transport between models and copies which would distinguish between the copy and the simulacra, but must resort to myth to accomplish this task.

This returns us to the Bergsonian issue of selecting among tendencies. The criterion for properly choosing among tendencies consists in selecting the tendency which contains difference as such. Platonism is no different in this respect. Insofar as Plato locates difference "between" the two lines of descent, he proves unable to determine which line should be selected. Hence the difficulty in determining why fishing ought to belong to arts of acquisition rather than of production. What is missing here is the *reason* for placing fishing in one rather than the other. As a result, models remain external to their copies and we are left unable to distinguish between copies and simulacra.

In the case of Kant, the problem arises as a result of the exteriority between concepts and intuitions. According to Deleuze,

> the mistake of dogmatism is always to fill that which separates, that of empiricism is to leave external what is separated, and in this sense there is still too much *empiricism* in the *Critique* (and too much dogmatism among the post-Kantians). (*DR* 170; italics mine)

In demonstrating this, Deleuze remarks that

> it is Salomon Maïmon who proposes a fundamental reformulation of the *Critique* and an overcoming of the Kantian duality between concepts and intuition. Such a duality refers us back to the extrinsic criterion of constructibility and leaves us with an external relation between the determinable (Kantian space as a pure given) and the determination (the concept in so far as it is thought). That the one should be adapted to the other by the intermediary of the schematism only reinforces the paradox introduced into the doctrine of the faculties by the notion of a purely external harmony: whence the reduction of the transcendental instance to a simple conditioning and renunciation of any genetic requirement. In Kant, therefore, difference remains external and as such empirical and impure, suspended outside the construction "between" the determinable intuition and the determinant concept. (*DR* 173)

The difficulty here is that so long as the difference between concepts and intuitions is treated as being merely an external difference, we are left without the means of explaining how complete determination is arrived at between determinable intuitions and determining concepts. Or, alternatively, we are left without the means of determining how a synthesis of the two is effected. To be sure, it is precisely this problem which the schematism is meant to solve; yet the solution of the schematism only seems to exacerbate the problem insofar as the notion of temporal determinations only begs the question by assuming *conceptual* determinations of time carried out by the imagination. Without this account of synthesis, our explanation of experience remains abstract and incomplete and we are unable to determine the conditions of real experience. For instance, we are able to explain, in Kantian terms, the notion of objectivity in general, but when it comes to a form of objectivities such as sadism or masochism, we find ourselves completely at a loss. One might object that it is precisely this which constitutes the difference between possible and actual experience. However, it is precisely the *form* of possible experience that Deleuze is objecting to. So long as the form is external to its matter, we are unable to see how it could condition experience. Since we can only refer to the empirical given to explain such a phenomenon, we find ourselves locked once again in all the aporias characterizing the complementary accounts of sadism and masochism. While the issue of empirical concepts is not normally seen as a problem for Kant, the question arises as to how it is possible for concepts and intuitions to be related to one another at all if the two differ in kind. Following Solomon Maïmon, upon whom Deleuze relies heavily for his critique of Kant, if concepts differ in kind from intuitions, then it would seem impossible to relate the two together by anything other than an external relation.[4] In this respect, Kant too falls prey to the empiricist fallacy. However, here, as we will see, the error will arise in that Kant treats concepts and intuitions as differing in kind and thus being externally related, rather than discerning the manner in which they only differ in degree.

Insofar as Kant's critical philosophy, and transcendental philosophies like his, privilege identity, they are led to accept only an empirical notion of difference which leaves the relation between models and copies, concepts and intuitions, external and unintelligible. Moreover, the difference between concepts and intuitions is for Deleuze a difference in degree rather than in kind. It is for this reason that these positions are led to the problem of their connection. *Here we see elements of Deleuze's rationalism as opposed to his alleged empiricism in that Deleuze is led to rationalize intuitions themselves.* For Deleuze, the difference between a concept and an intuition is the difference between a clear intuition and a confused perception. In short, it is not a difference in kind at all, but a variation on a principle. I will develop this point in greater detail later. What bears noting here is that for Deleuze concepts *do not* subsume intuitions at all, which means that Deleuze is able to avoid the problem of how the clear and confused are related to one another altogether. Hence, we might say that the philosophical position of empiricism is unable to account for experience as a type, while transcendental philosophies, which privilege the general or abstract in the form of self-identical concepts and models, are unable to account for real or concrete experience formed as a result of synthesis.

Between Conditioning and Genesis

Deleuze's project will consist in finding a third way between these extremes, but this will require overcoming the assumptions of representation and finitude upon which these premises are based. Deleuze must show how intuition is productive in such a way that he is able to comprehend how it is possible to conceive lawlike intuitions that are not subsumed under concepts. Deleuze does not waste much time with empiricism. He seems assured that there are principles governing experience, that there are essences, and he thus rejects nominalistic and empiricist accounts of our experience. On the other hand, he does question the way in which these essences have been conceived. This criticism finds its definitive formulation in the claim that transcendental philosophies leave conditions external to that which they condition . . . that they restrict themselves to a perspective of mere conditioning. In *Nietzsche and Philosophy* Deleuze will claim that

> Kant lacked a method which permitted reason to be judged from the inside without giving it the task of being its own judge. And, in fact, Kant does not realise his project of immanent critique. Transcendental philosophy discovers conditions which still remain external to the conditioned. Transcendental principles are principles of conditioning and not of internal genesis. We require a genesis of reason itself, and also a genesis of the understanding and its categories. (*NP* 91)

Initially we may believe that Deleuze seeks a genetic account because he has some sort of aesthetic preference for becoming over stasis, genesis over conditioning. Yet this is an entirely banal and unconvincing reason for adopting such a position. Such "reasons" only persuade those who are already convinced . . . which is to say those who are not interested in philosophy. Rather, we must seek concrete and necessary reasons supporting why a genetic account is to be desired over one of mere conditioning.

If Deleuze is compelled to reject an account of simple conditioning in favor of a genetic account, then this is because transcendental accounts based on conditioning somehow fail to ground that which they seek to found. As Deleuze argues,

The error of all efforts to determine the transcendental as consciousness is that they think of the transcendental in the image of, and in the resemblance to, that which it is supposed to ground. In this case, either we give ourselves ready-made, in the "originary" sense presumed to belong to the constitutive consciousness, whatever we were trying to generate through a transcendental method, or, in agreement with Kant, we give up genesis and constitution and we limit ourselves to a simple transcendental conditioning. But we do not, for all this, escape the vicious circle which makes the condition refer to the conditioned as it reproduces its image. (*LS* 105)

Do we not here discover the origin of all the problems surrounding classical essentialism with respect to determining membership to the extension of an essence? The empiricist fallacy as it pertains to transcendental philosophy is an extensionalist fallacy in that it conceives individuals as belonging to the extension of an essence or thinks them as subsumed under an essence. Essentialism has always been plagued by the problem of the border case, of the example whose membership cannot be clearly determined as belonging to or not belonging to the essence in question. If this is the case, then it is because the essence is itself based on an arbitrary and privileged example against which other instances are measured. Here we find the core reason supporting Deleuze's critique of Plato. If allusion to simulacra undermines the relation between models and copies, then this is because the order of simulacra announces a difference *other* than that found in the relationship of a model to a copy or in resemblance between copies. A simulacrum is a difference *without* a model.

We cannot yet be certain that this is Deleuze's criticism of classical essentialisms that discern the being of essence as a form containing individuals as a content. Deleuze's argument here is both subtle and perplexing. Initially one is inclined to question why it should constitute a criticism at all. Given that transcendental philosophy is to account for the conditions under which knowledge or experience is possible, and given that we can only arrive at a knowledge of these conditions through the analysis of experience, it would seem to be natural that the conditions should resemble that which they condition. Moreover, why should the fact that the condition resembles the conditioned be objectionable at all? To suggest that we ought to reject accounts of conditioning insofar as they are based on resemblance is also to claim that there is something a priori objectionable in the resemblance relation. Yet Deleuze does not seem to provide any reason for this a priori objectionability. He simply announces it.

In reality, Deleuze's argument is quite different. It is not the re-semblance relation that Deleuze objects to, but the reference relation involved in transcendental philosophy. To repeat, "we do not, for all this, escape the vicious circle which makes the condition *refer* to the conditioned as it reproduces its image" (*LS* 105; modified). There is both a logical and a critical problem with respect to the reference relation as it manifests itself in transcendental philosophy. Logically the problem arises as a paradox involving signification and denotation, or in this case consciousness (the condition/conditioning) and experience (the conditioned). As Deleuze argues in *The Logic of Sense,*

> The presupposed primacy of signification over denotation, however, still raises a delicate problem. When we say "therefore," when we consider a proposition as concluded, we make it the object of an assertion. We set aside the premises and affirm it for itself, independently. We relate it to the state of affairs which it denotes, independently of the implications which constitute its signification. To do so, however, two conditions have to be filled. It is first necessary that the premises be posited as effectively true, which already forces us to depart from the pure order of implication in order to relate the premises to a denoted state of affairs which we presuppose. But then, even if we suppose that the premises A and B are true, we can only conclude from this that the proposition in question (let us call it Z)—we can only detach it from its premises and affirm it for itself independently of the implication—by admitting that Z is, in turn, true if A and B are true. This amounts to a proposition, C, which remains within the order of implication, and is unable to escape it, since it refers to a proposition, D, which states that "Z is true if A, B, and C are true . . .," and so on to infinity . . . In short, the conclusion can be detached from the premises, but only on the condition that one always adds other premises from which alone the conclusion is not detachable. This amounts to saying that signification is never homogenous; or that the two signs "implies" and "therefore" are completely heterogeneous; or that implication never succeeds in grounding denotation except by giving itself a ready-made denotation, once in the premises and again in the conclusion. (*LS* 16)

In this context, Deleuze is discussing the relationship between the three elements of the proposition, or denotation, manifestation, and signification. Deleuze argues that denotation is only possible on the basis of manifestation (the I along with its beliefs and desires) insofar as entities are only pointed out in the world on the basis of a perspective that originates from a particular subject. However, manifestation, in turn, is dependent on signification insofar as the possibility of causing particular images associated with the word to vary, of substituting one image for another in the form "this is not that, it's that," can be explained only by the constancy of the signified concept. Similarly, desires would not form an order of demands or even of duties, distinct from a simple urgency of needs, and beliefs would not form an order of inferences distinct from simple opinions, if the words in which they were manifested did not refer first to concepts and conceptual implications rendering these desires and beliefs significative. (*LS* 16)

The nature of the problem now becomes evident. If denotation is dependent on manifestation, and manifestation is dependent on signification, but signification ends up being dependent on denotation, we find ourselves in a vicious circle within which we cannot ground that which we were initially seeking to ground . . . namely, the truth of what we say.

In this case, it turns out that signification, which is supposed to ground denotation, is thought in reference to or in resemblance with denotation. In other words, signification only becomes thinkable by giving itself a ready-made denotation. Signification comes to be thought in terms of a particular case or privileged example that comes to illicitly fill the content of the universal. But if signification is thought in reference to denotation, then somewhere, at some point in a signifying chain of implications, it assumes the truth of a ready-made denotation such that at least one term in any signifying chain turns out to be arrived at apart from the conditions which are supposed to render denotation possible.

This is precisely the argument Deleuze is advancing with respect to transcendental philosophy. In transcendental philosophy the conditions are supposed to account for what makes experience possible. However, insofar as transcendental philosophies of this sort adopt an account of simple conditioning that leaves the conditions external to that which is conditioned, they cannot avoid thinking these conditions in reference to the conditioned in such a way that we claim these conditions are "true" insofar as we take experience to be true. *In other words, the conditions are supposed to account for the possibility of truth within experience, yet the conditions themselves get their justification insofar as experience is taken to be true.* It is not difficult to discern once again a Bergsonian critique at work here. Having adopted a purely external concept of difference as difference between conditions and the conditioned, transcendental philosophy finds that it can only establish a difference in degree rather than kind between the condition and the conditioned.

Later we shall see that this is because *both* intuitions *and* concepts are rational structures for Deleuze such that an intuition is just a confused concept from the perspective of finite experience. For the moment we need only note that Deleuze is here arguing that the concept *is*, for all intents and purposes, the denotation. As a result, it fails to arrive at the conditions rendering experience possible. In this respect, it is not that Deleuze rejects transcendental philosophy, but that he criticizes a certain kind of transcendental thought for not being transcendental enough.

This first logical problem leads to a more critical or transcendental problem. Having established that transcendental accounts based on conditioning collapse because they always refer to a denotation that cannot be accounted for in terms of these conditions alone, it now becomes possible to directly question the status of these conditions themselves. In a Kantian framework, at least, the conditions of experience are supposed to be the conditions of all possible experience. However, if these conditions are only arrived at by reference or resemblance to conditioned experience, then this thesis is radically called into question and calls for a critique of the category of possibility itself. According to Deleuze,

> The possible is opposed to the real; the process undergone by the possible is therefore a "realisation" . . . Every time we pose the question in terms of possible and real, we are forced to conceive of existence as a brute eruption, a pure act or leap which always occurs behind our backs and is subject to a way of all or nothing. What difference can there be between the existent and the non-existent if the non-existent is already possible, already included in the concept and having all the characteristics that the concept confers upon it as a possibility? Existence is *the same* as but outside the concept. Existence is therefore supposed to occur in space and time, but these are understood as indifferent milieux instead of the production of existence occurring in a characteristic space and time. (*DR* 211)

Here Deleuze reveals a profound affinity to stoic thought, which was concerned with concrete, immanent reality rather than abstract forms.[5] This point holds equally for Deleuze. Like the stoics, Deleuze too refuses to grant a pride of place to intellectual or intelligible being over concrete reality. However, we must not assume that this means Deleuze reduces all of being to nominal individuals. Rather, Deleuze will instead seek to discover intelligibility within the concrete itself.

Applying this argument to Kant, we could say that the categories serve as the structure of possibility, while the pure forms of space and time are the medium within which possibility is realized. The problem here, then, is that we become unable to explain how a posteriori or realized experience adds anything to the concept. In short, the actualized reality of a possibility seems to contribute nothing to our understanding save presence of that possibility in the flesh . . . Which is to say, realization of a possibility merely renders that possibility visceral without adding anything to the content of the concept or possibility. However, this is not yet Deleuze's definitive argument. Deleuze goes on to argue that

> to the extent that the possible is open to "realisation," it is understood as an image of the real, while the real is supposed to resemble the possible. That is why it is difficult to understand what existence adds to the concept when all it does is double like with like. Such is the defect of the possible: a defect which serves to condemn it as produced after the fact, as retroactively fabricated in the image of what resembles it. (*DR* 212)

Where the relation between transcendental condition (as structure of possibility) and conditioned experience (the real) becomes indiscernible, it becomes impossible to determine whether these conditions are indeed conditions of all possible experience, or rather retroactive constructions of real, lived, and consequently conventional and arbitrary experience. In other words, what we call the possible is treated as something forever governing the structure of the real, even though it is drawn from a contingent moment in the real and is illicitly universalized to cover all experience. Deleuze is thus alluding to our tendency to conflate what we recognize or are accustomed to with what is possible. Possibility serves as a limiting concept defining the horizon of the real, but insofar as the possible is modeled on the real it seems to illegitimately limit the possible. Here, following Bergson, we must distinguish two senses of the possible. On the one hand there is possibility as that which defines what can be and what cannot be, while on the other hand there is possibility in terms of that which nothing prevents from being. It is the former sense of possibility that marks the target of Deleuze's critique.

Here we encounter a genuine transcendental problem. Given that we cannot arrive at the conditions of all possible experience without assuming some sort of ready-made denotation, and given that it is necessary to arrive at some account of these conditions lest we fall into all the problems surrounding empiricist positions based on the given or diversity, how is it possible for transcendental philosophy to get off the ground at all? In other words, transcendental philosophy seems to offer us the best possibility for establishing an account of internal difference free of the nominalistic problems of empiricism and the dogmatism of metaphysics, of distinguishing difference, of theorizing determination as such; yet we need an account of conditions that avoids all these fallacies which Kant (and we might add German idealism and phenomenology to the list as well) seem to encounter.

Between Chaos and Individuation: The Forced Vel of Representational Philosophy

What is it then that leads transcendental philosophy into this vexing state of affairs? Why is it ineluctably compelled to treat difference in terms of an external difference between the condition and the conditioned, rather than in terms of an internal difference generating experience itself? At the outset of this chapter I drew attention to Deleuze's claim that philosophy has been in the grip of an Image of thought that is moral in character. However, the claim that this image is moral is not immediately self-evident and will require extended explication at a later point in this book. More pertinently, Deleuze claims that transcendental philosophy has been subject to a false alternative which has forced it to take up an external account of difference between conditions and the conditioned. As Deleuze remarks,

> What is common to metaphysics and transcendental philosophy is, above all, this alternative which they impose on us: *either* an undifferentiated ground, or groundlessness, formless nonbeing, or an abyss without difference and without properties, *or* a supremely individuated Being and an intensely personalized Form. Without this Being or this Form, you will have only chaos . . . In other words, metaphysics and transcendental philosophy reach an agreement to think about *those determinable singularities only which are already imprisoned inside a supreme Self or a superior I.* It seems therefore entirely natural for metaphysics to determine this supreme Self as that which characterizes a Being infinitely and completely determined by its concept and which thereby possess the entire originary reality. In fact, this Being is necessarily individuated, since it relegates to nonbeing or to the bottomless abyss every predicate or property which expresses nothing real, and delegates to its creatures, that is, to finite individualities, the task of receiving derived predicates which express only limited realities. At the other pole, transcendental philosophy chooses the finite synthetic form of the Person rather than the infinite analytic being of the individual; and it thinks natural to

determine this superior I with reference to man and to enact the grand
permutation Man-God which has satisfied philosophy for so long. The
I is coextensive with representation, as the individual used to be coextensive with Being. But in both cases, we are faced with the alternative
between undifferentiated groundlessness and imprisoned singularities.
(*LS* 105–6)

No doubt the Self of metaphysics that Deleuze refers to here is some
variant of God or even the demiurge of Plato, while the Person of
transcendental philosophy is none other than the famous transcendental
subject. In short, Deleuze seems to locate the assumption of a finite
perspective at the center of both metaphysics and transcendental
philosophy which privileges the primacy of the individuated subject
as the condition for individuated Being in general. As a result, the
productive power of Being or the structure of possibility is illegitimately
restricted to the subject in such a way as to lead to all of the paradoxes
surrounding internal and external difference. However, as I suggested
in the introduction, the assumption of finitude leads to all the
problematics surrounding representation. Insofar as the finite subject
is governed by the passivity of receptivity and the activity (spontaneity)
of (conceptual) thought, it encounters the *quid juris* question of how
one can be related to the other. It is this that leads to the assumption
that the two must differ in kind. Because I can think my concepts at
will, while I must await my intuitions in sensibility, it is held that the two
must form entirely different orders of cognition. As we will see later,
matters change radically when the perspective of finitude is no longer
assumed.

However, more fundamentally, both metaphysics and transcendental philosophy are led to this impasse because they restrict themselves
to the alternative of either an undifferentiated abyss, a pure chaos, *or* a
supremely individuat*ed* Being. Here we encounter the interminable discourse of the senses which are said to be unreliable, misleading, chaotic,
indeterminate. In short, the senses, intuition, are held to be everything
rational, conceptual cognition is not . . . which is to say they are held to
be a rhapsody of irrational flux. From the vantage of the senses, of empirical flux, it is the Self or Person, which is individuat*ed*, that maintains
itself in its identity through the power and structure of its thought, and
which thus represents an island of order within chaos. As Deleuze puts
it with respect to Kant,

What is the fate of a philosophy which nevertheless conserves the essential (that is, the form), and is satisfied with raising to the transcendental

a mere empirical exercise in an image of thought presented as originary? It is not only the dimension of signification that is given ready-
made, whenever sense is conceived as a general predicate; and it is not
only the dimension of denotation that is given in the alleged relation
between sense and any determinable or individualizable object whatsoever. It is the entire dimension of manifestation, in the position of a transcendental subject, which retains the form of the person, of personal
consciousness, and of subjective identity, and which is satisfied with creating the transcendental out of the characteristics of the empirical. What
is evident in Kant, when he directly deduces the three transcendental
syntheses from corresponding psychological syntheses, is no less evident
in Husserl when he deduces an originary and transcendental "Seeing"
from perceptual "vision." (*LS* 98)

There are two problems at work here. First, the Self or Person thus
appears as the invariant within variance. For this reason, the Self or Person
which is treated as invariant comes to be understood as the condition
under which Being is individuated, whether it be in the form of God
bestowing essences or a transcendental subject organizing experience.
However, insofar as the domain of appearances comes to be treated as
the variant and the domain of the Self or Person comes to be treated as
the invariant, an external difference between the Self and appearances,
the individuated and the chaotic, comes to be established.

Second, in treating the form of sense as identical with that of the
general predicate, we seem inevitably led to a dualistic ontology as it
pertains to the relationship between the subject and the predicate. Take
the proposition "Socrates is just." If we take this to be a proposition
stating the sense of justice, how are we to think the ontological relation
between the subject and the predicate? The difficulty seems to lie in
the fact that the being of Socrates is singular and irreplaceable, while
the being of justice seems to be such that it is non-localized and can be
exemplified in a number of different individuals. This seems to lead
to the conclusion that there are two types of being: the being of individual entities which are all singular and irreplaceable, and the being of
predicates or general universals that can be exemplified in a number of
different cases. In short, I can equally well ask "What is Socrates?" and
"What is justice?" But this leads to the difficult and insoluble question
of how the two orders of being are related.

It is this problem that will lead Deleuze to adopt a stoic conception
of sense. From the stoic point of view, sense is not to be located in the
predicate affixed to the subject, but in the verb. Consequently, when
stating the sense of the proposition "the tree turns green," we do not

locate the sense in the general predicate "green" but rather uncover the sense by stating that "the tree greens." Initially this move might appear bizarre, but if we look closer we will see that it undermines the whole problem of predication. When treating sense in terms of verbs, we avoid the entire problem of attribution in that we are now able to locate the sense in the being alone to which it pertains. We no longer say that greenness is and the tree is, but that the tree greens.[6] Consequently there are not two orders of beings, but one order of being organized around events. This allows Deleuze to assert the univocity of being without worries of a gap or separation between being and beings in that he is able to claim that being is. Being is here conceived of as the event that gathers together all other events in a unity or open whole. Unfortunately these points will not receive here the detailed treatment they deserve.

At this point, the precise nature of the transcendental problem Deleuze is dealing with becomes clear. In the case of empiricism, metaphysics, and transcendental philosophy, the empiricist fallacy arises as a result of being unable to give a proper account of individuation. Empiricism fails to explain the individuation of beings because it falls prey to all the difficulties of nominal or material definition which tend to erase rather than disclose the being of difference presiding over appearances or phenomena. On the other hand, metaphysics and transcendental philosophy are only able to proceed by granting themselves a ready-made individuat*ed* being in the form of the Self or the Person (in much the same way that signification finds itself assuming a ready-made denotation), rather than an account of individuation *as such*. It is in precisely this sense that metaphysics and transcendental philosophy can be said to restrict themselves to accounts of simple conditioning. Whether we are talking about otherworldly essences or the conditions of possible experience, these essences and conditions are thought of as merely conditioning that which they enter into communication with in an external and indifferent manner. As Deleuze puts it,

> When we define signification as the condition of truth, we give it a characteristic which it shares with sense, and which is already a characteristic of sense. But how does signification assume this characteristic? How does it make use of it? In discussing the conditions of truth, we raise ourselves above the true and the false, since a false proposition also has a sense or signification. But at the same time, we define this superior condition solely as the possibility for the proposition to be true. The possibility is nothing other than the *form of possibility* of the proposition itself . . . Kant even invented two new forms of possibility, the transcendental

and the moral. But by whatever manner one defines form, it is an odd procedure since it involves rising from the conditioned to the condition, in order to think of the condition as the simple possibility of the conditioned. Here one rises to a foundation, but that which is founded remains what it was, independently of the operation which founded it and unaffected by it. Thus denotation remains external to the order which conditions it, and the true and the false remain indifferent to the principle which determines the possibility of the one, by allowing it only to subsist in its former relation to the other. One is perpetually referred from the conditioned to the condition, and also from the condition to the conditioned. (*LS* 18–19)

Insofar as sense gets conceived (1) in terms of conditioning and (2) in terms of the form of truth, it ends up modeling itself on the very phenomena it seeks to explain in such a way that the conditioned remains indifferent to that which conditions it. By a strange sleight of hand, the conditions end up merely doubling that which they ought to account for in a way that is both redundant and suspect. But more fundamentally, since these conditions are conceived under the *form* of truth, they become entirely abstract and unable to account for the production of the false. Accounts based on conditioning can only account for experience in the most general sense such that real or actual experience becomes merely accidental. Moreover, such accounts prove unable to account for the power and efficacy of the false in any other terms but lack, absence, and negation. In other words, they are unable to explain the power and meaning of the false *as such*, but can only account for it in terms of what it is not.

The solution to a deep mystery of Deleuze's thought comes into relief here. In nearly all of Deleuze's texts one finds detailed discussions of the problem of individuation. In *Bergsonism* he devotes an entire chapter to it when discussing the *élan vital*. In *Difference and Repetition* he devotes two chapters to it at the end of the text. In *The Logic of Sense* he devotes four entire series to it (two series for static genesis, and two for dynamic genesis). Finally, in *The Fold: Leibniz and the Baroque*, he devotes yet another chapter to individuation. It is likely that these instances can be multiplied. At any rate, the question of individuation has all the appearances of being a central and crucial concern in Deleuze's thought. Yet strangely, Deleuze's extended discussion of individuation has received very little attention in the secondary literature. Often it goes undiscussed at all. When it is discussed commentators generally devote only a few pages to it. Badiou doesn't worry himself about it at all. No doubt, the lack of discussion surrounding individuation arises because often the purpose of Deleuze's account of individuation is enigmatic and appears critically suspect.

On the one hand, Deleuze more often than not proceeds abruptly into a discussion of the process of individuation without explaining to his readers why such an account is necessary. On the other hand, Deleuze often sounds as if he has crossed from critical philosophy, which restricts itself to claims about the conditions for the possibility of experience along with their limits, to speculative claims that seem to speak beyond the limits of experience. This is especially the case in *Difference and Repetition,* where one is utterly baffled as to why Deleuze feels compelled to discuss individuation in detail, to discuss how individuals are actualized, when he seems to have adequately solved the problems of difference and repetition in the first two chapters of the text. Yet it is precisely Deleuze's critique of empiricism and the Image of thought which obligates him to give an account of individuation capable of avoiding the defects of external difference and of accounting for the conditions of real rather than *all possible* experience. In other words, Deleuze is obligated to give us an account of the genesis or constitution of forms of experience that shows how we are able to move from the conditions of a being to the actualization of a being if he is to explain how the problems of empiricism can be avoided. As Deleuze puts it,

> For the condition of truth to avoid this defect, it ought to have an element of its own, distinct from the form of the conditioned. It ought to have *something unconditioned* capable of assuring a real genesis of denotation and of the other dimensions of the proposition. Thus the condition of truth would be defined no longer as the form of conceptual possibility, but rather as the ideational material or "stratum," that is to say, no longer as signification, but rather as sense. (*LS* 19)

Rather than simply conditioning experience, such an account would theorize the unfolding, development, or production of experience in and through experience. Once again we see how Bréhier's reading of stoic ontology is relevant here. In situating sense in the verb and events, the stoics are able to avoid treating sense as a transcendent model and posit it as immanent to the facts out of which it is exuded.

Here it is clear that the Kantian problematic or conception of critical philosophy is reversed. Like Kant, Deleuze restricts himself to experience or establishes his thought in terms of explaining the conditions which render experience actual. The aim is not simply to describe experience but to give an *account* of experience. For, as we saw in the case of sadism and masochism, the given is not sufficient to account

for the sense of experience but is rather that which must be accounted
for. However, unlike Kant, Deleuze argues for the openness, the end-
lessness of experience in such a way that we can no longer define the
limits of experience a priori. As a result, we fall prey to a transcendental
illusion not when we go beyond the limits of experience, but rather
when we illicitly universalize and naturalize a specific actualization of
real experience. Such an account would remain transcendental in that
it would still refer to genetic conditions as the transcendental factors
enabling this production of experience. As we will see later, Deleuze,
following Maïmon, locates these conditions in the differentials (in the
sense of calculus) of experience, which allows him to (1) pose a continuity between the sensible and the intelligible such that the sensible is
the intelligible and the intelligible is sensible; (2) posit a real genesis
of experience capable of going all the way to the singular individual
without a gap between concepts and intuitions; and (3) undermine the
opposition between the finite and the infinite.

The crucial difference between such an account and an account
based on conditioning is that the former would account for the actual
production of the given, rather than simply the conditioning of the giv-
en in a homogeneous medium (space and time) according to abstract
and self-identical categories or forms. Unlike a category of the understanding or a form, a differential is not *opposed* to the particular but is
continuous with it *and* is intelligible. Thus, far from being a sense-data
empiricist who bases the formations of being on the irrational surds of
experience, Deleuze is in fact a hyper-rationalist who discovers intelligibility even in the apparent chaos of the matter of intuition. In short,
in an obscure manner that we will not be able to fully clarify here, the
differentials are not *applied to* experience, but *are* the very medium of
experience. Maintaining this point is crucial for Deleuze's project. The
differentials are not representations of sensations, but are the genetic
conditions of sensations. Hence Deleuze can proudly say:

> The elementary concepts of representation are the categories defined as
> the conditions of possible experience. These, however, are too general
> or too large for the real. The net is so loose that the largest fish pass
> through. No wonder, then, that aesthetics should be divided into two
> irreducible domains: that of the theory of the sensible which captures
> only the real's conformity with possible experience; and that of the the-
> ory of the beautiful, which deals with the reality of the real in so far as it
> is thought. Everything changes once we determine the conditions of real
> experience which are not larger than the conditioned and which differ
> in kind from the categories: the two senses of the aesthetic become one,

to the point where the being of the sensible reveals itself in the work of art, while at the same time the work of art appears as experimentation. (*DR* 68)

Transcendental empiricism reconciles the two halves of the aesthetic insofar as the aesthetic of receptivity, of sensibility, of the denoted, is also a produced or authentic creation. In other words, receptivity is no longer receptivity, but has become spontaneity, productivity. Later we will see why this is so, but for now we merely point it out. It is also able to account for the conditions of real, rather than possible experience, because it treats diversity or the given as the result of a genesis from differentials rather than the passive recipient of conditioning by abstract categories.

In light of this, illumination is shed on the relationship between the two chapters on difference and repetition and the chapters on individuation in *Difference and Repetition*. In Kant, the first *Critique* proceeds through an analytic of intuition, the categories, and finally to an account of the various modes of synthesis. In Deleuze an analogous structure is at work. The chapter on difference corresponds to the transcendental aesthetic, while the chapter on repetition corresponds to the transcendental analytic. We can thus represent the analogy between the structure of Deleuze's project and Kant's as shown in table 2.

In other words, rather than passing through the intermediary of the categories, Deleuze proceeds directly to the synthesis of difference through repetition as a way of accounting for the genesis or structure of experience. This shift is significant, for as Deleuze says, repetition is not based on generality, but is a repetition of the singular (*DR* 1). Insofar as repetition is always a repetition of the singular, Deleuze is able to articulate the conditions of real rather than all possible experience. Here experience is no longer pervaded by generality and sameness, but instead takes on the singularity and creativity proper to it. However, this creativity is no longer a singular irrationality, but is rather a novel

	Aesthetic	Analytic	Syntheses
Kant	Time/space	Categories	Axioms, anticipations, analogies
Deleuze	Difference in itself	The three modes of repetition	(Indi)-different/cia-tion

Table 2. Schematic representation of the similarities and differences between Deleuze's and Kant's critical projects.

intelligible structure. Finally, the chapters on individuation provide an
account of the actualization or genesis of experience resulting from the
syntheses of repetition exercised upon difference or the differentials
composing the experience. If the account of repetition is not sufficient
to account for the production of experience, this is because Deleuze
must demonstrate that repetition does not simply condition experience passively, but rather, he must show how experience is unfolded
genetically in a process of actualization. In other words, he must demonstrate how these syntheses account for the givenness of the given for
experience.

Variations of Difference: The Topological Essences of Intuition

However, do we not here fall once again into all the aporias of
nominalism in a form even more radical than that described by the
classical empiricists? In other words, in seeking to account for the
conditions of real rather than *all possible* experience, do we not fall into
another type of nominalism which repeats, once again, all the difficulties
we encountered in the first place? Recall our criticism of transcendental
philosophy and empiricism for not being able to account for the internal
differences constituting or determining a phenomenon like masochism.
In giving ourselves the task of accounting for real experience, do we
not inevitably end up treating each actualized or generated being as a
nominal entity, different from all the rest? And if this is the case, does
not Deleuze find himself in the position of being unable to account
for the principle underlying phenomena like masochism as well? A
moment's reflection is sufficient to demonstrate that this is only the
case if we continue to conceive of the relationship between the real
and the conditions of the real in terms of matter and form, or external
difference.

In accounting for real rather than all possible experience, what
Deleuze is after is not an account of each individual entity, but rather
a set of *variations* capable of defining a series or set of beings. In short,
the variations of difference must be conceived as a unity of difference
by virtue of having a common principle of production underlying the
variations. In other words, the conditions of real experience are what
might be called morphological, topological, or genetic essences which
are capable of accounting for a series of variations which we find in real
experience. Here we find, once again, one of the guiding threads of
Deleuze's choice of calculus in thinking the production of experience.

As Mary Tiles points out, the calculus thinks the being of a being in its production rather than its static completion. It is this that distinguishes post-Cartesian mathematical thought from Euclidean thought. As Tiles remarks,

> The pressures which brought down the edifice of classical, Aristotelean finitism did indeed come from within mathematics and physics. Ultimately they derive from the demand for a numerical, practically applicable handling of continuous magnitudes and in particular of continuous change (including, of course, motion).[7]

It is precisely these continuous changes that Deleuze attempts to think with his genetic conditions or topological essences. Of great interest here is the fact that what can be thought mathematically far outstrips what can be intuited. Thus, for instance, Tiles refers to "pathological" functions discovered by Fourier whose function could be algebraically expressed in terms of infinite sums but whose graphs could not be pictured.[8] The very possibility of such functions suggests that there is something deeply amiss with the Kantian claim that all thought must be in the service of intuition and the Heideggerian privilege of finitude. Mathematics far outstrips the capacities of finite intuition. The Heideggerian might claim that mathematics represents the greatest inflection of "enframing," yet it is nonetheless the case that mathematics is a real possibility of human experience and thought.

Deleuze describes something like a topological or morphological essence in his early essay on Bergson when he remarks that

> the different colors are no longer *under* a concept, but the nuances or degrees of the concept itself, degrees of difference itself and not differences of degree. The relation is no longer one of subsumption, but of participation. White light is still a universal, but a concrete universal, which enables us to understand the particular because it is itself at the extreme of the particular. Just as things have become the nuances or degrees of the concept, the concept itself has become the thing. It is also a universal thing, we could say, since the objects are sketched therein as so many degrees, but a concrete thing, not a kind or a generality. ("BCD" 54)

These genetic essences contain within them all the possible variations of the phenomena in question on the basis of a sort of topological diagram capable of expressing the becoming of the essence, but are also no larger than that for which they serve as a condition, for they are able to specify the precise conditions under which this particular form of diversity is produced. Furthermore, given that the concept is itself treated as a thing (Deleuze here sounds reminiscent of Hegel), the conditions of experience neatly evade the form-matter binary, effectively closing off the possibility of treating concepts in terms of external differences. For the moment, I must defer discussion of these genetic essences to a later chapter in this book, since they require a detailed analysis of the process of individuation. Right now, it is sufficient to note that these morphological essences neatly evade the forced choice between nominalism and realism in a way that allows us to maintain the best of both worlds. Moreover, this account allows Deleuze to navigate the aporia surrounding the active and the passive, the conditioned and the conditioning.

Nonetheless, it seems that there is yet another problem which Deleuze must contend with. What are we to make of the difference between external and empirical difference and internal and transcendental difference? Does not Deleuze reproduce an external and thereby empirical difference *between* external and internal difference in his attempt to formulate a genetic account of real experience? It is perhaps this question, above all, which differentiates Deleuze's position from that of Bergson. In Bergson it is always a question of dividing between two or more tendencies, one containing all the differences in kind, the other containing all the differences of degree. For Bergson, it is always a matter of time as opposed to space, of matter opposed to memory, of living matter opposed to inert matter. As a result, Bergson perpetually finds himself caught within dualisms, in such a way that the gulf between the internal and the external comes to appear insurmountable.

To be sure, Deleuze perpetually attempts to demonstrate that Bergson does in fact establish a monism; but the manner in which this demonstration proceeds is surprising. Whenever Deleuze takes up the issue of Bergson's monism, he always proceeds with caution, claiming that "Bergson does not himself say this, but he seems to suggest that." Moreover, when discussing his works on Bergson he claims:

> I suppose the main way I coped with it at the time [being forced to write histories of philosophy] was to see the history of philosophy as a sort of buggery or (it comes to the same thing) immaculate conception. I saw myself as taking an author from behind and giving him a child that would be his own offspring, yet monstrous. It was really important for it to be his own child, because the author had to actually say all I had him saying. But the child was bound to be monstrous too, because it resulted from all sorts of shifting, slipping, dislocations, and hidden emissions that I really enjoyed. I think my book on Bergson's a good example. (*N* 6)

Given Deleuze's hesitation in discussing Bergson's monism, along with his claim that his writings on Bergson are a good example of what he means by creating a monstrous child, it seems clear that the question of how extensive difference is generated from intensive or internal difference is more Deleuze's than Bergson's. Consequently, in what follows, we shall have to trace this movement in order to demonstrate how Deleuze avoids falling prey to implicating an external difference between extensive difference and intensive difference. This discussion will also have the much more important consequence of explaining how Deleuze is able to account for the Image of thought itself, and the critique that follows from it. In other words, it is necessary that a genetic account of the Image of thought be given as well . . . that an account be given of why such an image characterizes our experience, and of why we necessarily fall prey to it.

In light of the foregoing, it now becomes possible to see that Deleuze's position is not based on a renunciation of transcendental thought and an affirmation of the empirical. Rather, in a manner somewhat reminiscent of phenomenology, transcendental empiricism paradoxically offers itself as a radical critique of empiricism with the aim of articulating a transcendental philosophy which no longer traces the transcendental from the empirical. However, it is precisely here, at the site of this project, that one of the central tensions of Deleuze's thought arises. On the one hand, Deleuze locates empiricism as the place of transcendental illusion. On the other hand, Deleuze claims that philosophy must be empiricist if it is to escape this error. If Deleuze is not openly contradicting himself, then it is clear that he must be attributing two distinct senses to the term *empiricism*. Or is it that empiricism is the skeptical fallout of our inability to completely execute the project of transcendental philosophy?

Following Maïmon, we can say that mathematical thought evades the oppositions between the finite and the infinite, the passive and the active, the spontaneous and the receptive. Mathematical thought is akin to the thought of God, to infinite thought, in that it seems to produce its objects of thought in the very act of thinking them. Not only does mathematical thought allow me to intuit objects that I have never intuited in receptive experience, but it also allows me to think objects that *cannot* be intuited in receptive experience, as in the case of "pathological" functions and actually infinite sets.

In this connection, Mary Tiles's example of irregular, pathological functions whose graphs cannot be drawn is to the point. These mathematical properties have important philosophical consequences that ought not to be ignored, and which it would be dishonest to ignore on

the basis of having already made a choice for a certain conception of
intuition and thinking or what constitutes authentic experience: First,
they tend to undermine the dogma shared by both empiricism and Kant
which holds that knowledge must be founded in intuition. This holds
for phenomenology as well. Kant had argued that mathematical judgments would not be possible if they did not find support in intuition.
Yet an examination of mathematics itself reveals that so little of our
mathematical reasoning is actually founded on intuition in this way as
to undermine the strongest argument supporting Kant's claims about
synthetic a priori judgments and the Copernican revolution. Second,
the ability to think objects that have not been experienced through receptivity tends to undermine the distinction between spontaneity and
receptivity, pointing the way to conceiving of intuition itself as productive. Finally, mathematical thought tends to undermine the opposition
between the finite and the infinite by enabling us to think the infinite
and engage in a mathematics of the infinite, thereby calling into question the limits that Kant and phenomenology have defined for experience in terms of the premise of finitude as the ground from which
philosophy must begin.

However, while mathematics suggests a way of conceiving intuition
such that it is no longer comprehended as irrational, unintelligible receptivity, it is nonetheless true that very little of our experience has the
luminous clarity possessed by mathematical thought. Consequently,
if we are to claim that the phenomena of experience *are* differentials
(in the sense of calculus) and thus intelligible, then we must explain
why conscious experience nonetheless so seldom expresses this intelligibility. In short, we must show how finitude differs in *degree*, not kind,
from the infinite. This, then, will be the empirical moment of transcendental empiricism. While all experience may be produced by differentials—may be the integration of differentials—not all experience can
be deduced or constructed in mathematical thought by subjects such as
ourselves. Thus transcendental empiricism implies an experimentalism
and a limited skepticism. Yet how these two positions can be reconciled
with one another is yet to be demonstrated. We must unravel this apparent paradox and articulate why transcendental thought must become
empirical if the fallacy of empiricism is to be avoided.

As I hope to show, the necessity of this gesture arises from Deleuze's critique of the primacy of the subject and its self-presence to
itself, which entails that we can no longer rely on the supremely individuated contents of the Self to determine or arrive at the conditions of
real experience. It is here that Deleuze diverges from phenomenology,
though it could still be argued that his position is in fact a radicalization

of phenomenology. As a result of this critique of the subject, it follows that we can only arrive at insight into the conditions of experience on the basis of a unique and special *experience* of difference. Consequently, our first task will be to determine what Deleuze conceives by difference, and then to develop a "phenomenology" of this experience which gives us access to the conditions of real experience. Once these two tasks are completed, we will then show why these conditions cannot be traced back to the giving intuition of a subject (Husserl). The completion of this project will culminate in the final chapter, where we outline Deleuze's account of individuation and show how it gives rise to the empiricist illusions characterizing the Image of thought.

Bergsonian Intuition and Internal Difference

Internal Difference

From the foregoing, we are able to determine why Deleuze paradoxically characterizes his position as both a transcendental *empiricism* and a *transcendental* empiricism. On the one hand, it is necessary that his position be a transcendental *empiricism* insofar as we cannot methodologically begin with the assumption of a supremely individuated world, of a world already given whether in the form of the subject or the object, without falling into all the difficulties of external difference and mere conditioning on the part of the understanding. Overcoming such a perspective requires education, inquiry, learning, and thus constitutes a sort of empiricism. As Deleuze puts it,

> Nothing can be said in advance, one cannot prejudge the outcome of research: it may be that some well-known faculties—too well known— turn out to have no proper limit, no verbal adjective, because they are imposed and have an exercise only under the form of common sense. It may turn out, on the other hand, that new faculties arise, faculties which were repressed by that form of common sense. For a doctrine in general, there is nothing regrettable in this uncertainty about the outcome of research, this complexity in the study of the particular case of each faculty: on the contrary, transcendental empiricism is the only way to avoid tracing the transcendental from the outlines of the empirical. (*DR* 143–44)

If we are to avoid merely repeating a set of subjective presuppositions underlying the constitution of our own personhood and relation to objectivity, then it is necessary that we adopt some sort of empiricism which avoids judging the outcome of research and inquiry in advance.

What, according to Deleuze, are these subjective presuppositions? How can we recognize them?

> What is a subjective or implicit presupposition: it has the form of "Everybody knows . . .". Everybody knows, in a pre-philosophical and pre-

conceptual manner . . . everybody knows what it means to think and to be . . . As a result, when the philosopher says "I think therefore I am," he can assume that the universality of his premises—namely, what it means to be and to think—will be implicitly understood, and that no one can deny that to doubt is to think, and to think is to be . . . *Everybody knows, no one can deny,* is the form of representation and the discourse of the representative. When philosophy rests its beginning upon such implicit or subjective presuppositions, it can claim innocence, since it has kept nothing back—except, of course, the essential—namely the form of discourse. (*DR* 129–30)

It is not a question of truth or falsity, but, as Deleuze says, the *form of discourse*. The presuppositions may be true or they may be false; we do not know, because such claims are not yet grounded in their essential being. And this lack of knowing, this not knowing, is the essential point. As Deleuze will say elsewhere, "What a profound and intelligent man says has value in itself, by its manifest content, by its explicit, objective, and elaborated signification; but we shall derive little enough from it, nothing but abstract possibilities, if we have not been able to reach other truths by other paths" (*PS* 21). Such truths have value because they are clear and explicit, and thus easily make sense. But they make sense, they are explicit, they are easily recognized, precisely because they are based on subjective presuppositions or what "everyone knows." In other words, these claims are only clear and explicit because they reflect a form of discourse, because they *repeat* a form of discourse.

As a result, far from being based on some sign of truth, they are instead based on recognition. "The ideas of the intelligence are valid only because of their explicit, hence *conventional,* signification" (*PS* 16; my italics). Only the practice of a sort of empiricism can protect us from such subjective presuppositions, because only empiricism assumes that it does not know in advance. This, of course, does not mean that empiricism does not itself fall prey to subjective presuppositions. But empiricism, at least, fosters an attitude which attempts to avoid judging the outcome of research in advance.

On the other hand, such an approach must also be transcendental insofar as it seeks to determine the conditions under which beings are individuated, their internal being or essence, and not simply their empirical outlines traced from subjects and objects. "If philosophy is to have a positive and direct relation with things, it is only to the extent that it claims to grasp the thing itself in what it is, in its difference from all that it is not, which is to say in its *internal difference*" ("BCD" 42–43).

We shall have to determine what Deleuze means by "thing"—a term which is misleading insofar as it suggests we are interested in the composite *given* in experience—but for the moment it is sufficient to note that what is of importance is the transcendental difference, the internal difference, presiding over the genesis of experience. What is this essence? "It is a difference, the absolute and ultimate Difference. Difference is what constitutes being, what makes us conceive being" (*PS* 41).

> But what is an absolute, ultimate difference? Not an empirical difference between two things or two objects, always extrinsic . . . It is something in a subject, something like the presence of a final quality at the heart of a subject: an internal difference, "*a qualitative difference* that there is in the way the world looks to us . . ." . . . The essences are veritable monads, each defined by the viewpoint to which it expresses the world, each viewpoint itself referring to an ultimate quality at the heart of the monad. (*PS* 41; modified)

What we seek is not the empirical difference characterizing the thing extrinsically in terms of something else, but the internal difference presiding over the genesis of a world. Hence the paradoxical term *transcendental empiricism*. On the one hand, we cannot anticipate what these differences will be in advance and must thus resort to a sort of empiricism. On the other hand, these differences are not what is *given* in experience, but rather, as Deleuze says elsewhere, that by which the given is given.

Bergsonian Intuition

From the standpoint of inquiry, Deleuze places us in a very awkward position. On the one hand, the level of empirical or *actualized* experience presents us with nothing but composites or differences in degree, and thus is not a suitable domain for determining the conditions under which experience of a particular type is possible.

> Things, products, results are always *mixtures*. Space will never show, intelligence will never find, anything but mixtures, a mixture of the closed and the open, of the geometrical order and the vital order, of perception and affection, of perception and memory . . . And what must be understood is that no doubt the mixture is a blend of tendencies which differ in nature, but, as such, it is a state of things in which it is impos-

> sible to establish any difference of nature. The mixture is what we see
> from the point of where nothing differs in nature. ("BCD" 45)

When we begin with the composites or mixtures characterizing *actualized* experience, we cannot help but discover homogeneity, differences in degree, identity, sameness, resemblances. We find ourselves unable to determine internal differences characterizing phenomena such as memory, perception, the animal and the vegetable. Each comes to appear as if it only differed in magnitude from the other. We end up confusing memory with perception and perception with memory in such a way that we are no longer able to say what either is.

Deleuze refers to this approach to determining the conditions under which experience is possible as the fallacy of "tracing the transcendental from the empirical." Take the example of Kant:

> Of all philosophers, Kant is the one who discovers the prodigious domain
> of the transcendental. He is the analogue of a great explorer—not of
> another world, but of the upper and lower reaches of this one. However,
> what does he do? In the first edition of the *Critique of Pure Reason* he de-
> scribes in detail three syntheses which measure the respective contribu-
> tions of the thinking faculties, all culminating in the third, that of recogni-
> tion, which is expressed in the form of the unspecified object as correlate
> of the "I think" to which all the faculties are related. It is clear that, in this
> manner, Kant traces the so-called transcendental structures from the em-
> pirical acts of a psychological consciousness: the transcendental synthesis
> of apprehension is directly induced from an empirical apprehension and
> so on. In order to hide this all too obvious procedure, Kant suppressed
> this text in the second edition. Although it is better hidden, the tracing
> method, with all its "psychologism," nevertheless subsists. (*DR* 135)

One would be mistaken to think that it is the three syntheses in the A edition's deduction that Deleuze is objecting to here. While the syntheses of apprehension, reproduction, and recognition do indeed appear all too psychologistic and leave us baffled as to how Kant can, on their basis, establish the synthetic a priori propositions he seeks, this criticism is secondary. Rather, if Deleuze is led to criticize Kant for tracing the transcendental from the empirical, it is insofar as this leads Kant to postulate an "unspecified" notion of the object and the subject which allows him to maintain their self-identity. In short, Kant is able to establish the *quid facti* question that concepts apply to intuitions, but not the *quid juris* question of *how* concepts can apply to intuitions. According to Deleuze, Kant, who proposes to give us the conditions of experience, ends up reducing all of experience to differences of degree in that he demands that all experience must unfold in the homogeneous mediums of space and time, and is unable to provide the sufficient reason for real experience in the myriad forms that it takes. If this is the case, then it is because, as we shall see, the difference between concepts and intuitions is a difference in degree rather than kind. Everything becomes an abstract object or an abstract subject in such a way that all differences among subjects and objects become accidental and secondary. Nor can we begin with the primacy of a self-identical subject, with an analysis of the structure of lived experience, with the immanence of the contents of our consciousness to ourselves. For here, again, we arrive at all the difficulties of reducing experience to simple differences in degree. Unable to refer to the domain of actualized empirical experience in the form of objects or the contents of a transcendental consciousness, we seem to be at a loss as to where to begin. What is needed is some point of beginning that breaks up the unity of the object while still serving as its sufficient condition and which calls into question the primacy of the person.

In his two early works "Bergson's Conception of Difference" and *Bergsonism* we find the beginnings of such an approach in what Deleuze calls the *method* of intuition. We ought not to assume that by "intuition" Deleuze means the direct and immediate apprehension by a knowing subject of itself, of its conscious states, of other minds, of an external world, of universals, of values, or of rational truths. In seeking to explain how we come to "know" internal difference, Deleuze does not *appeal* to an immediate intuition shared by all of us, but rather treats intuition as a *practice* or method. If, on the contrary, Deleuze advanced his position on the basis of an appeal to intuition as an immediate given, then we would find ourselves returned to all the difficulties of tracing the transcendental from the empirical, of determining the transcendental in terms of the given, since what is immediate is the empirical or the mixtures characterizing experience. Strangely, then, intuition, for Deleuze, is mediated insofar as it involves a plurality of acts of cognition (*B* 14). In contrast to the notion of intuition as immediate knowledge, Deleuze claims that

> *intuition* is the method of Bergsonism. Intuition is neither a feeling, an inspiration, nor a disorderly sympathy, but a fully developed method, one of the most fully developed methods in philosophy. It has its strict rules, constituting that which Bergson calls "precision" in philosophy. (*B* 13)

While Deleuze's concept of intuition shares affinities with what has been called "intuition" throughout the history of philosophy, it differs in the crucial respect that it must be practiced and performed, that it requires a discipline and "training," rather than being an immediate given. In this respect, it is much closer to phenomenological methods of analysis than traditional appeals to intuition. On the other hand, intuition is not Deleuze's final word regarding "method."

> All methods have an object. What then is the object of intuition as method, as practice? . . . Intuition is the *jouissance* of difference. But it is not only the pleasure of the result of the method, it is the method itself. As such, it is not a unique act, it proposes to us a plurality of acts, a plurality of efforts and directions. Intuition in its first impulse [*effort*] is the determination of differences of nature. And since these differences are between things, it is a matter of a veritable distribution, of a problem of distribution. Reality must be divided according to its articulations, and Bergson cites Plato's famous text on carving and the good cook. ("BCD" 43)

Intuition cannot be said to be an immediate relationship to reality or being because it presupposes a plurality of acts requiring an effort and therefore involves mediations. Rather, in a manner reminiscent of Plato, intuition is instead a method of division, a way of making divisions proper to being. When practicing intuition or this method of division, it is not simply any difference that matters or is of concern. For instance, we are not concerned with the differences between tables and chairs or blue and green. These differences are of course important, but do not themselves constitute the object of intuition. They are external differences or differences "between," and thus not the proper objects of intuition. "Intuition . . . methodologically, already presupposes *duration*" (*B* 13).

Internal Difference and the Intensive Multiplicity of Duration

What we seek is not difference as it manifests itself between two things, but difference in itself, difference differing from itself, difference as it can only be contained within duration or time unfolding itself. Such difference is movement, but in a very specific sense. "Movement is no longer the character of something, but has itself taken on a substantial character, it presupposes nothing else, no moving object" ("BCD" 48). What is this movement that no longer requires an object? How are we to conceive it?

> Movement is qualitative change and qualitative change is movement. In short, duration is what differs, and what differs is no longer what dif-

fers from something else, but what differs from itself. What differs has become itself a thing, a *substance*. Bergson's thesis could be expressed in this way: real time is alteration, and alteration is substance. Difference of nature is thus no longer between two things or rather two tendencies, difference of nature is itself a thing, one tendency opposing itself to the other. ("BCD" 48)

Consequently, movement here is not change of position in three-dimensional space, but qualitative transformation or continuous variation. What is it about movement, qualitative change, or duration such that it differs from itself without contradicting itself, giving rise to alterity, or negating itself? So long as we think this form of movement in terms of change of place, we will not be able to understand the nature of Deleuze's claim because change of place is only a change in degree, since change in space still remains a spatial change. Moreover, in change of place the being remains the same without undergoing any substantial change. Rather, we must think duration or movement as the continuous, qualitative alteration that a tendency undergoes in the process of its moving. Bergson elucidates this point masterfully in a long passage from *Time and Free Will:*

> Think of what you experience on suddenly perceiving a shooting star: in this extremely rapid motion there is a natural and instinctive separation between the space traversed, which appears to you under the form of a line of fire, and the absolutely indivisible sensation of motion or mobility. A rapid gesture, made with one's eyes shut, will assume for consciousness the form of a purely qualitative sensation as long as there is no thought of the space traversed. In a word, there are two elements to be distinguished in motion, the space traversed and the act by which we traverse it, the successive positions and the synthesis of these positions. The first of these elements is a homogenous quality: the second has no reality except in a consciousness: it is a quality or an intensity, whichever you prefer. But here again we meet with a case of endosmosis, an intermingling of the purely intensive sensation of mobility with the extensive representation of the space traversed. On the one hand we attribute to the motion the divisibility of the space which it traverses, forgetting that it is quite possible to divide an *object,* but not an *act:* and on the other hand we accustom ourselves to projecting this act itself into space, to applying it to the whole of the line which the moving body traverses, in a word, to solidifying it: as if this localizing of a *progress* in space did not amount to asserting that, even outside consciousness, the past co-exists along with the present![1]

Movement, when apprehended from the inside as act, manifests itself as indivisible while nonetheless containing qualitative change. On the other hand, when we apprehend movement externally, in terms of the space traversed, we treat the object as self-identical and discern change only as a change from one place to another. The difference between one place and another is only an external difference, and thus not the internal, determining, difference we are seeking. Position, change of position, is not a difference that touches the being of the being, but only externally relates the being to other beings in the homogeneous medium of space.

What is important is that the act, the alteration, the qualitative motion, be thought in its continuity. In other words, the entire motion belongs to the act in such a way that we cannot really say that the motion contains parts, contradictions, negations, or alterity with itself. For instance, when I move my hand from point A to B it is internally experienced as one complete continuity which contains difference while being indivisible. By contrast, when I view the movement externally, from the point of view of space, I discern it only as passing through a number of points such that it could halt or change trajectory at any one of these points without changing what it is. Viewed internally, it is a pure alteration that differs from itself without the various moments being external to themselves.

Here we find yet another affinity between Deleuze and the stoics. As Bréhier points out, the stoics conceive causality not as mechanical transfers of force between entities, but as an internal force characterizing the duration or history of the object in the process of its unfolding.[2] Is this not the internal act or duration of Bergsonian becoming? Deleuze expresses this becoming of duration as an identity of difference and difference of identity.

> When I say "Alice becomes larger," I mean that she becomes larger than she was. By the same token, however, she becomes smaller than she is now. Certainly, she is not bigger and smaller at the same time. She is larger now; she was smaller before. But it is at the same moment that one becomes larger than one was and smaller than one becomes. This is the simultaneity of a becoming whose characteristic is to elude the present. Insofar as it eludes the present, becoming does not tolerate the separation or the distinction of before and after, or of past and future. It pertains to the essence of becoming to move and to pull in both directions at once: Alice does not grow without shrinking, and vice versa. (*LS* 1)

It is not because becoming is inherently contradictory that it moves in both directions at once. As we have seen, contradiction and opposition are quite foreign to the duration because of its continuous nature. The notions of contradiction and opposition require distinct terms, while a tendency contains no distinct terms.

Moreover, the notions of contradiction and opposition are purely representational in character and thus empiricist. As Deleuze puts it,

> Representation [is] defined by certain elements: identity with regard to concepts, opposition with regard to judgment, resemblance with regard to objects. The identity of the unspecified concept constitutes the form of the Same with regard to recognition. The determination of the concept implies the comparison between possible predicates and their opposites in a regressive and progressive double series, traversed on the one side by remembrance and on the other by an imagination the aim of which is to rediscover or re-create (memorial-imaginative reproduction). Analogy bears either upon the highest determinable concepts or on the relations between determinate concepts and their receptive objects. It calls upon the power of distribution present in judgment. As for the object of the concept, in itself or in relation to other objects, it relies upon resemblance as a requirement of perceptual continuity. (*DR* 137–38)

For minds accustomed to thinking of representation in terms of "man's glassy essence," this definition might appear perplexing insofar as it seems to offer no reference to consciousness. However, Deleuze is led to define representation in this way insofar as both philosophies of reflection and classical or pre-critical philosophies make the same set of assumptions regarding the relationship between concepts and objects. In both cases, the relationship between concepts and objects is defined in terms of recognition, which is perhaps the central defining feature of empirical consciousness. This manifests itself clearly in the cases of the concepts of opposition and contradiction. In both cases, these concepts contain the notion of negativity deep within them. Hence, opposition is defined as a relation between two things that are not like one another, while contradiction implies a symmetrical relation between two terms entering into a negative relation.

But here it is clear that it is only from the standpoint of empirical consciousness that the notion of negativity can arise. Only from the perspective of empirical consciousness, defined by recognition and a collaboration of the faculties of memory and sensibility, do things seem to pass away and come to be. But this passing-away and coming-to-be can only result from the affirmation of an object in the past such that it can appear to be negated. In other words, it is an effect of affirmation.

Put differently, an object from past experience comes to be affirmed normatively as the model of experience and is used to judge subsequent experience. On the basis of this affirmation, experience comes to be comprehended on the basis of coming-to-be and passing-away rather than on continuous transformation. On the other hand, viewed from the perspective of duration, becoming manifests itself as a continuity without negation. Becoming is not paradoxical because it contains contradiction and opposition within it, but rather, because becoming as act or in its internal nature contains the entire series in which the becoming unfolds in an identity with itself, it takes on this paradoxical nature. Such becomings are never purely present, but rather maintain themselves or insist over an expanse of time. The simplicity of the act is what allows us to call it "substance," while it is the alterity of the act as it unfolds in a series that allows us to say that it differs from itself. We thus find another parallel between Deleuze's thought and differential calculus. From the standpoint of coming-to-be and passing-away, experience describes a continuously unfolding motion internal to its changing velocities that is not a change in position but rather a qualitative transformation.

Intensive and Extensive Multiplicities

Deleuze thus refers to duration, which contains all the differences in kind or internal differences, as that which changes in nature whenever it is divided, and he calls it a multiplicity. A multiplicity is neither one nor multiple, but a sort of unity representing a heterogeneous becoming.

> Duration divides up and does so constantly: that is why it is a *multiplicity*. But it does not divide up without changing in kind, it changes in kind in the process of dividing up: this is why it is a nonnumerical multiplicity, where we can speak of "indivisibles" at each stage of the division. There is *other* without there being *several*; number exists only potentially. (*B* 42)

Here Deleuze and Bergson follow Aristotle in their solution of Zeno's paradoxes. Where Zeno conceived of space and time as being *actually* composed of an infinite number of points and instants, thus rendering the concept of motion incoherent, Aristotle, Bergson, and Deleuze treat time and space as only being potentially infinite. In short, the positions and instants of time and space do not preexist the acts of dividing them. It is for this reason that Deleuze claims that the whole is open rather than a closed totality. However, here it bears noting that while I may not be able to intuit it, when we speak of entities like lines and number series, we do not conceive of them as being only potentially infinite—which would be to confuse epistemic properties with ontological properties of mathematical entities—but as actually infinite. In this respect, we might express some reservations about the manner in which Deleuze and Bergson endorse Aristotle's solution to the continuum problem set forth by Zeno. It is on precisely this issue that Badiou will issue his challenge to Deleuze. Where Deleuze-Bergson endorses a potential infinity as a way of countering the philosophies of finitude, Badiou sides with actual infinity, which becomes possible to think in light of Cantor's advances in set theory. Unfortunately, I am unable to deal with this issue in greater detail here, but merely note it as a problem.

Perhaps the best way to think multiplicities is in terms of the concept of structure. What is definitive of structure is not the notion of signifiers or language, but rather the idea of a set of elements characterized only in terms of their *relations* to other elements or in terms of relational identities. We could also say that the central characteristic of structure is the *immanence* of elements with respect to one another in relations of reciprocal conditioning. Insofar as the elements are all mutually dependent upon one another for their being, we cannot say that a structure is many. However, insofar as the structure consists of a set of ordered relations and elements which are in some sense distinct, we also cannot say that the structure is one. In other words, structures know no center.

Deleuze distinguishes between two sorts of multiplicities:

> One is represented by space (or rather, if all the nuances are taken into account, by the impure combination of homogeneous time): It is a multiplicity of exteriority, of simultaneity, of juxtaposition, of order, of quantitative differentiation, of *difference in degree;* it is a numerical multiplicity, *discontinuous and actual.* The other type of multiplicity appears in duration: It is an internal multiplicity of succession, of fusion, of organization, of heterogeneity, of qualitative discrimination, or of *difference in kind;* it is a *virtual and continuous* multiplicity that cannot be reduced to numbers. (*B* 38)

In clarifying the difference between these two sorts of multiplicities, Deleuze refers to the mathematician Riemann.

> Riemann defined as "multiplicities" those things that could be determined in terms of their dimensions or their independent variables. He distinguished *discrete multiplicities* and *continuous multiplicities.* The former

contain the principle of their own metrics (the measure of one of their parts being given by the number of elements they contain). The latter found a metrical principle in something else, even if only in phenomena unfolding in them or in the forces acting in them. (*B* 39)

In the case of discrete or spatial multiplicities, the metric is contained within the multiplicity. It is for this reason that we can say that space and objects present only differences in degree rather than differences in kind. A movement from place to place is still a spatial change. If I divide an object, I get more objects. A patch of red divided in two is still two patches of red. On the other hand, in the case of a virtual, continuous, or durational multiplicity, the multiplicity contains a variety of different dimensions which change in kind when elements are added or removed. These elements subsist together in a fusional unity and contain the principle of heterogeneity without alterity.

In light of the preceding, we can now understand what takes place in the method of division involved in intuition. When I seek to divide the composites or mixtures making up my experience, I am not dividing it between two differences in kind (which, according to the principles of continuous multiplicities, would yield another difference in kind), but rather *between* differences in kind *and* differences in degree. In short, intuition brackets differences in degree which contain their metric within themselves and selects differences in kind. The aim is to trace the path of the tendencies (differences in kind) belonging to duration, to determine the nature of its differentiation, to follow it in its becoming. This is clearly evident in Bergson's remarks about the shooting star. On the one hand, there are representational and spatialized differences which yield only differences in degree, while on the other hand there is pure duration, qualitative motion, alteration which contains all the differences in kind as acts or tendencies which differ from themselves.

> If we consider all the definitions, descriptions and characters of duration in Bergson's work, we realise that difference of nature, in the end, is not *between* these two tendencies. Finally, difference of nature is itself *one* of these tendencies, and is opposed to the other. What in effect is duration? Everything that Bergson says about duration always comes back to this: duration *is what differs from itself.* Matter on the contrary is what does not differ from itself, what repeats. ("BCD" 47–48)

We lay aside the side that repeats identically or the differences in degree which repeat without producing a new kind, the side that does not differ from itself, in order to determine the tendencies characterizing the phenomenon in question. These tendencies are forces, potentials, differentials, or movements which develop themselves through a process of actualization, and which serve as the internal conditions for the phenomenon.

Conditions of Real Experience

It is now clear why these internal differences serve as the conditions of experience. And, more importantly, why they are the conditions of *real* rather than possible experience. If tendencies, durations, continuous multiplicities are transcendental conditions of experience, it is because they are the acts internal to experience which make it be through a process of actualization. Unlike Kantian conditions which are conditions of all possible experience, these conditions are no broader than that which they condition. Nevertheless, these conditions are not the given insofar as experience itself presents nothing but composites, mixtures, differences in degree.

> Experience itself offers us nothing but composites. But that is not where the difficulty lies. For example, we make time into a representation imbued with space. The awkward thing is that we no longer know how to distinguish in that *representation* the two component elements which differ in kind, the two pure *presences* of duration and extensity. We mix extensity and duration so thoroughly that we can now only oppose their mixture to a principle that is assumed to be both nonspatial and non-temporal, and in relation to which space and time, duration and extensity, are now only deteriorations. (*B* 22)

It is because experience presents us with nothing but composites, mixtures, differences in degree, and because thinking in terms of these mixtures leads us to problems on the order of transcendental illusions, that we must go beyond what is given in experience to the transcendental conditions governing the production of experience.

> There is some resemblance between intuition as method of division and transcendental analysis: If the composite represents the fact, it must be divided into tendencies or pure presences that only exist *in principle* [*en droit*]. We go beyond experience, toward the conditions of experience (but these are not, in the Kantian manner, the conditions of all possible experience: They are the conditions of real experience). (*B* 23)

Unlike Kantian conditions, Deleuzian conditions are not external to that which they condition, but are rather genetic conditions of experience which produce that which they serve as necessary conditions for. In one respect, then, the conditions are identical to that which they produce. Where Kantian conditions condition the matter of intuition and remain external to it, Deleuzian conditions generate this matter of intuition and are internal to it. Here we might think of the equation for a circle. The equation for the circle is not external to the circle, but is instead that by which the circle becomes or is produced in an act of unfolding. In other words, experience, which presents only mixtures, is an *expression* of these tendencies. As Deleuze puts it in his 1956 essay on Bergson,

> In order to reach true differences, we must rejoin the point of view where the mixture divides itself. It is tendencies that are dually opposed to each other, that differ in nature. It is the tendency that is the subject. A being is not the subject, but the expression of the tendency, and furthermore, a being is only the expression of a tendency in so far as this is contrasted with another tendency. It is in this way that intuition presents itself as a method of difference or division: that of dividing the mixture into two tendencies. This method is something other than a spatial analysis, more than a description of experience and less (in appearance) than a transcendental analysis. It certainly raises itself to the conditions of the given, but these conditions are tendency-subjects, they are themselves given in a certain way, they are lived. Moreover, they are at the same time the pure and the lived, the living and the lived, the absolute and the lived. The essential thing is that the foundation be a foundation, but that it is nevertheless *experienced* . . . We must not raise ourselves to the conditions of all possible experience, but to conditions of real experience: Schelling already gave himself this aim and defined his philosophy as a superior empiricism. This formula suits Bergson just as well. If these conditions can and must be grasped in an intuition, it is precisely because they are conditions of real experience, because they are no broader than the conditioned, because the concept they form is identical to its object. ("BCD" 46)

We can thus say that the given is an expression, product, or result of a combination of tendencies such that it actualizes these tendencies. It is for this reason that the conditions of experience are no broader than that which they condition, that they are unique to that which they condition. Finally, it follows from this that they are conditions of real rather than all possible experience, since they are no broader than that which they condition.

For this reason, Deleuze is able to claim that

> it is strange that aesthetics (as the science of the sensible) could be
> founded on what *can* be represented in the sensible. True, the inverse
> procedure is not much better, consisting of the attempt to withdraw the
> pure sensible from representation and to determine it as that which
> remains once representation is removed (a contradictory flux, for ex-
> ample, or a rhapsody of sensations). Empiricism truly becomes transcen-
> dental, and aesthetics an apodictic discipline, only when we apprehend
> directly in the sensible that which can only be sensed, the very being *of*
> the sensible: difference, potential difference and difference in intensity
> as the reason behind qualitative diversity. It is in difference that move-
> ment is produced as an "effect," that phenomena flash their meaning
> like signs. The intense world of differences, in which we find the reason
> behind qualities and the being of the sensible, is precisely the object of a
> superior empiricism. (*DR* 56–57)

To found aesthetics on what "can" be represented is to decide in advance
what can be presented within the sensible. This procedure consists in
reducing the sensible to what is homogeneous within the sensible or to
discrete, extensive multiplicities. From the point of view of empiricism,
this is indeed a strange position in that it purports to know in advance
what cannot be known. Only by thinking in the most abstract terms, the
most general terms, by thinking in terms of possibility, does the sensible
present itself in this way. Moreover, while Deleuze's project consists of
an attempt to think the sensible in continuity with the intelligible, it is
nonetheless the case that the vast majority of our experience is made
up of passive receptivity. While all experience is for Deleuze intelligible
in principle, the principles governing most of our experience remain
unconscious. On the other hand, the empiricist position which would
begin with the given, with the flux of experience, isn't much better
insofar as "flux" is just another abstract universal characterizing all of
experience without qualifying any experience in particular. This is the
flaw of Dionysian and empiricist approaches to Deleuze which take
him as the herald of becoming, chaos, and flux. Deleuzian becoming
is not a chaos, but the unfolding of differentials that are intelligible
entities. The Dionysians take Deleuze to be the champion of never-
ending becoming without being able to qualify anything in particular.
As a result, their discourse becomes empty and monotonous in that it
is unable to qualify anything singular or specific. Such a perspective is
no less generalist than the Kantian forms of intuition. In contrast to the
Dionysian version of Deleuze, it is the genitive "of" in the phrase "being

of the sensible" which is all-important. This phrase is ambiguous in that it simultaneously suggests sensible being and that which engenders sensibility within being. As such, it is well suited for overcoming the exteriority of condition and conditioned that Deleuze seeks. To say that something is the being of the sensible is to identify it neither with the sensible as given, nor with the general form belonging to the sensible *as such.* Rather, the being of the sensible is that which makes the diversity of experience be as it is, which produces it in its being, which allows it to manifest itself. It is essence, intensity, internal difference such that it inheres in the sensible while nonetheless differing from it. One might object to the use of the term *essence,* citing Deleuze's constructivism in *What Is Philosophy?* which he coauthored with Guattari. However, it must be borne in mind that not all constructivisms are opposed to essence. Mathematicians construct proofs and mathematical entities, but this does not undermine the essential nature of their objects and render them merely conventional. If we retain the term *essence,* then this is to emphasize the rationalist dimension of Deleuze's thought that has tended to be occluded by undue emphasis on the experimentalist dimension of his thought. Emphasis on Deleuze's experimentalism has distorted accounts of his metaphysics by drawing attention away from the problems his concepts are responding to.

The being of the sensible is none other than duration, tendency, or act. In this respect, Deleuze is able to claim that transcendental empiricism reconciles the two halves of aesthetics (the theory of the sensible and the theory of beauty) insofar as it is able to explain how the being of the sensible allows for a genesis of experience (thus treating experience as an aesthetic production in the sense of artistic production), which in turn creates a domain of experience or the given (the aesthetic in the sense of sensible receptivity). In other words, we are entitled to say that transcendental empiricism is the experience of experience producing experience, on the condition that we understand that the term *experience* here plays on two registers of signification, between experience as transcendental lived condition, and experience as the given diversity of the sensible.

Topological Essences and Singular Styles of Being

At this point a number of problems arise. First, on the basis of this account, how can Deleuze avoid falling into a sort of radical nominalism? In other words, how can Deleuze avoid treating each object to be explained in terms of its self-identity? Moreover, insofar as Deleuze argues that the conditions of experience are no broader than the conditioned, that they stand in a relation of genesis rather than external conditioning, that they are internal to the form of experience that expresses them, how can he avoid turning each individual thing into a singular essence which abolishes the value of this account of essence altogether? For example, if I assert that each singular entity is its own essence, is it any longer possible for me to speak of "sadism" or "masochism," or am I now restricted to speaking of the art of Sacher-Masoch and the Marquis de Sade in opposition to all positions that would treat these essences as general structures of perversion?

Second, and in a closely related vein, what explanatory power does Deleuze's account of intuition have here? In other words, what explanatory value does Deleuze's notion of a condition no broader than the conditioned have? What do these conditions explain? We have said that these conditions explain real experience, that they are the genetic principles underlying the diversity of experience. Yet on the surface this is not saying much. In the case of Kant, the notion of a condition explains how we can make universal and certain claims regarding experience despite the fact that this knowledge is not itself given in experience (a posteriori). By contrast, Deleuze's transcendental empiricism, insofar as it purports to explain the conditions of real experience, *seems* to abolish these aspirations of universality and necessity in favor of the contingent and singular. If these conditions are conditions of the singular and contingent, how do they add anything to our understanding of that which is singular and contingent? In other words, how are they not merely redundant? Moreover, if these conditions restrict us to the singular and contingent, then why do we not fall back into the Dionysian reading of Deleuze? Is Deleuze's transcendental empiricism just Humean skepticism in disguise?

Third, how can Deleuze avoid the fallacy of tracing the transcendental from the empirical? If we are situated within experience, if experience is what is given, and if experience is what is real and therefore what is to be explained, then how can the tendencies we discover in experience, the internal differences which are the being of the sensible, avoid tracing the transcendental from the empirical? Does not Deleuze place too much weight on actualized experience? Are not the conditions we discover within experience always doomed to be found after the fact (since experience is ever changing) and therefore to being little more than history? Does not Deleuze fall prey to characterizing experience in advance, as Kant does when he attempts to determine the conditions of all possible experience, in a different way by restricting experience to all actual or real experience?

It is clear that all three of these problems are interrelated. We find ourselves perplexed by the problem of the relationship between conditions and the conditioned because we assume that experience is made up of nothing but nominal beings and that consequently the conditions of such experience, when said to be conditions of real experience, must themselves be nominal. Similarly, Deleuze appears to end up tracing the transcendental from the empirical insofar as the relevance of the conditions can only be defined in terms of the *identity* of the real or concrete experience. We might characterize one of Deleuze's aims as that of establishing the necessity of the contingent, the singular aesthetic conditions lying behind its conditioned, but this also seems to lead to the paradoxical position of relying on the identity of the actual. Insofar as Deleuze also seeks to demonstrate that identity is produced as an effect of difference, this puts him in the difficult position of simultaneously attempting to demonstrate how effects of the same, similar, and identical are produced, while also relying upon these effects as given. The crucial questions to ask in the context of these problems are (1) what is the "thing" which the condition is perfectly tailored to, (2) what does it mean to claim that the conditions of experience are no broader than that which they condition, and (3) what is meant by real experience?

In fact, it is a mistake to believe that for Deleuze the aim of intuition is to account for *this* given, *here* and *now*. Rather, the object of intuition is not the ephemeral event in the form of an actualized happening characterizing a state of affairs, but rather what might be called a style, diagram of becoming, or morphological essence. Here, once again, the differential sheds light on what Deleuze is up to. We can think of the object as a value generated by the function, whereas the function is a style of becoming. Where becoming conceived in terms of coming-to-be and passing-away is always broader than the duration it purports to describe, the function is able to reach all the way to the individual event and continuous transformation at any moment in the history or process of its unfolding. A morphological essence does not characterize a thing, but a possible world, a system of appearances, a way of being; for instance, the worlds of Proust, Joyce, or Kafka, but also the unique patterns of seashells one finds on Nagshead beach in North Carolina or the migration patterns of birds.[3] To be sure, one of Deleuze's central preoccupations throughout his work is the being *of* the event, as is clearly evident from *The Logic of Sense* and *The Fold: Leibniz and the Baroque*. However, he is always careful to distinguish between what happens as a spatiotemporal actualization of an event, and the Ideal event as the being of the happening.

> Events are ideal. Novalis sometimes says that there are two courses of events, one of them ideal, the other real and imperfect—for example,

ideal Protestantism and real Lutheranism. The distinction however is not between two sorts of events; rather, it is between the event, which is ideal by nature, and its spatio-temporal realization in a state of affairs. The distinction is between *event* and *accident*. Events are ideational singularities which communicate in one and the same Event. They have therefore an eternal truth, and their time is never the present which realizes them and makes them exist. Rather, it is the unlimited Aion, the Infinitive in which they subsist and insist. Events are the only idealities. (*LS* 53)

When Deleuze calls for a transcendental philosophy capable of accounting for the conditions of real experience, he is not referring to this or that object, but rather to the conditions under which a world is produced. A world must be seen as an event, and any particular object must be seen as an effect of the structure of this world. This is already evident from Deleuze's remarks about the nature of essence in *Proust and Signs*. In this context, Badiou has expressed matters perfectly:

> One starts to go wrong as soon as one imagines that the constraint exercised by concrete cases makes of Deleuze's thought a huge description or collection of the diversity characterizing the contemporary world. For one presumes then that the operation consists in thinking the case. This is not so: the case is never an object for thought; rather, intrinsic to the destination that, ultimately automatic, is thought's own, intrinsic to the exercising "to the very end" of thought's power, the case is what forces thought and renders it impersonal.[4]

The concrete case or real being is never the object of thought, of intuition, but rather is the opportunity for intuition. What we seek in the case is not an adequate description of the case (which would very likely be impossible), but rather the style or morphological essence that inheres throughout a series of cases. We seek to determine the world, structure, or system to which the case belongs.

> The real theme of a work is therefore not the subject the words designate, but the unconscious themes, the involuntary archetypes in which the words, but also the colors and the sounds, assume their meaning and their life. Art is a veritable transmutation of substance. By it, substance is spiritualized and physical surroundings dematerialized in order to refract essence, that is, the quality of an original world. This treatment of substance is indissociable from "style." (*PS* 47)

Consequently, we can say that the object, the theme, the thing which the concept is identical to is not what is given in experience, but is rather the essence or style functioning as the principle of that experience or world.

This point of view is not restricted to *Proust and Signs*. As Deleuze puts it in "Bergson's Conception of Difference,"

> Movement is qualitative change and qualitative change is movement. In short, duration is what differs, and what differs is no longer what differs from something else, but what differs from itself. What differs has become itself a thing, a *substance*. Bergson's thesis could be expressed in this way: real time is alteration, and alteration is substance. Difference of nature is thus no longer between two things or rather two tendencies, difference of nature is itself a thing, one tendency opposing itself to the other. ("BCD" 48)

It is not the given which is the thing, but rather the tendency, the movement, the act. As such, the concept is not identical to the object given in experience, but rather to the tendency insofar as it functions as a style or essence of a possible world. The concept is the thing, not a re-presentation of the thing. As Deleuze puts it in *Difference and Repetition*, "Only an empiricist could say: concepts are indeed things, but things in their free and wild state, beyond 'anthropological predicates' " (*DR* xx–xxi). Concepts, for Deleuze, are therefore an ontological rather than an epistemological category. A concept is not, according to Deleuze, something that people have in their minds, but is rather a way of being . . . namely, the being of an intensive multiplicity. In this respect, Deleuze reveals an important affinity to Plato.

A style or essence is what we might refer to as an identity of difference, or an identity produced through difference. It is not a type or kind, but rather a rule of production, a genetic factor. It is an identity that maintains itself through *topological variations*. It is for this reason that we speak of morphological essences or diagrams of becoming.

We can think about style in terms of the difference between Euclidean and topological geometries. Taking the example of a triangle as a being composed of three singularities or points along with three relations, a Euclidean view emphasizes the static form possessed by the triangle, its formal identity, while a topological point of view emphasizes the dynamisms or adventures the relations between these singularities are able to undergo. Thus, for instance, a Euclidean view is prone to emphasize the different types of triangles such as right, isosceles, and equilateral triangles, while topology thinks the manner in which these triangles can be transformed into one another and other shapes through operations of stretching, pulling, and twisting. In this respect, topological thought is similar to Husserlian free variation, with the difference that the aim here is not to discover the invariant essence without which the being could not be what it is, but rather to see what sorts of variations a set of singularities is able to undergo while maintaining a structural identity. Both points of view are in a sense "structural"; however, the former seeks to determine what it can understand of a triangle under its fixed form, while the latter seeks to determine what it can understand of the structure by setting it in variation. From a topological point of view, no particular ideal triangle is of central concern (here topology agrees with geometry in making actual triangles secondary to ideal or ideational triangles); rather, what is of concern is the relational or structural identity of relations among singularities characterizing the triangle as it undergoes variation. Consequently, unlike a Euclidean formalist approach, a topological approach would claim that there is a topological identity between right, isosceles, and equilateral triangles. Rather than focusing on the properties of each of these triangles (which is not unimportant), a topological approach seeks to determine the sorts of variations a structure can undergo through stretching, folding, bending, twisting, and so on, up to the point where the structure undergoes a structural mutation forming another structural identity (for instance, the point at which a triangle becomes a quadrilateral by folding one of its tips). The notion of topological variation is extremely fruitful for all structural domains. In any domain containing singularities and differential relations, we can imagine such variations and treat them as variations on a theme or style.

That Deleuze has something like this in mind is clear from a number of passages within his texts. For instance, in "Bergson's Conception of Difference" he remarks that

> the specificity of temporal difference is to make the concept into a concrete thing, because things are so many nuances or degrees which present themselves at the heart of the concept. It is in this sense that Bergson has placed difference, and with it the concept, in time . . . The distinctions between subject and object, body and spirit, are temporal, and in this sense are a matter of degree. Thus we can see how the virtual becomes the pure concept of difference, and what such a concept can be: such a concept is *the possible coexistence of degree or nuances.* ("BCD" 54)

Such a difference is called "temporal" because it refers to variations undergone in a topological space. As a variation, the difference must not be thought as *a* difference—which is only a nuance or degree of the concept—but as the becoming of these nuances or inflections. It is in this sense that the difference is temporal. The difference is thought in its unfolding variation. Here we encounter an echo of Deleuze's Spinozism in that the concept is not thought as a set of possibilities which lack actualization, but as that in which whatever can be affirmed *is* affirmed of being. The concept holds none of its degrees in reserve, but produces them all. Time is the unfolding of whatever can be affirmed at a particular point in time. It contains all the degrees or nuances of difference because these are the variations that can be undergone by the tendency. Moreover, we are able to understand here the somewhat mysterious thesis that continuous or durational multiplicities undergo a difference in kind each time they are divided. To divide a continuous multiplicity is to either subtract or add relations or singularities so as to bring about a mutation in the topological identity which brings about an accompanying qualitative change. Additionally, we are able to understand why Deleuze claims that identity is a product of difference, rather than difference a product of identity. In the first place, topological structures differ in themselves. In other words, the value of all the terms within the structure is only determinable in relation to the other terms. Second, the variations that the relations and elements can undergo produce effects of identity rather than assuming them from the outset. Once we address Deleuze's account of reciprocal determination, we will see exactly why this is so. For the moment, we need only note that the singularities composing the topology only take on their identity with respect to each other. Finally, we can comprehend why Deleuze holds that structural criticism or interpretation is both creative and apodictic. On the one hand, it is creative insofar as the interpretive work always depends upon a fundamental decision or risk surrounding what sorts of variations the structure of the text must undergo. Will I stretch it, fold it, twist it? On the other hand, it is apodictic in that it refers to relations and singularities necessarily embodied in the text.

Although Deleuze himself never makes reference to the notion of topological essences, the theme can be seen to clearly run throughout his work. Thus, in *Difference and Repetition* Deleuze remarks that

> "shortest" may be understood in two ways: from the point of view of conditioning, as a schema of the imagination which determines space in accordance with the concept (the straight line defined as that which in all parts may be superimposed upon itself)—in this case the difference remains external, incarnated in a rule of construction which is established "between" the concept and the intuition. Alternatively, from the genetic point of view, the shortest may be understood as an Idea which overcomes the duality of concept and intuition, interiorises the difference between straight and curved, and expresses this internal dif-

ference in the form of a reciprocal determination and in the minimal
condition of an integral. The shortest is not a schema but an Idea; or it
is an ideal schema and no longer the schema of a concept. In this sense,
the mathematician Houel remarked that the shortest distance was not
a Euclidean notion at all, but an Archimedean one, more physical than
mathematical; that it was inseparable from a method of exhaustion, and
that it served less to determine the straight line than to determine the
length of a curve by means of the straight line. (*DR* 174)

Between the two topological variations of the straight and the curved
characterizing "line-ness" as such, a differential relation obtains which
allows for a third property to be produced, characterized in terms of
exhaustion. The predicate "shortest" here refers to a variation of lines
as they are lived in an experience of distance. In the difference between
the straight and the curved an intelligible structure is uncovered internal
to the straight. Thus, the shortest is similar to a limit discovered in the
straight pertaining to distance, akin to the operation of integration in
an equation. Insofar as a topological identity is produced between the
variations a structure can undergo, Deleuze is also able to maintain
the being of concrete universals which are no longer opposed to
particulars. Deleuze often denotes these universals with the qualifier
"white." Hence,

Ideas contain all the varieties of differential relations and all the distributions of singular points coexisting in diverse orders "perplicated"
in one another. When the virtual content of an Idea is actualised, the
varieties of relation are incarnated in distinct species while the singular
points which correspond to the values of one variety are incarnated in
the distinct parts characteristic of this or that species. The Idea of color,
for example, is like white light which perplicates in itself the genetic
elements and relations of all the colors, but is actualised in the diverse
colors with their respective spaces; or the Idea of sound, which is also
like white noise. There is even a white society and a white language, the
latter being that which contains in its virtuality all the phonemes and relations destined to be actualised in diverse languages and in the distinctive parts of a given language. (*DR* 206)

When Deleuze refers to "white society" he is not talking about Caucsians,
but rather the Idea or topological structure of society insofar as it contains all its possible nuances or degrees of difference through variation
insofar as it is determined by a set of tendencies and their relations. It is
in this respect that the concept becomes a concrete universal.

Where universals defined by divisions in a genus according to specific differences (which function roughly as the intension of the concept) find that they encounter a gulf between the specific differences of the concept arrived at by tracing oppositions and individuating differences belonging to the singular being, the notion of a concrete universal as a topological entity containing all its variations encounters no such problem. Because a topological essence is composed of all the degrees of difference or structural variations, it passes all the way from "white noise" or the chaos of the undetermined to individuating difference. As a result, Deleuze would claim that there is no concept of the color red, but only of white light, of which red is a variation. If red does not form a proper Deleuzian concept, then this is not because it is not real but because it does not mark the joints of being. Red marks a difference in degree from other colors, whereas color as such is a difference in kind. It is precisely in this sense that Deleuze's position evades the alternatives of realism and nominalism.

The distinction between the intension and extension of concepts common to both nominalistic and realistic accounts of concepts also mirrors that of mental content and objective reference of the concept. Here, already, Deleuze would object to illicitly treating concepts as mental entities. Nominalistic positions tend to begin with the extension of a concept and seek to explain the production of conceptuality through processes of abstraction. Individual things being the only things given and which can properly be said to exist, the question becomes one of how general ideas can be produced on the basis of resemblance. By contrast, realist positions, noting that extension seems only to be arrived at on the basis of the intension of the concept, and that some sort of universality seems to necessarily serve as a condition for the possibility of resemblance or similarity relations, grant an existence or reality proper to the concept or universal itself. In this respect, the universal is said to have a constitutive and purely mental existence grasped through intellectual or categorial intuition, or it is said to exist in some extraworldly or transcendent somewhere. Deleuze's position fits neither of these characterizations. While it might first appear that Deleuze's concept of the concept refers it to its extension, this is not the case insofar as the given is given by the Idea and its variations without being identical to it, nor being its origin. Like Platonic forms, Deleuzian Ideas are a condition of Beings. Unlike Plato, these Ideas do not stand opposed to the individuals they generate. On the other hand, they do not have a purely mental existence because the concept itself is a thing, because it is a real condition of experience, because the subject itself is a temporal determination in a continuity between subjects and objects.

3

Transcendental Empiricism: The Image of Thought and the "Phenomenology" of the Encounter

Deleuze Contra Bergson

There can be little doubt that Deleuze is deeply indebted to Bergson. This influence can be discerned everywhere in the way Deleuze makes use of division in his major texts. In *Difference and Repetition* it manifests itself in the division between difference containing all the differences in kind and repetition as the principle of differences of degree. Moreover, it manifests itself in the way he makes use of a Bergsonian concept of a properly ontological memory in the second synthesis of repetition (which I will not be able to discuss until later in this book in relation to the problematic of time). This method of division manifests itself again in Deleuze's distinction between causes and effects in *The Logic of Sense*. We even discern it at work late in his career in *Foucault,* in the use he makes of the distinction between seeing and speaking.

We also see Bergsonism at work in the three dimensions of a Deleuzian concept. According to Deleuze,

> *Duration, memory, élan vital form three clearly distinct aspects of the concept.* Duration is difference with itself; memory is the coexistence of degrees of difference; the *élan vital* is the differentiation of difference. The three stages define a schematism in Bergson's philosophy. The meaning of memory is to give the virtuality of duration an objective consistency which makes it a concrete universal, which enables it to realise itself. When virtuality realises itself, which is to say differentiates itself, it is through life and in a vital form; in this sense it is true that difference *is* vital. But virtuality could only differentiate itself using the degrees which coexist in it. Differentiation is only the separation of what coexists in duration. The differentiations of the *élan vital* are, more profoundly, the degrees of difference itself. ("BCD" 55)

With respect to the first moment, we trace the differences in kind belonging to a composite or a mixture. In the second moment, we trace all the degrees of difference belonging to the virtual tendency. Finally, in the third moment, we trace, in a virtual diagram, the point at which difference in kind or nature converges with difference in degree in the actualization of experience.

> This broadening out, or even this going-beyond does not consist in going beyond experience toward concepts. For concepts only define, in the Kantian manner, the conditions for all possible experience in general. Here, on the other hand, it is a case of real experience in all its peculiarities. And if we must broaden it, or even go beyond it, this is only in order to find the articulations on which these peculiarities depend. So that the conditions of experience are less determined in concepts than in pure percepts. And, while these percepts themselves are united in a concept, it is a concept modeled on the thing itself, which only suits that thing, and which, in this sense, is no broader than what it must account for. For when we have followed each of the "lines" beyond the turn in experience, we must also rediscover the point at which they intersect again, where the directions cross and where the tendencies that differ in kind link together again to give rise to the thing as we know it. It might be thought that nothing is easier, and that experience itself has already given us this point. But it is not as simple as that. After we have followed the lines of divergence *beyond the turn,* these lines must intersect again, not at the point from which we started, but rather at a virtual point, at a virtual image of the point of departure, which is itself located beyond the turn in experience; and which finally gives us the sufficient reason of the thing, the sufficient reason of the composite, the sufficient reason of the point of departure. So that the expression "beyond the decisive turn" has two meanings: First, it denotes the moment when the lines, setting out from an uncertain common point given in experience, diverge increasingly according to the differences in kind. Then, it denotes another moment when these lines converge again to give us this time the virtual image or the distinct reason of the common point. Turn and return. (*B* 28–29)[1]

It is precisely this movement of turn and return which characterizes *Difference and Repetition, The Logic of Sense,* and *Foucault.* In *Difference and Repetition* this movement manifests itself in Deleuze's account of indi-different/ciation, which explains how difference and repetition are synthesized in the production of sensibility. In *The Logic of Sense* this movement manifests itself in the centrally important and seldom-discussed accounts of the static ontological and logical geneses, which explain the "differenciation" of the proposition into the propositional dimensions of denotation, manifestation, and signification. In *Foucault* it appears once again in the account of how power links the heterogeneous domains of speaking and seeing. Just as there are three distinct moments of the concept in Bergson, we might say that there are also three distinct moments of the concept in Deleuze as well. Deleuze's account of different/citation will be discussed in greater detail in the final chapter. For the moment it is sufficient to point out that "differentiation" refers to the virtual domain of relations, singularities, or problems, and the unusually spelled "differenciation" refers to the actualization of these problems in solutions defining species and parts. For instance, the genome would be the virtual domain of differentiation and the actualized organism would be the differenciation of this genome as an instance of a species characterized by a particular organization of parts (cf. *DR* 184–85).

Nevertheless, it would be a mistake to claim, as so many have, that Deleuze's method is Bergsonian. In the first place, Deleuze explicitly calls the notion of method into question. As Deleuze puts it in *Nietzsche and Philosophy,*

> Thinking, like activity, is always a second power of thought, not the natural exercise of a faculty, but an extraordinary event *in* thought, *for* thought itself. Thinking is the n-th power of thought . . . But it will never attain this power if forces do not do violence to it. Violence must be done to it *as* thought, a power, *the force of thinking,* must throw it into a becoming-active. A constraint a training of this kind is what Nietzsche calls "Culture." Culture, according to Nietzsche, is essentially training and selection. It expresses the violence of the forces which seize thought in order to make it something affirmative and active. We will only understand the concept of culture if we grasp all the ways in which it is opposed to method. Method always presupposes the good will of the thinker, "a premeditated decision." Culture, on the contrary, is a violence undergone by thought, a process of formation of thought through the action of selective forces, a training which brings the whole unconscious of the thinker into play. (*NP* 108; *DR* 165–66)

There is no sure and certain method for thinking, but only the constraint of the encounter which forces us to think. The selection of forces for thought is not carried out by a sovereign subject exercising its will to think, but rather it is as if we were selected by these forces. In short, there is something fortuitous in thought which cannot be produced through a simple act of will. In this connection, two questions present themselves. First, what exactly does Deleuze understand by thought? Normally we think of thought as a voluntary activity that we are free to initiate at will. What does it mean to claim that thought requires a fortuitous encounter? Second, what problem does this conception of thought respond to? Why is it necessary to conceive thought in this way?

Much of Deleuze's conception of thought arises from his engagement with Proust. "In opposition to the philosophical idea of 'method,'" writes Deleuze, "Proust sets the double idea of 'constraint' and of 'chance.' Truth depends on an encounter with something that forces us to think and to seek the truth" (*PS* 16). If method shows itself to be inadequate, it is because it (1) presupposes an affinity with the truth or good will on the part of the thinker, (2) presupposes the nature of what it sets out to know or understand, and (3) supposes a strict difference between the knowing subject and the object known. It presupposes that it *can* know, what it is to know, and that what it knows is independent of its own subjective peculiarities and such. In part, then, Deleuze contrasts an existential conception of thought based on a startling encounter of an amorous or violent nature with an academic conception of knowledge. Thought emerges from a lived encounter that disrupts habit and functions like a trauma or an amorous encounter that calls to be comprehended. Knowledge, by contrast, seeks recognition so that it might prevent such encounters and establish the smooth continuity of experience.

> This is not a call for wild and undisciplined creation that would renounce all method out of hand and advocate instead a sort of vulgar associationism. Creation itself is bound to the fortuitous nature of an encounter or event, which undermines the possibility of willfully creating. Association, far from delivering us to difference, tends to cover it over in explicated space.
>
> Good sense is based upon a synthesis of time, in particular the one which we have determined as the first synthesis, that of habit. Good sense is good only because it is wedded to the sense of time associated with that synthesis. Testifying to a living present (and to the fatigue of that present), it goes from past to future as though from particular to general. However, it defines this past as the improbable or the less probable. (*DR* 225)

This first synthesis of time, *habitus,* upon which good sense is founded, is precisely that of association. As such, association cannot be adequate for characterizing what Deleuze understands by thought. Rather than an associationist stream of consciousness, there is a discipline of the encounter, a necessity, which must be attended to in opposition to the smooth continuity of day-to-day experience. The mark of the encounter is that it interrupts experience, does it a violence, calls its assumptions into question. This is why the encounter must be opposed to habit and association, both of which strive to establish the continuity of experience. In this respect, we might say that the Deleuzian encounter performs a sort of involuntary transcendental *epoche*. Where the phenomenological *epoche* is performed by the transcendental subject, the Deleuzian *epoche* is a sort of performance on the part of being itself that is imposed upon me by an involuntary encounter. I am selected by the encounter, by being. I cannot perform this *epoche* myself, I cannot will it, I can only be open to it when it takes place.

It is for this reason that Deleuze's "phenomenology" of the encounter is anti-methodological and requires an apprenticeship in signs. Here the sign, of course, is the encounter. It is anti-methodological because it relies on the constraint of the contingent encounter as the condition under which thought is engendered in thinking. It is not the immanent and self-conscious ego possessing sovereign power over its ability to think which exercises the power to think, but rather the unconscious thinking under the constraint of the encounter. On the other hand, such thought requires an apprenticeship or training in signs to engender an openness to the encounter, to prevent it from covering over the difference which manifests itself with the subjects and objects resulting from the syntheses of *habitus*.

In light of this, we can see how Deleuze's position diverges from Bergsonian intuition. In *Bergsonism* Deleuze remarks that "to open us up to the inhuman and the superhuman (*durations* which are inferior or superior to our own), to go beyond the human condition: This is the meaning of philosophy, in so far as our condition condemns us to live among badly analyzed composites, and to be badly analyzed composites ourselves" (*B* 28). To open ourselves up to superior and inferior durations is to open ourselves up to greater and lesser rhythms of time or difference which go beyond our own subject-centered experience. Intuition is the means by which we are supposed to reach this aim. "Intuition is not duration itself. Intuition is rather the movement by which we emerge from our own duration, by which we make use of our own duration to affirm and immediately recognize the existence of other durations, above or below us" (*B* 33). In order to clarify what it means to open ourselves up to durations superior and inferior to our own, Deleuze remarks that

> the flowing of the water, the flight of the bird, the murmur of my life
> form three fluxes; but only because my duration is one of them, and also

the element that contains the two others. Why not make do with two fluxes, my duration and the flight of the bird, for example? Because the two fluxes could never be said to be coexistent or simultaneous if they were not contained in a third one. The flight of the bird and my own duration are only simultaneous insofar as my own duration divides in two and is reflected in another that contains it at the same time as it contains the flight of the bird: There is therefore a fundamental triplicity of fluxes. It is in this sense that my duration essentially has the power to disclose other durations, to encompass others, and to encompass itself ad infinitum. (*B* 80)

Here we begin to see what problem Deleuze's conception of thought responds to. If thought must emerge out of an involuntary encounter, then this is because thought must not be opposed to being, but unfolds within being. This point shall be discussed in more detail later, but for the moment suffice it to say that this is the first step in establishing a shift from treating finitude as the beginning point of philosophy to establishing thought within the infinite. Through intuition we open ourselves up to durations greater and smaller than our own in the form of the bird or the water insofar as these durations are contained within a third duration. In other words, intuition comes to discover immanence, where immanence is no longer immanence to my consciousness, but rather where my consciousness discovers itself as one more element within a field of immanence. However, we are right to be suspicious of the optimism of such a claim. In the first place, it is surprising that Bergson-Deleuze speaks of the duration of birds, water, and the subject. Here Bergson seems to clearly trace what is transcendental (duration) from the empirical. In fact, this manner of speaking does not seem to noticeably change traditional subject-object ways of conceiving the world, as is evident from Bergson's assertion that the other two durations are contained in the duration of consciousness. In fact, this is one of the pervasive problems with the manner of speaking in terms of composites and mixtures characterizing experience. It lends itself too easily to tracing the transcendental from the empirical, and thereby illicitly asserting the necessity of the empirical.

Second, and more seriously, there is Bergson's methodological stance regarding intuition itself.[2] In this connection, Bergson remarks that

the intuition we refer to then bears above all upon internal duration. It grasps a succession which is not juxtaposition, a growth from within, the uninterrupted prolongation of the past into a present which is already blending into the future. It is the direct vision of the mind by the mind—nothing intervening, no refraction through the prism, one of whose facets is space and another, language. Instead of states contiguous to states, which become words in juxtaposition to words, we have here the indivisible and therefore substantial continuity of the flow of inner life. Intuition, then, signifies first of all consciousness, but immediate consciousness, a vision which is scarcely distinguishable from the object seen, a knowledge which is contact and even coincidence.[3]

While Bergson wishes to assert that intuition is a direct relation of mind to mind, it is clear that the practice of intuition cannot meet this condition insofar as an analysis of mind is already a reflective mediation of experience that distances the experience as analyzed from the experience as lived. Thus, for instance, in *Time and Free Will* we find Bergson distinguishing between a real and authentic subject and a sedimented and artificial subject. Is this not the fantasy of a subject free of mediation, capable of autonomous and immediate self-relation? By speaking of intuition as a methodology, Bergson speaks as if there is an external difference between the practice of intuition and duration. Second, this implies that intuition is a sovereign power of the subject that can be exercised at any time we might wish. The first issue reproduces all the problems surrounding the questions of external and internal difference. It raises the whole problem of how we can avoid implicitly treating the divisions made through intuition in a merely arbitrary way. On the other hand, by treating intuition as a power of a sovereign subject, Bergson seems to risk reproducing all the problems of the relation between the subject and object, as well as falling back into the conventional nature of a good will on the part of the thinker which only finds itself reflected in the products of its inquiry. In other words, it is not at all clear that intuition is sufficient to open us to the inferior and superior durations that are characteristic of immanence. One might protest that for Bergson both the subject and the object are temporal determinations of duration. Yet from the standpoint of the practice of intuition itself, it is not at all clear that this is the case. One might also point out that intuition requires an "effort," and that effort, at least, has some resemblance to a violence exercised on thinking. But the violence Deleuze speaks of with respect to the encounter is contingent, constraining, and involuntary, whereas all methods can be said to properly involve some anticipation of what they seek.

There can be no doubt that Bergson has a central place in Deleuze's thought. Bergson also helps us to orient what Deleuze means by an internal difference as opposed to external and extrinsic difference.

Nonetheless, Bergson cannot be said to be Deleuze's final word on methodology and difference. By contrast, Deleuze's "phenomenology" of the encounter comes to define what it means to think a relation to difference, a knowledge of difference, that is no longer determined by the power of the sovereign subject and the assumptions of *doxa* defined by the "everybody knows." In other words, the question with respect to Bergson is that of whether or not his methodology is informed by what Deleuze refers to as the "Image of thought." That such is the case seems plausible from Bergson's claim that the tendencies express the conditions under which the object is possible, as well as from the implicit sovereignty exercised by the subject in its effort of intuition. In the first instance Bergson seems to assume the identity of the object, while in the second he seems to assume the identity of the subject. In both cases Bergson seems to assume a good will on the part of the thinker in the pursuit of truth. That is, he seems to assume that the thinker has a natural affinity with the truth.

The Image of Thought

In contrast to Bergsonian intuition, Deleuze's "phenomenology" of the encounter is an account of thought which strives to avoid the assumptions of the moral Image of thought. This aim of presenting an account of thought which is no longer based on the moral Image of thought arises out of the project of determining the conditions under which thought is possible. Although Deleuze criticizes the moral Image of thought for being based on moral presuppositions and for being politically conservative, the proximal justification for Deleuze's criticism is not its moral character, but rather the inability of the Image of thought to properly account for the phenomenon of thought and to break with *doxa*. Based on the assumptions of representation and recognition, the moral Image of thought finds that it cannot arrive at the differences that inhabit thought, but can only reflect itself and its own presuppositions.

> Common sense shows every day—unfortunately—that it is capable of producing philosophy in its own way. Therein lies a costly double danger for philosophy. On the one hand, it is apparent that acts of recognition exist and occupy a large part of our daily life: this is a table, this is an apple, this the piece of wax, Good morning Theatetus. But who can believe that the destiny of thought is at stake in these acts, and that when we recognise, we are thinking? (*DR* 135)

Proceeding on the assumption that the object of thought is the self-identical thing, the Image of thought finds that it can only dumbly repeat the identity of the object (a = a, a table is a table) without introducing a difference into thinking. It is in this model of thought that philosophies governed by relations between form and content, model and copy, come to dominate ontology. However, the very fact that *there are* simulacra, that *there are* differences that are neither those pertaining to models nor copies, is sufficient to demonstrate that something here remains unthought. In short, something escapes the model of models and copies that is designed to be metaphysically exhaustive. However, if there is a form of difference that is not the difference between models and copies or that of resemblance, then there is something amiss in our conception of difference. Consequently, the importance of the simulacrum lies not in the valorization or celebration of the pretender, the fake, the illusory, but in the fact that it reveals a form of difference other than that surrounding relations of genus, species, and individuals. The simulacrum is the *symptom* that something is amiss with the traditional model of difference. As such, it demands a transcendental strategy for determining the conditions under which it is possible. Deleuze, thus, is not suggesting a *preference* for simulacra over models and copies, but instead pointing to something that escapes this model and thus demands a rethinking of the model in principle.

Taking up a Derridean strategy, we might say that the encounter which disrupts and calls recognition into question is not the exception to thought, but rather its defining feature. Just as the absence pervading writing is the ever-present possibility of both speech and empirical writing, their defining or determining feature, so too is the disruption of the encounter the defining feature of thought. By contrast, thought ought, by right (*quid juris*), to contain difference within itself. It ought to introduce difference into thinking, such that thought is able to break with both objective and subjective presuppositions characterizing the Image of thought. That which brings me to think is not the recognized, not what I'm accustomed to, not the habitual, but that which differs and is uncanny. There is a violence proper to thought. This is not a violence exercised by thought, but rather a violence undergone in thinking.

What, then, is this Image of thought which Deleuze seeks to criticize and move beyond? In *Difference and Repetition* Deleuze maps and criticizes eight postulates belonging to the Image of thought and offers an alternative account of thought which would be a thought without image. Put in the most simple terms, the Image of thought is an image or set of assumptions about what it means to think. It would be a mistake to think that Deleuze is objecting here to an empirical state of affairs that is sometimes present and at other times absent. The Image of thought is not a momentary historical state of affairs, but that which haunts all thought. Deleuze is fortunately free of this sort of naive positivism. As such,

> the Image of thought must be judged on the basis of what it claims in principle, not on the basis of empirical objections. However, the criticism that must be addressed to this image of thought is precisely that it has based its supposed principle upon extrapolation from certain facts, particularly insignificant facts such as Recognition, everyday banality in person; as though thought should not seek its models among stranger and more compromising adventures. (*DR* 135)

On the one hand, a critique of the Image of thought is not concerned with how the Image of thought manifests itself in this or that social and historical instance, but rather with what the Image of thought claims *as such*, in principle, in its essence. There is a sense in which the Image of thought is itself constitutive of thought or is a perpetual danger *internal* to thought in a manner similar to Kant's transcendental illusions, which arise not from some lack of adequation between representation and presentation, but within the structure of thought itself. On the other hand, the error of the Image of thought consists in tracing the transcendental from the empirical, of improperly thinking the conditions under which experience is possible, of conceiving the genetic conditions of experience in terms of resemblance to actualized experience.

The consequences of this notion of the Image of thought are clear. When Deleuze claims that "the conditions of a true critique and a true creation are the same: the destruction of *an* Image of thought which presupposes itself and the genesis of the act of thinking in thought itself" (*DR* 139; italics mine), it would be an empiricist, naturalist, and positivist mistake to conclude that the Image of thought is overcome once and for all. The indefinite article qualifying the Image of thought above is enough to establish this point. But more importantly, if the Image of thought is to have the status of a quasi-transcendental illusion, if it is in a sense constitutive of thought, then there can be no question of departing from the Image of thought once and for all. After all, can we seriously believe that it would be possible to live in a world without recognition and such that we are not perpetually seduced into treating recognition as the model of what it means to think? The Image of thought is not a Foucaultian *episteme* or structure of power, but a constitutive dimension of thought. We shall see later how this image is born of the "transcendental illusion" consisting of the erasure of difference arising as thought explicates itself in extensities or spacings. For the moment, *it suffices to recognize that the Image of thought is internal to thought, that it inhabits thought, and not that it is imposed upon thought from without.* However, while the Image of thought might inhabit thought, it is always possible to depart from this image insofar as conventional values are called into question, set into motion, and adventures of a thought without image take place. It is precisely these adventures that Deleuze's account of the encounter seeks to explain.

We have already encountered one of the assumptions of the Image of thought in the form of the implicit or subjective presupposition that everyone knows. Expressed in its philosophical form, the subjective presupposition that everyone knows manifests itself in the form of a good will on the part of the thinker who is said to have a natural affinity with the truth. In total, Deleuze elaborates and criticizes eight postulates of the Image of thought, but these postulates can be said to follow from three central assumptions that could be said to constitute the transcendental structure of the Image of thought. "To the extent that it holds in principle, this image presupposes a certain distribution of the empirical and the transcendental, and it is this distribution or transcendental model implied by the image that must be judged" (*DR* 133). Insofar as the Image of thought is entitled to make certain claims in principle, it constitutes a sort of transcendental structure whose conditions of genesis or individuation must themselves be determined. Defenders of Deleuze often overlook this condition of his thought. If we are to take Deleuze's assertion of the univocity of Being seriously, then we cannot treat the Image of thought as an external force imposing itself from the outside without falling into an opposition between being and appearance that would betray this univocity.

The first element of the model of the Image of thought consists in the presupposition of recognition. Deleuze gives recognition a precise transcendental articulation which does not simply consist in defining what it does empirically.

> There is indeed a model, in effect: that of recognition. Recognition may be defined by the harmonious exercise of all the faculties upon a supposed same object: the same object may be seen, touched, remembered, imagined or conceived . . . No doubt each faculty—perception, memory, imagination, understanding . . . —has its own particular given and its own style, its peculiar way of acting upon the given. An object is recognised, however, when one faculty locates it as identical to that of another, or rather when all the faculties together relate their given and relate

themselves to a form of identity in the object. Recognition thus relies upon a subjective principle of collaboration of the faculties for "everybody"—in other words, a common sense as a *concordia facultatum;* while simultaneously, for the philosopher, the form of identity in objects relies upon a ground in the unity of a thinking subject, of which all the other faculties must be modalities. (*DR* 133)

The defining feature of representation is a sort of cross-modal relation between the different faculties which establishes the identity of the object in question. From the perspective of representation or identity, each of the faculties, when taken alone, is unreliable. Perception or sensibility contains confused and contradictory perceptions like the simultaneity of becoming where someone appears to become both larger and smaller at one and the same time, or the size of a man when viewed from afar who is both large and small. Memory is unreliable insofar as it contains additions and subtractions betraying its origins in the present. Imagination, when exercised alone, is prone to all sorts of flights of fancy and dissimulations. However, if cross-modal relations or a harmonious exercise of the faculties can be established, then at least the faculties can be made to correct one another and converge upon a single and self-identical object in a proper relation of adequation. Nonetheless, it is clear that this sort of transcendental approach works in reverse. Rather than explaining how the empirical object is generated from the conditions of experience, it treats the form of the empirical given as that which the conditions must inevitably be shackled to. The identical object is the referent of these activities and the condition under which their collaboration is possible. Rather than moving from the conditions to the object in a genetic account, such an approach moves from the object to the conditions and thus traces the transcendental from the empirical.

It is precisely this maneuver which constitutes the activity of tracing the transcendental from the empirical, and which forever ties such approaches to the empirically contingent, conventional, or doxastic. In other words, recognition illegitimately universalizes the empirically contingent and simply gives an external account of the collaboration of the faculties to account for this arbitrary identity after the fact. Rather than determining the necessity of the contingent *as* contingent, it treats what *can* be recognized as the form of all that is.

It will only give rise to local skepticism—or indeed, to a generalised method—on condition that thought already has the will to recognise what essentially distinguishes doubt from certitude. The same goes for dubitable as for certain things: they presuppose the good will of the thinker along with the good nature of thought, where these are understood to include an ideal form of recognition as well as a claimed affinity with the true, that *philia* which predetermines at once both the image of thought and the concept of philosophy. (*DR* 139)

The model of recognition assumes from the outset what it means for something to be true, what the truth is, and thus traces itself from the empirical instance which it takes to be true simply because it is familiar.

We might refer here to texts like Foucault's *The Order of Things* or Kuhn's *The Structure of Scientific Revolutions* in establishing this point. What is interesting in these texts is not the empiricist and positivistic thesis that the configurations of knowledge are variable over time. The champion of the progress of knowledge could easily admit a thesis such as this. Rather, what is intriguing here is the manner in which the structures of these configurations of knowledge render themselves invisible through a sort of universalization of what it means to know. It is as if there is a constitutive, a priori blindness to the contingency of our knowledge. The entire world comprehends itself in terms of this knowledge, thus minimizing the gap between world and thought. However, it is likely that this blindness is in part a fortunate state of affairs. A stance that perpetually maintained its distance from the contingency of the order of knowledge would be a stance that was unable to act.

Nonetheless, by treating the conditions of this knowledge in terms of their most abstract form (the form of objectivity in general), the would-be transcendental philosopher paradoxically ensures that the most particular, the most contingent, the most historically determined form of knowledge will be universalized. "The *form* of recognition has never sanctioned anything but the recognisable and the recognised; *form* will never inspire anything but conformities" (*DR* 134; italics mine). "Concepts only ever designate possibilities. They lack the claws of absolute necessity—in other words, of an original violence inflicted upon thoughts; the claws of a strangeness or an enmity which alone would awaken thought from its natural stupor or eternal possibility" (*DR* 139). It is here that the task of determining the conditions under which real experience is possible shows its necessity. It is not that Deleuze denies these forms of recognition defining empirical experience. Recognition is all too real as a cognitive phenomenon. Instead, what he rejects is their illicit universalization. Formalism always sanctions the universalization of that which is historically produced in such a way that the production of the produced, the fact that it was produced, becomes invisible. Formalism sanctions the decontextualization of the produced. It is only in terms of a transcendental philosophy that would determine the conditions of real experience that such illicit universalization could be avoided.

The model of recognition underlying the Image of thought is itself based on two further assumptions. The first of these consists in what Deleuze calls "common sense," while the second consists in "good sense." For Deleuze, common sense does not refer to a basic know-how that all sensible people have, but rather the conditions under which such a claim to know-how is possible. This condition manifests itself in the form of an unspecified unity and identity on the part of the subject and an unspecified identity on the part of the object. "This is the meaning of the Cogito as a beginning: it expresses the unity of all the faculties in the subject; it thereby expresses the possibility that all the faculties will relate to a form of object which reflects the subjective identity" (*DR* 133). If recognition demands that all the faculties converge on the same object, then this condition can only be met on the basis of an identity of the subject within which these faculties can converge. Hence, the subject is made to mirror the object in its identity, once again revealing the manner in which the conditions are being traced by virtue of their resemblance to the empirical.

However, "the objection will be raised that we never confront a formal, unspecified, universal object but only this or that object delimited and specified by a determinate contribution from the faculties" (*DR* 133). Common sense explains the abstract form of possibility, but does not yet account for the empirical *realization* of the possibility of recognition. For this reason, common sense refers to good sense as the means by which it is realized.

> For while common sense is the form of the unspecified object which corresponds to it, good sense is the form of distribution from the point of view of empirical selves and objects qualified as this or that kind of thing (which is why it is considered to be universally distributed). Good sense determines the contribution of the faculties in each case, while common sense contributes the form of the Same. (*DR* 133–34)

Where common sense contributes identity, good sense contributes the distribution of the faculties for each empirical instance. Thus, for instance, it is good sense that distributes the relation between memory and perception by instantiating the rule that given a perception x, one is to recollect all memories y such that they resemble x. Through this distribution, good sense is able to maintain the identity of the object in both time and space according to a hierarchical distribution which qualifies the object as being a "this" or a "that."

According to Deleuze, in effecting this distribution, good sense maintains an essential relation to time.

> Good sense is based upon a synthesis of time, in particular the one which we have determined as the first synthesis, that of habit. Good sense is good only because it is wedded to the sense of time associated with that synthesis. Testifying to a living present (and to the fatigue of that present), it goes from past to future as though from particular to general. However, it defines this past as the improbable or the less probable. (*DR* 225)

The first synthesis of time or *habitus* constitutes the living present through a synthesis of differences constituting retentions and expectations. "A change is produced in the mind which contemplates: a difference, something new *in* the mind. Whenever A appears, I expect the appearance of B" (*DR* 70). For instance, when I encounter a series of ticks and tocks in a clock, the first synthesis of time draws these differences together in such a way that given a tick I come to expect a tock. What is important here is not the individual ticks or tocks, but the relations that come to exist between them. Of course, it will be recalled that an external difference is an empirical difference or a difference between two or more elements. Given that the difference between these ticks and tocks is purely external, it must be contingent. This form of synthesis is based on the pre-givenness of already actualized ticks and tocks, and thus does not explain to us how the given comes to be given.

The necessity of this form of synthesis arises from the fact that time would present no succession if it were only composed of instants without relations of before and after among these instants.

> The imagination is defined here as a contractile power: like a sensitive plate, it retains one case when the other appears. It contracts cases, elements, agitations or homogenous instants and grounds these in an internal qualitative impression endowed with a certain weight . . . This is by no means memory, nor indeed an operation of the understanding: contraction is not a matter of reflection. Properly speaking, it forms a synthesis of time. A succession of instants does not constitute time any more than it causes it to disappear; it indicates only its constantly aborted moment of birth. Time is constituted only in the originary synthesis which operates on the repetition of instants. This synthesis contracts the successive independent instants into one another, thereby constituting

the lived, or living, present. It is in this present that time is deployed. To it belong both the past and the future: the past in so far as the preceding instants are retained in the contraction; the future because its expectation is anticipated in this same contraction. The past and the future do not designate instants distinct from a supposed present instant, but rather the dimensions of the present itself in so far as it is a contraction of instants. The present does not have to go outside itself in order to pass from past to future. Rather, the living present goes from the past to the future which it constitutes in time, which is to say also from the particular to the general: from the particulars which it envelops by contraction to the general which it develops in the field of its expectation (the difference produced in the mind is generality itself in so far as it forms a living rule for the future). In any case, this synthesis must be given a name: passive synthesis. Although it is constitutive it is not, for all that, active. It is not carried out by the mind, but occurs *in* the mind which contemplates, prior to all memory and all reflection. (*DR* 70–71)

It bears noting that this passage ought to be enough to count as evidence against Badiou's claim that Deleuze's thought constitutes a sort of return to classical philosophy or onto-theology. In a manner vaguely reminiscent of Derrida, the present is not the first term, but is rather constituted out of a field of traces and syntheses forming what might be thought of as "text." Paradoxically, the present is never present, but is an effect of syntheses of retention and anticipation. Such a synthesis is passive in that it is not based on the active usage or employment of the faculties, but occurs "automatically," as it were. It is this distinction between the active and the passive that Deleuze seeks to undermine in arguing that passive synthesis occurs *in* the mind rather than being carried out *by* the mind. Despite the fact that such a synthesis occurs in the mind, we thus cannot say that it is based on the sovereign power and self-presence of the subject. As such, the first passive synthesis is not an *activity* of intentional consciousness, but precedes any intentionality and renders intentionality possible in the first place. In this way, the distinction between subject and object is blurred in that the first passive synthesis precedes both subjects and objects.

Contrary to Badiou's thesis that Deleuze's thought rejects the critical turn and strives to articulate a metaphysics without the subject, it is instead the case that Deleuze tries to complete the critical project by subjecting critique itself to a critique. In arguing that the subject is an eject of passive synthesis—a product—Deleuze effectively undermines the premise of finitude in that he begins from the point of view of the infinite and proceeds to derive finite subjects. We shall see how exactly this is so later in this book. This critique has an essential relationship to time, the discussion of which I will have to defer until the next chapter. What is important here is that "mind" has become a name of synthesis rather than a transcendental unity of apperception. While Kant's transcendental unity of apperception also calls into question Descartes' substantialization of the subject, what is in question here is not so much rational psychology, but the premise of finitude underlying Kant's critical project. On the other hand, if the defining difference between classical and critical philosophies is taken to be the difference between two respective attitudes toward the infinite and the finite and whether the two differ in degree or in kind, then Deleuze does fall into the category of classical thought. For Deleuze is above all a thinker of the infinite.

Finally, it should also be pointed out that Deleuzians who seek to locate Deleuze's account of difference solely in the first synthesis of time end up falling prey to the empiricist fallacy of external difference and therefore canceling difference. It is true that the first synthesis produces something new, but it also covers over or cancels the new. The relations between instants in a unity of retentions and anticipations is a set of external relations between instants rather than internal differences determining the being of the given. The first synthesis of time is the ground of good sense, which the phenomenology of the encounter strives to overcome.

Now, the reason good sense is based on the first synthesis of time is that *habitus* is the ground under which a distribution of empirical subjects and qualified objects in a temporal ordering moving from the less to the more general is made possible. In short, the first synthesis of time is the ground upon which the moral Image of thought is produced. From the perspective of good sense, the past is treated as a reservoir of singular events that have happened only once, and are thereby singular, while the future is understood in terms of generality or the form of possibility. If the future is understood in terms of generality, this is because expectation, formed from the first synthesis of time, is always general in character, expecting not this or that particular thing, but rather that things will continue in their resemblance to the past, as they generally have already. *Habitus* thus pre-delineates the set of possibilities to be realized in the unfolding of time. We *expect* that the sun will rise tomorrow, while we know that it rose yesterday. We anticipate what the other side of the object will look like, even though we have not yet seen it. Thus, in the dimension of retention the event only occurs once and is irreplaceable, while in that of anticipation events take on the character of generality. We can easily see how this is a necessary component of recognition, for it is none other than the assumption that the future will continue to resemble the current state of affairs, that the future will continue to be *recognizable*. It is in this respect that the moral Image of thought is essentially conservative. The moral Image of thought tends to exclude radical departures from patterns that have been inferred from the past.

If the moral Image of thought, the model of recognition, represents an inadequate model of thought then it is because recognition itself fails to induce thought. To be sure, recognition involves all sorts of cognitions and processing; but it would be philosophically and conceptually irresponsible to simply identify thought with cognition. Thought does not simply involve mental acts but is that which requires us to go beyond what is familiar. To identify thought with cognition would be purely empirical and therefore nominal insofar as it would vaguely identify thought with any movement of the mind, rather than identifying the distinguishing feature which characterizes thought alone. On the other hand, there are all sorts of different modes of cognition (imagining, wishing, sensing, remembering, fantasizing), such that simply identifying thought with recognition would amount to being unable to know where to locate thought at all. Finally, the notion of thought seems to imply all sorts of upheavals, perplexities, and questions, while that of recognition seems to imply a passive complacency and continuity which thus sets it at odds with what we refer to as thought. Beginning with a passage from Plato's *Republic,* Deleuze writes,

> "Some reports of our perceptions do not provoke thought to reconsideration because the judgment of them by sensation seems adequate, while others always invite the intellect to reflection because the sensation yields nothing that can be trusted.—You obviously mean distant appearances, or things drawn in perspective.
> —You have quite missed my meaning . . .". [4] This text distinguishes two kinds of things: those which do not disturb thought and (as Plato will later say) those which *force* us to think. The first are objects of recognition: thought and all its faculties may be fully employed therein, thought may busy itself thereby, but such employment and such activity have nothing to do with thinking. Thought is thereby filled with no more than an image of itself, one in which it recognises itself the more it recognises things: this is a finger, this a table, Good morning Theatetus. Whence the question of Socrates' interlocutor: is it where we have difficulty in recognising, that we truly think? (*DR* 138)

The recognized does not provoke thought because it recognizes only itself; it recognizes only what it expects. As a result, a model of thought based on recognition is doomed only to rediscover itself. Rather, if we are to understand the nature of thought, we must seek out those events which disturb the complacency of recognition, which call it into question, which perplex and startle us.

4

First Moment of the Encounter: The *Sentiendum*

Imperceptible Encounters

Given Deleuze's account of recognition and good and common sense, the criteria he must meet to avoid these assumptions are daunting. With respect to recognition, Deleuze must avoid assuming a cross-modal or harmonious exercise of the faculties. With respect to common sense, Deleuze must avoid assuming the unspecified form of the subject and the object. Finally, with respect to good sense, he must avoid assuming an empirical distribution of selves and objects based on the living present or the synthesis of *habitus*.

It is for this reason that Deleuze opposes a violence of the senses to that of recognition and a discordant exercise of the faculties to that of the harmonious use of the faculties. Later we shall determine just how it is possible to distinguish among the faculties, but for the moment I will focus here on this discordant use of the faculties. This violence or force which forces us to think has the triple role of calling into question the conservative structure of the living present or *habitus,* of introducing a difference into thought, and of engendering thought within thought. For thought is essentially rare and is incapable of engendering itself. If thought must be engendered within thought, this is because the subject, formed from syntheses of *habitus,* is powerless to begin thinking on its own because the subject always only recognizes itself in its attempt to think. For this reason it is necessary that

> something in the world forces us to think. This something is an object not of recognition but of a fundamental *encounter.* What is encountered may be Socrates, a temple or a demon. It may be grasped in a range of affective tones: wonder, love, hatred, suffering. In whichever tone, its primary characteristic is that it can only be sensed. In this sense it is opposed to recognition. In recognition, the sensible is not at all that which can only be sensed, but that which bears directly upon the senses in an object which can be recalled, imagined or conceived. The sensible is referred to an object which may not only be experienced other than by

sense, but may itself be attained by other faculties. It therefore presupposes the exercise of the other faculties in a common sense. The object of encounter, on the other hand, really gives rise to sensibility with regard to a given sense . . . It is not a quality but a sign. It is not a sensible being but the being *of* the sensible. It is not the given but that by which the given is given. It is therefore in a certain sense the imperceptible [*insensible*]. It is imperceptible precisely from the point of view of recognition—in other words, from the point of view of an empirical exercise of the senses in which sensibility grasps only that which also could be grasped by other faculties, and is related with the context of a common sense to an object which also must be apprehended by other faculties. (*DR* 139–40)

Transcendental empiricism is an empiricism insofar as it must rely on the force of an encounter to engender thought. Here it is not the object of the encounter that is important. The aim is not to represent the object, or to draw a sensation from the object. Rather, the object of the encounter is the occasion of thought, but not that which is to be thought. It is in this respect that transcendental empiricism diverges from classical empiricism in that its object is that which is, in a certain sense, imperceptible.

In order to understand why this is so, we must recall that qualities are produced through the first synthesis of time or *habitus*. Insofar as the notion of a quality implies homogeneity, identity, sameness, and insofar as time without synthesis implies nothing but an ever-flowing flux of differences, quality must be a product of the first synthesis of time. If this is the case, then it is because the concept of quality involves identity, an individuation, which requires a leap beyond the given in duration. To think quality is to think the one that insists in the many. It is not to think this red here, but redness as a common quality of many red thises. In contrast to the quality recognized which is characterized by familiarity, the encounter has the property of being both contingent and necessary.

> In opposition to the philosophical ideal of "method," Proust sets
> the double idea of "constraint" and of "chance." Truth depends on
> an encounter with something that forces us to think and to seek the
> truth. The accident of encounters and the pressure of constraints are
> Proust's two fundamental themes. Precisely, it is the sign that constitutes the object of an encounter and works this violence upon us. It is
> the accident of the encounter that guarantees the necessity of what is
> thought. (*PS* 16)

These claims can be equally attributed to Deleuze. In fact, where the encounter and the force of signs are concerned, Deleuze is much more profoundly Proustian and Nietzschean than he is Bergsonian in his "methodological" outlook. The encounter is contingent insofar as it might not have happened at all, insofar as it might have happened otherwise. Like Lacan's conception of trauma, the encounter exceeds our powers of anticipation and thus explodes the symbolic or system of possibility that characterizes so much of our organism. However, it evokes the necessity of thinking by engendering thought within thought that refuses being ignored. Where thought tied to recognition is concerned, we remain trapped within the grip of an abstract system of possibilities which fails to establish the necessity of that which is thought. By contrast, thought tied to the encounter contains all the necessity of the concrete insofar as it *commands* us to think. The encounter is thus imperative in nature. It is that which we *must* think or that which we cannot avoid thinking or that which it falls to us to think.

Why does Deleuze attribute to the encounter this paradoxical quality of being both imperceptible and being that which can only be sensed? If the encounter is imperceptible, it is only so from the standpoint of recognition, which employs a harmonious exercise of the faculties upon the same object and distributes the contribution of each faculty for each case of recognition. Insofar as recognition cancels difference by effecting a movement from particular to general according to good sense, it becomes blind to the encounter. Rather than seeing the encounter as announcing a new domain of being to be mapped and explored, the moral Image of thought instead treats the encounter as a deviation from the norm, resulting from an error. Good sense is precisely an attempt to protect ourselves from the violent and wounding effects of the encounter, to ward off encounters and be done with them. Good sense dreams of an end to the violence of surprise.

On the contrary, the encounter pertains to sensibility alone and thus presupposes no harmonious exercise of the faculties or distribution of their use. In other words, the encounter does not measure the requirements of the *sentiendum* against the requirements of recognition. Instead, the encounter is an encounter with difference *as such*, with internal difference, with difference as it manifests itself for the sensibility alone. Difference is no longer shackled to external and empirical differences *between* the faculties, *between* the subject and object, *between* objects, but instead becomes the internal difference or tendency characterizing sensibility as duration itself. If this is so, then it is because the encounter is not an encounter with an identical object, but with a difference which cannot be situated in the topos of recognition. We might say that under the constraint of the encounter, we discover a variation within the topological or morphological essence belonging to the faculty of sensibility itself.

The *Sentiendum*, or That Which Can Only Be Sensed

However, the discovery of this internal difference is not unfolded in terms of the continuity of the tendency characterizing sensibility or quality, but rather in terms of the limit of this tendency. Moreover, we see why this point is crucial if we are to treat the difference between infinitude and finitude as a difference in degree, rather than a difference in kind. If this position is to be coherent, then Deleuze must offer some means of determining limits from within infinity. In short, we must account for how the "illusion" of finitude can be produced as an effect. This is the significance of Plato's contradictory perceptions such as the simultaneity of becoming found in growing smaller and larger in one and the same becoming. These contradictory or paradoxical perceptions allow us to define the limits of a faculty and therefore determine what properly determines that faculty.

> Sensibility, in the presence of that which can only be sensed (and is at the same time imperceptible) finds itself before its own limit, the sign, and raises itself to the level of a transcendental exercise: to the "nth" power. Common sense is there only in order to limit the specific contribution of sensibility to the conditions of a joint labour: it thereby enters into a discordant play, its organs become metaphysical. (*DR* 140)

Not only do the contradictory perceptions disclose a domain of sensibility which goes beyond that found in recognition (thus announcing its transcendental exercise apart from the selection effected in recognition), but they also allow us to determine the degrees of difference belonging to the faculty in question. This first aspect allows us to determine the difference in kind belonging to the faculty such that we no longer fall prey to the error of treating faculties like sensibility or memory as only differing in degree from one another, while the second allows us to determine all the degrees of difference belonging to the faculty in question. What we discover in this exercise of the faculty is a differential structure that traces the degrees of difference in much the same way that an equation traces the graph of a curve.

What is of concern in the analysis of the encounter is not the concrete encounter itself—which is discarded in the process of explicating the sign which forces us to think—but rather the transcendental exercise of the faculty, its internal logic and structure. The aim is not to represent the encounter, but rather to engage the encounter as the occasion of thought. And we should not doubt for a moment that these faculties are truly transcendental for Deleuze, that they are true conditions of experience.

> Despite the fact that it has become discredited today, the doctrine of the faculties is an entirely necessary component of the system of philosophy . . . Each faculty must be borne to the extreme point of its dissolution, at which it falls prey to triple violence: the violence of that which forces it to be exercised, of that which it is forced to grasp and which it alone is able to grasp, yet also that of the ungraspable (from the point of view of its empirical exercise). This is the threefold limit of the final power. Each faculty discovers at this point its own unique passion—in other words, its radical difference and its eternal repetition, its differential and repeating element along with the instantaneous engendering of its action and the eternal replay of its object, its manner of coming into the world already repeating. (DR 143)

Hence, for example, *The Logic of Sense* discovers a faculty of language which consists of that which can only be spoken, but which is at the same time silence or the unspeakable. The limit defining language becomes the possibility of nonsense, while the differences contained in language are those of sense. In this case, the object of transcendental inquiry is not this or that particular language, but rather language *as such*, the internal differences which constitute the specific being of language. In other words, *The Logic of Sense* is concerned with the conditions under which language is possible. These are not conditions pertaining to all possible experience, because not all experience is characterized by language; but they are also not conditions characterizing just one specific case of language to the exclusion of all others.

If such an account is referred to as providing the conditions of concrete or real experience, it is because it no longer assumes the collaboration of the faculties (which would likely tie language to either its representative or referential function), but instead delivers us to the being of language as such. Deleuze is here able to simultaneously arrive at language as such, at the being of language, *and* to give a formulation of language that merges with individual languages themselves. Individual languages are like points defined on the curve that is language as such. They maintain continuity with the being of language, while being singular inflections of this being.

To be sure, Deleuze begins with concrete cases in thinking the be-ing of language (in *The Logic of Sense* these cases consist of the stoics and the works of Lewis Carroll), but these cases serve to engender thought within thought, rather than serving as cases to be represented. The aim is not to represent Carroll, but to discover the forces of nonsense and sense in his literature as constitutive features of language. What is sought in each case is the transcendental dimension characterizing the phenomenon in question.

Deleuzian Faculties and the Joints of Being

From this we can also see just how broad Deleuze's notion of "faculty" is. Perhaps one of the reasons that the term *faculty* is approached with distrust and suspicion lies in the fact that this notion is often associated with the psychology of the subject, with the primacy of a transcendental ego. Faculties are understood to be faculties *of* a subject, which suggests a form of psychologism. Recognizing this problem, transcendental philosophies often attempt to solve it by positing a transcendental subject or cogito, distinct from individual subjects, which would transcend individual psychology and be invariant for all minds. This, of course, leads to the problem of whether minds are truly universal in this way. Moreover, language is clearly not something that is dependent exclusively upon the subject. Subjects may be necessary conditions for the *actualization* of language, but are not sufficient for this actualization. For one of the defining features of language is precisely that it is trans-individual or intersubjective. In treating language as a faculty, Deleuze is not asserting a Chomskyan thesis about deep and innate grammar, but rather attributing to it the status of a domain of difference, of a structure, of a tendency.

Speaking somewhat cryptically, we might say that faculties do not belong to subjects (if for no other reason than Deleuze's critique of the subject), but rather subjects are precipitated from faculties. In fact, granting that Deleuze must indeed reject finitude as a corollary to his critique of representation, it follows that he cannot treat the subject as a metaphysically primitive term, but must instead give an account of how subjects are possible. Consequently, these faculties are none other than the tendencies characterizing being. They are the differentials or joints of being itself, and not faculties of a subject's mind. It is for this reason that Deleuze qualifies faculties with the genitive "of" when referring to the "being of the sensible," "the being of language," "the being of mem-ory," and so on. In all of these cases, the tendency is not identical to sensibility, language, or memory as we find them in our experience, but rather is that by which sensibility, language, or memory is given. They are the genetic conditions allowing for the givenness of the given.

Finally, on the basis of this we can also see how Deleuze avoids shackling the encounter or the tendency it expresses to the distribution in time effected by good sense. What is of concern where the tendency is concerned is not the linear distribution between the particular and general, between the universal and particular, but rather the internal logic of the tendency, its topological or morphological essence. The morphological essence is neither general nor particular, but rather singular. It contains all the degrees of difference without presupposing any particular order or hierarchy among them. In other words, such conditions are no broader than that which they condition insofar as they pertain to this domain of difference alone. In this way Deleuze is able to claim that the noetic stands in a relation of continuity with *aisthesis* in that *aisthesis* is a differential inflection of the noetic, of the differential, or a degree of difference within the articulation of being. It is for this reason that the relevant epistemological opposition characterizing Deleuze's thought is not that between the active spontaneity of concepts and the passive receptivity of intuitions—which fails to account for how the givens of experience are given or generated—but rather between the distinct-obscure and clear-confused (*DR* 213). It is only through an essentialization of finitude that we are led to treat the opposition between active thought and passive intuition as decisive. Taking mathematics as a paradigm in which thought is able to produce its object in intuition like God, Deleuze instead argues that all intuition is productive and creative. This is the secret meaning of Deleuze's call to unify the two sundered halves of the aesthetic. Deleuzian intuition is productive intuition. Deleuzian affects are rules or differentials for the production of lived qualities.

However, while intuition may be productive, only a comparatively small region of intuition is clear for human beings. While we may be able to discover the genetic factors or principles governing mathematical intuition, the genetic factors characterizing the vast majority of our experience remain confused and obscure. The zone of objects we are able to produce through thought alone is relatively small. Consequently, experience presents us with a zone of clarity like the sound of waves crashing, while leaving the genetic factors producing this intuition obscure and unconscious. It is this obscurity which produces the unavoidable illusion that intuition is characterized by passive receptivity in affection. For Deleuze all intuition is productive, and we are led to believe it is passive insofar as most of the principles governing its production are unconscious.

Signs of the Transcendental

From the foregoing, we can discern why Deleuze refers to the encounter as a sign rather than a quality. In defining signs Deleuze remarks:

> By "signal" we mean a system with order of disparate size, endowed with elements of dissymmetry; by "sign" we mean what happens within such a system, what flashes across the intervals when a communication takes place between disparates. The sign is indeed an effect, but an effect with two aspects: in one of these it expresses, *qua* sign, the productive dissymmetry; in the other it tends to cancel it. The sign is not entirely of the order of the symbol; nevertheless, it makes way for it by implying an internal difference (while leaving the conditions for its reproduction still external). (*DR* 20)

Leaving aside the idiosyncrasy of Deleuze's definition of signals (usually signals are associated with information, rather than notions of series), a sign is taken to be those events or effects that are produced by "flashing between" the intervals of the system. Here Deleuze's definition resembles the Lacanian or even Saussurean thesis that meaning is produced as an effect of signifiers (not signifieds) playing off one another. Deleuze clarifies this definition later when he states that

> *signs* as we have defined them—as habitudes or contractions referring to one another—always belong to the present. One of the great strengths of Stoicism lies in having shown that every sign is a sign of the present, from the point of view of the passive synthesis in which past and future are precisely only dimensions of the present itself. A scar is the sign not of a past wound but of "the present fact of having been wounded": we can say that it is the contemplation of the wound, that it contracts all the instants which separate us from it into a living present. Or rather, that we find here the true meaning of the distinction between natural and artificial: natural signs are signs founded upon passive synthesis; they are signs of the present, referring to the present in which they signify. Artificial signs, by contrast, are those which refer to the past or the future as distinct dimensions of the present, dimensions on which the present might in turn depend. Artificial signs imply active syntheses—that is to say, the passage from spontaneous imagination to the active faculties of reflective representation, memory and intelligence. (*DR* 77)

It is clear that the *sentiendum* is indeed a sign of the present insofar as it belongs to the sensibility, insofar as it is the being *of* the sensibility, which pertains to the present. Insofar as it is a sign announcing the being of the sensible, it is an indication of the differential through which the encounter was produced. However, it falls outside of the stoic articulation of signs which Deleuze articulates. On the one hand, we cannot say that the *sentiendum* is a "natural sign" insofar as it does not result from the contractions of difference belonging to *habitus*. As we have seen, the encounter necessarily evades the smooth continuity of *habitus*. For the same reason, on the other hand, we cannot say that it is an artificial sign because it is neither based on the synthesis of *habitus*, nor is it a matter of the active synthesis of recognition, since it evades and calls into question recognition. The signs belonging to the encounter are not conventions of a linguistic community. As a result, there must be a third type of sign which is neither natural nor artificial. Although Deleuze does not name it, such a sign would be a transcendental sign. To say that such a sign is a transcendental sign is not to say that the sign is a sign of something transcendent to experience—the transcendental ought not to be confused with the transcendent—but rather that it is a sign of the transcendental conditions of real experience or the genetic factors out of which the diversity of the given is produced.

If the encounter is a sign rather than a quality, this is because it expresses or indicates a tendency or faculty as its condition. The encounter is the sign of a limit, which in turn indicates a domain of difference belonging to that faculty alone. Our initial impulse might be to equate the domain of difference with Husserlian regions of phenomena, but as we will see later, the genetic conditions of experience do not resemble actualized experience characterizing the phenomenal field. The encounter is not a quality because it does not refer to a homogeneity conditioning experience, but is instead a sign *expressing* that which belongs to the faculty in question alone. As a sign it differs from that which it indicates just as smoke differs from fire. Despite Deleuze's prohibitions against method, we can nonetheless deduce a methodological choice from the nature of the encounter. However, here the question is not one of methodological accuracy, but of authenticity in taking up the encounter such that we are constituted as a subject. In other words, to refuse the encounter by covering it over with *habitus*, to push recognition as opposed to the difference that has announced itself, is to fall into Deleuze's equivalent of inauthenticity or bad faith. In this connection, authenticity would not be an attitude a person adopts toward her true self or way of temporalizing herself, but rather the manner in which she relates to her trauma which is "in her more than herself." The trauma thus shatters habitualized identity *and* renders it possible for the first time. In this connection there is an entire ethics of the event surrounding Deleuze's thinking of the encounter.

On the one hand, when confronted with a paradoxical encounter we can descend back into the empirical and explain it in terms of a failure of recognition. For instance, when we are led to believe that a man is small when seen from far away, we might explain this error by pointing out that our memory had not sufficiently contributed its share to this experience by reminding us that it is not in the nature of men to appear like ants, thus leading us astray. On the other hand, we can capitalize on the encounter by treating it as an opportunity to determine the nature of the faculty in which it manifests itself or shows itself as a sign. The first approach treats the referent as the primary term of importance, while the second seeks to determine the nature of the tendencies out of which these are actualized. Put differently, we can use the encounter as an opportunity to question the conditions under which such paradoxical encounters are possible, or ask "what must be proper to sensibility, what must sensibility be like, what internal logic must it follow for such phenomena to be possible?" In the first approach we ignore the limit suggested by the paradoxical instance of the encounter, while in the second we treat it as both the condition and the indication of thought. We treat the encounter as the sign of what is to be thought. This, for instance, is precisely what Derrida does in his essay "Signature, Event, Context," when he resolves not to reject performatives performed on stage and to instead determine what the fact that performatives can be performed on stage at all shows us about language *as such*.

We see here how Deleuze departs from both Bergsonian intuition and philosophies of reflection. On the one hand, the method of division is no longer exercised by a sovereign subject containing a good will and an affinity with the truth, but is rather announced through being itself in the contingency of an encounter. "We never know in advance how someone will learn: by means of what loves someone becomes good at Latin, what encounters make them a philosopher, or in what dictionaries they learn to think" (*DR* 165). On the other hand, Deleuze's position is at odds with philosophies of reflection such as Kantianism, German idealism, and phenomenology because all of these positions, in one way or another, trace the transcendental from the outlines of the empirical and assume a model of external difference between subjects and objects. It is not because Kant is a state thinker, or because Hegel is a thinker who shackles everything to totalities, that Deleuze rejects Kant and Hegel, but rather because they trace the transcendental from the empirical and assume an external model of difference. Kant and Hegel do not assert the primacy of recognition because they are state thinkers bent on justifying only established values; rather, they assert the primacy of established values because they begin with the model of recognition . . . And, as we shall see later, they do so for necessary and unavoidable reasons.

5

Second Moment of the Encounter: The *Memorandum*

The Ontological Structure of Problems and the Encounter

The encounter has the effect of forcing us to pose a problem. "That which can only be sensed (the *sentiendum* or the being of the sensible) moves the soul, 'perplexes' it—in other words, forces it to pose a problem: as though the object of encounter, the sign, were the bearer of a problem—as though it were a problem" (*DR* 140). It would therefore be wrong to suppose that the encounter is an encounter with a positive reality or a something. What is important in the encounter is not the object or concrete experience, but the problem. The problem is the true referent of the encounter, supposing that encounters have referents. Through the encounter we are led to discover the problem in such a way that we cannot determine whether we are the ones who have posed the problem or if the problem has always already been posed. We come into being with problems, just as problems seem to eternally preexist us. Put in negative terms, we can see why the *sentiendum* forces us to pose a problem. From the perspective of recognition governed by the living present or *habitus* composed of expectations and retentions, the *sentiendum* introduces a gap, explosion, event, or discontinuity which calls into question the smooth functioning of the living present. The *sentiendum* problematizes the living present and questions the continuity it sets up as a result of the first synthesis of time. Consequently, while I discover a difference other than an external difference between terms in the encounter, this difference is not an encounter with a determinate quality, but is a problematic difference.

However, this is a purely negative characterization of the *sentiendum* insofar as it defines it in terms of what it is not and shackles it to the primacy of recognition or the living present. The *sentiendum* is here merely treated as the absence of recognition, and the problematization which occurs is that of how to return to the continuity of expectation. Thus, for instance, Dewey's *Logic of Inquiry* treats the encounter as a failed hypothesis that gives us the opportunity to engage in further inquiry, refine our hypotheses, and reestablish the continuity of anticipation and actualization. This hardly represents a departure from the moral Image of thought. Rather, one of the central activities involved in the posing of problems consists in the diagnosis and critique of false problems.

> We always find two aspects of the illusion: the natural illusion which involves tracing problems from supposedly pre-existent propositions, logical opinions, geometrical theorems, algebraic equations, physical hypotheses or transcendental judgments; and the philosophical illusion which involves evaluating problems according to their "solvability"—in other words, according to the extrinsic and variable forms of the possibility of their finding a solution. It is then fatal that the ground should itself be no more than a simple external conditioning. A strange leap on the spot or vicious circle by which philosophy, claiming to extend the truth of solutions to problems themselves but remaining imprisoned by the dogmatic image, refers the truth of problems to the possibility of their solution. What is missed is the internal character of the problem as such, the imperative internal element which decides in the first place its truth or falsity and measures its intrinsic genetic power: that is, the very object of the dialectic or combinatory, the "differential." Problems are tests and selections. What is essential is that there occurs at the heart of problems a genesis of truth, a production of the true in thought. (*DR* 161–62)

When problems are treated in terms of preexistent forms of some type, or according to a criterion of solvability, they are understood in terms of recognition, the Image of thought, a preestablished model. Yet the encounter, like the simulacrum, is precisely a difference without model, a difference that evades the model. If problems are understood in terms of their intrinsic solvability, then they are understood in an empirical sense, which in turn leads us to transcendental accounts based on conditioning rather than genesis, external difference rather than internal and essential difference. For this reason, the perplication which takes place in the *sentiendum* forces us to problematize recognition, to determine the manner in which it is based on poorly analyzed composites and mixtures, to rediscover true differences in nature or kind lying beneath the differences in degree belonging to recognition. It is in this respect that the *sentiendum* forces us to pose a problem. The *sentiendum* functions as a sort of imperative calling us to trace the conditions under which it is possible, to rediscover the tendencies inhabiting it, to trace the synthetic structure or topological essence out of which our experience is given.

Ontological Memory: The Being of the Past

Upon entering the activity of posing the problem, we are no longer in the domain of sensibility, but within the domain of Memory.

> Must problems or questions be identified with singular objects of a transcendental Memory, as other texts of Plato suggest, so that there is the possibility of a training aimed at grasping what can only be recalled? Everything points in this direction: it is indeed true that Platonic reminiscence claims to grasp the immemorial being *of* the past, the *memorandum* which is at the same time afflicted with an essential forgetting, in accordance with the law of transcendental exercise that what can only be recalled should also be empirically impossible to recall. (*DR* 140)

It will immediately be objected that here Deleuze is treating the relationship between the *sentiendum* and the *memorandum* in terms of convergence, and is thus returning to the model of recognition. However, to object in this way is to speak loosely. A relation does not yet constitute a harmony, and the relation involved in the *memorandum* is one of force, not convergence. Here memory is not functioning in convergence with sensibility, but discordance. If there is an essential discord at work here, then it is because memory is no longer functioning on behalf of a resemblance between past experience and a present sensation, but now functions autonomously to pose problems. In other words, the *sentiendum* of the sensibility forces Memory into its superior exercise, such that it departs from sensibility. It is here that we witness a disharmonious or asymmetrical exercise of the faculties, opposed to the harmonious exercise found in recognition which is based on resemblance between past and present. To be sure, the faculties continue to communicate with one another, but it is now a communication based on force and violence, rather than convergence and harmony upon a selfsame object within an identical subject. Where the latter exercise of the faculties is based on a self-identical referent which is external to the faculties in question, the former is the functioning of the faculties independent of any being whatsoever.

It is for this reason that Deleuze is quick to distinguish transcendental memory from empirical memory.

There is a considerable difference between this essential forgetting and an empirical forgetting. Empirical memory is addressed to those things which can and even must be grasped: what is recalled must have been seen, heard, imagined or thought. That which is forgotten, in the empirical sense, is that which cannot be grasped a second time by the memory which searches for it (it is too far removed; forgetting has effaced or separated us from memory). Transcendental memory, by contrast, grasps that which from the outset can only be recalled, even the first time: not a contingent past, but the being of the past as such and the past of every time. In this manner, the *forgotten* thing *appears* in person to the memory which essentially apprehends it. It does not address memory without addressing the forgetting within memory. (*DR* 140)

That which is grasped in the *memorandum* is the past *as such,* the being *of* the past, rather than this or that contingent memory. This form of memory differs from empirical memory in that it is ontological rather than subjective. In fact, in *Bergsonism* Deleuze even goes so far as to claim that

there must be a difference in kind between matter and memory, between pure perception and pure recollection, between the present and the past . . . We have great difficulty in understanding a survival of the past in itself because we believe the past is no longer, that it has ceased to be. We have thus confused Being with being-present. Nevertheless, the present *is not;* rather, it is pure becoming, always outside itself. It *is* not, but it acts. Its proper element is not being but the active or the useful. The past, on the other hand, has ceased to act or be useful. But it has not ceased to be. Useless and inactive, impassive, it *is,* in the full sense of the word: It is identical with being in itself. (*B* 55)

In other words, Deleuze equates transcendental or ontological memory with the ontological difference between Being and beings. If memory corresponds to being, then this is because (1) in its passivity it resides identically in itself, and (2) it is the condition under which any being is able to appear in that the becoming of the present only discloses itself in differentiating itself from the past. Beings compose the domain of the act, which is not, since it is always already passed away, while Being consists in Memory which maintains and preserves itself. Deleuze refers to this domain of experience as the "virtual," which he defines, following Proust, as that which is "real without being actual, ideal without being abstract." It is not difficult to discern the differential at work in this definition of virtuality. Nowhere in the being that is concretely becoming do we directly encounter the differential, which renders it ideal. The differential is a sign that can only be sensed. However, since the differential is carried all the way to the being of the individual being, it lacks abstraction. The wager is that differentials are capable of both accounting for geometrical *form* and going beyond the limitations of Euclidean thinking based on the opposition between form and content. Deleuze's thought is thus profoundly inspired by eighteenth-century advances in mathematics.

The virtual differentials are the genetic factors of being. They are that which preside over the genesis of individuals *and* which are capable of doing so because the differential is carried all the way to the individual. As Pierre Lévy puts it,

> The word "virtual" is derived from the Medieval Latin *virtualis*, itself derived from *virtus*, meaning strength or power. In scholastic philosophy the virtual is that which has potential rather than actual existence. The virtual *tends* toward actualization, without undergoing any form of effective or formal concretization. The tree is virtually present in the seed. Strictly speaking, the virtual should not be compared with the real but the actual, for virtuality and actuality are merely two different ways of being.[1]

It is important not to associate the virtual with images, the imaginary, or the unreal. The virtual, as Deleuze uses it, has nothing to do with what conventional discourse sometimes calls "virtual reality." For Deleuze, the virtual is not opposed to the real, but is on the side of the real. For this reason, it is better to think the virtual as opposed to the actual. The virtual is the condition under which the actual actualizes itself. Since images too must be actualized, they have a virtual dimension that lacks any resemblance to the actual as well (see *DR* 100–101, 208–21). The differentials are potential or virtual in that they preside over a becoming, a duration, which is not yet completed. In this respect they can also be said to be "symbolic" or structural in that they define a system of ideal relations and places allowing for lack to be produced at the level of actualized experience as an effect of structure.

However, this becoming is creative in that it creates its own form of being in unfolding. The adult oak tree is a unique actualization of the seed that cannot be comprehended without comprehending the *history* of the oak tree. In actualizing itself, the seed as potentiality finds itself in a problematic field defined by its relation to other elements in its environment as well as its genetic history. The uniqueness of the oak tree is the manner in which the oak tree lives as a solution to this problematic field.

It may seem strange to think of differentials as productive forces in this way. When we think of differential equations, we tend to think of static forms that represent the rule of a completed graph. However, as Tiles points out, these equations are to be thought as principles of movement, not statically completed Euclidean forms. Like the illusions of difference in degree described by Bergson, it is only the graph placed before our eyes that gives us the impression that there is no movement, that we are before a completed form. In reality, it is a violent rejection of Euclid that stands at the foundation of Deleuze's critique of Plato, Aristotle, and Kant. What is rejected in all these cases is the primacy of Euclidean static form as the telos of becoming or the reality of being. Deleuze rejects the invariance and eternity of these forms in favor of those invariances characterizing becoming in the differential.

In this respect it is surprising, given Kant's great admiration for both Leibniz and Newton, that he did not make more of the calculus rather than arithmetic and geometry. Is Kant's philosophy perhaps a reactionary attempt to save thought from the terrifying universe that had been opened up with the algebrization of geometry and the creation of calculus that opened the way to envisioning pathological functions and infinite sets? No doubt Kant believed that the calculus was continuous with these disciplines, but as the example of irregular functions demonstrates, this is not so. If irregular functions are important, then this is because they represent a form of movement that cannot be graphed or visualized in intuition. This means that there are possibilities of thought *not* in service of intuition which are also not dogmatic. For Kant, who had argued that all knowledge requires both concepts and intuitions—thus completing a long trajectory of philosophy which consisted in treating sensibility as passive and thought as active, that had already been inaugurated in Plato—this is disastrous. No wonder the rationalists had such disdain for the empiricists, all of whom were united in their rudimentary knowledge of mathematics and singular lack of contributions to physics. With the exception of Spinoza, the rationalists had discovered a form of knowledge in analytic geometry and calculus which exceeded the constraints of intuition and allowed them to think the infinite with the daring and innocence of which Koyré speaks. This is a knowledge open to humans and which exceeds the constraints of finitude. As we shall see, it is in this spirit that Deleuze begins not with the finitude of the subject, but with the open whole out of which subjects and objects are actualized.

Three questions present themselves to us here. First, what is the being *of* Memory which Deleuze speaks of here? Why is it simultaneously the forgotten and that which can only be remembered? Second, and more importantly, what entitles Deleuze to claim that there is such a memory? Is he not guilty here of a sort of humanization, an anthropomorphization, of Being? Is this notion of being not just a gross metaphor? And third, what work does this notion of memory do for Deleuze? Why does he feel compelled to adopt it?

Memory and the Passage of the Present

The first and second questions can be answered together. The reason that we are led to distinguish an originary domain of Being characterized by Memory is that it is necessary to account for the conditions under which it is possible for something to become or for the present to pass.

> Although it is originary, the first synthesis of time is no less intratemporal. It constitutes time as a present, but a present which passes. Time does not escape the present, but the present does not stop moving by leaps and bounds which encroach upon one another. This is the paradox of the present: to constitute time while passing in the time constituted. We cannot avoid the necessary conclusion—*that there must be another time in which the first synthesis of time can occur.* This refers us to a second synthesis. (*DR* 79)

Such a conclusion must have already occurred to readers in relation to my brief account of the living present or *habitus* given earlier. Given that the living present is only produced through a synthesis engendering retentions and expectations, and that otherwise time would appear like a mass of unconnected instants in which no instant would ever seem to pass at all because I would always find myself in just this instant, how is it that this synthesis can occur at all? In other words, if time preceding the first synthesis is merely a mass of disconnected instants, then how is it that the synthesis of these instants occurs? By all accounts, it seems like the first synthesis ends up presupposing the very thing which it sets out to demonstrate. When expressed more precisely, the problem arises because the notion of "instant" seems to imply the idea of that which effaces or erases itself in the process of its passing. As Descartes had already noticed in his Third Meditation, instants are external to one another such that there seems to be an infinite and unbridgeable gulf between any two instants rendering communication between them impossible. For this reason it seems that there must be a third term between instants allowing for their synthesis. Just as Descartes had seen fit to have God effect the communication of instants, so too does

Deleuze describe the foundation of this communication in memory or the pure past.

If instants are doomed to oblivion in the course of their passing, then it seems to follow that the first synthesis is impossible insofar as it is left without anything to synthesize. It is in this sense that we ask how it is possible for the present to pass, that we require an account of what allows the present to pass. For in the passage of the present, that which passes is not simply annihilated, but is preserved as that which has passed. From the perspective of recognition this question clearly seems absurd, since the present clearly passes. However, this really is no argument, since it just marks a refusal of thought similar to the belief that it is idiotic to ask why things fall when we clearly see that they *do* fall. This marks a failure to think transcendentally, it marks a sign that one has remained within the empirical, that one feels dogmatically entitled to the claims made about experience, despite the fact that experience itself offers nothing in the given to support such claims. After all, birds do not fall, they fly, which leads us to wonder why there should be this exception to the rule that airborne entities fall. When one pauses for a moment, the fact that the present in fact passes comes to seem quite remarkable. So long as we conceive time as a passing of instants, then we are condemned to an eternal present in which no instant is different from any other. At the very least, the phenomenon of passing requires that one instant be distinguished from another so that one might know that a present has passed. *Habitus* can no less account for this passing than the notion of time as a collection of instants because *habitus* requires a sense of this passing in order to effect its synthesis.

For this reason, the first synthesis must necessarily refer to a second synthesis which preserves or maintains that which passes.

> The first synthesis, that of habit, is truly the foundation of time; but we must distinguish the foundation from the ground . . . Habit is the foundation of time, the moving soil occupied by the passing present . . . It is memory that grounds time. We have seen how memory, as a derived active synthesis, depended upon habit: in effect, everything depends upon a foundation. But this does not tell us what constitutes memory. At the moment when it grounds itself upon habit, memory must be grounded by another passive synthesis distinct from that of habit. The passive synthesis of habit in turn refers to this more profound passive synthesis of memory: Habitus and Mnemosyne, the alliance of the sky and the ground. Habit is the originary synthesis of time which constitutes the life of the passing present; Memory is the fundamental synthesis of time which constitutes the being of the past (that which causes the present to pass). (*DR* 79–80)

Our initial reaction is to accept this argument while rejecting its meta-physical pretensions. After all, upon reflection it seems obvious that a synthesis such as that of *habitus* should rely on some sort of mnemonic recording device like Freud's mystic writing pad to preserve the differences which are destined to be synthesized, the difference between the trace and its reactivation. If this were not the case, how could subsequent "tocks" ever be brought together in the synthesis engendering their expectation? But why, we might ask, should we complicate things by claiming that this synthesis is based on a substantialized notion of the past? Couldn't we simply attribute this power to the brain or any similar recording device?

However, a moment's thought is sufficient to demonstrate that this criticism is bound to fail. In the case of the recording device, Descartes' problem still stands. If we attribute *habitus* and *mnemosyne* to the brain, we just end up reproducing the problem at the level of materiality. Here the brain is treated as the agent or being carrying out the first synthesis of time, and memory is attributed to the brain as that which allows the brain to do this. Memory is treated as something that is *in* the brain, while the first synthesis of time is treated as something that the brain does. But it soon becomes apparent that the brain too must preserve itself if it is to carry out these syntheses. But if this is the case, then memory cannot be *in* the brain, but rather the brain must in a sense be in memory; or, at the very least, in time. In fact, Deleuze is more than happy to grant this argument. "We are made of contracted water, earth, light and air—not merely prior to the recognition or representation of these, but prior to their being sensed. Every organism, in its receptive and perceptual elements, but also in its viscera, is a sum of contractions, of retentions and expectations" (*DR* 73). *Habitus* is not something per-taining simply to psychic life, to the little ticks we develop in the course of our development, but is the biological principle par excellence. As such, it pertains to the organization of the brain as well. It is for this rea-son that Deleuze is able to say that Memory is an originary dimension of being itself, or as we saw before, that memory *is* Being. When the brain itself, when matter itself, comes to be understood in terms of *habitus,* then it becomes dependent upon this dimension of Memory in effect-ing its syntheses. Memory becomes the ground upon which these syn-theses can effectuate themselves. For this reason, Deleuze's concept of Memory avoids the criticism of being anthropocentric. Rather, it is the treatment of Memory as a faculty belonging to the minds of individuals alone which constitutes an anthropocentric conception of Memory . . . and an empiricist one at that.

Here we get a sense of why Deleuze understands the *memorandum* as that which can only be remembered *and* that which is forever forgotten. Memory can only be remembered because it *is*. This is to say, Memory is only memorial because it is memory *as such*, because it is an originary dimension of experience serving as the condition for the possibility of the living present. Here ontological memory is not what *has been* or what was once present and is now past. As the being of the past it has never been present and therefore can *only* be remembered. Unlike empirical memory, it does not refer to a transcendent memory that can be both lived and recollected. In short, it is not a memory of *something*. Another way of saying this would be to say that Memory can only be remembered because Memory *as such* is precisely that which has never been present, which has never manifested itself in sensibility, which is *always already* past. To say that Memory, *mnemosyne*, or the *memorandum* can only be remembered is to say (1) that it is not lived in sensibility or as an actuality, and (2) that in remembering the memorial we place ourselves directly within memory or the past. In other words, memory is an ontological dimension of experience itself and is not the memory of once lived, but now past, empirical experiences. Deleuze thus pairs that which is remembered and memory as such.

It is also for this reason that *mnemosyne* constitutes the forgotten, that which is a priori forgotten. If it is forgotten, it is forgotten from the standpoint of empirical experience, which recognizes only subjects and objects. However, we also see that there is a transcendental forgetting which is grounded in the fact that each memory expresses the whole of the past while only clearly actualizing a level of the past. Like Heidegger's *aletheia*, each actualized experience possesses an essential forgetfulness. It is from the perspective of empirical memory that Memory *as such* is forgotten, for in empirical memory what we remember is this or that lived experience, and not the dimension of Memory *as such* which renders such remembering possible in the first place. In fact, we might say that this is a constitutive aspect of the ground itself. The ground always has the peculiar characteristic of being absolutely present as a condition rendering experience possible, while also being absolutely absent or forgotten insofar as it differs from any particular empirical experience. The ground perpetually recedes from that which it grounds so that the grounded may stand forth in prominence. Its proximity is the very thing that engenders its distance.

The Virtual Causality of Structure

This is both one of the most difficult and the most important aspects of Deleuze's thought. It is of central importance because much of what Deleuze claims becomes highly speculative or even absurd if his account of Memory cannot be defended. Given that Memory is equated with the virtual, and that the virtual is equated with the conditions of real experience or the dimension of the transcendental in general, we can see just how important Deleuze's concept of Memory is to his thought. Regardless of whether we wish to think difference as essence, structure, assemblage, machine, system, or whatever other term we might fetishize to the detriment of actual inquiry, all of these notions become incomprehensible in the absence of an ontological dimension like Memory or the virtual. For example, how can there be synchronous language at work in unfolding speech characterized by the irreversible arrow of time? The reason for this is that they all rely on the notion of a structural, essential, machinic, systematic, or assemblage-based causality which is static with respect to events they render possible, rather than dynamic like the causality belonging to actual entities which moves from actuality to actuality. We must oppose a structural causality to mechanical causality.

> One will notice that the process of actualization always implies an internal temporality, variable according to what is actualized. Not only does each type of social production have a global internal temporality, but its organized parts have particular rhythms. As regards time, the position of structuralism is thus quite clear: time is always a time of actualization, according to which the elements of virtual coexistence are carried out at diverse rhythms. Time goes from the virtual to the actual, that is, from structure to its actualization, and not from one actual form to another. ("HRS" 268–69)

So long as we conceive Being according to the Newtonian paradigm of actual objects all causing and effecting one another, the notion of structure, assemblage, machine, system, or essence (in the specific sense I am developing it here) becomes incomprehensible. This is because the world of causes and effects, of actual entities does not recognize the continuity of relations, their ontological efficacy, but only the ever-shifting movements of real beings transferring force to one another. We here encounter one of the fundamental reasons explaining why we tend to think of the world in terms of subjects or individuals and atomic objects, rather than the systems of relations organizing them. Insofar as experience is spatialized and composed of mixed composites and differences in degree, and insofar as Memory is essentially forgotten, the relations organizing and informing our experience become invisible or efface themselves. We fail to recognize a specifically structural causality. In this respect, it can honestly be said that Deleuze attempts to provide the ontology proper to structuralism. Where Ricoeur asserts that structuralism is a Kantianism without a transcendental subject, Deleuze demonstrates what this means.[2] However, where Kant leaves a gap between concepts and intuitions, structuralism dreams of a transcendental philosophy capable of carrying itself all the way to the individual. But here I get ahead of myself.

If, on the other hand, the sense of the *memorandum* proves incredibly difficult to comprehend, then this is because we are inclined to understand memory only in the empirical sense of a past that was once present, but is no longer. In a paradoxical way, the difficulty involved in comprehending Deleuze's concept of ontological or transcendental Memory actually serves as a confirmation of it. For in this way, we are brought forcefully before the forgetting involved in Memory and the manner in which our experience is pervaded by empiricist assumptions.

The First Paradox of Memory: Contemporaneity

It is not enough to simply say that *mnemosyne* constitutes the being *of* the past *as such,* and to claim that the *memorandum* brings us before this past. Rather, we must be able to determine the properties or dimensions which belong to Memory in its very being. In the absence of such an analysis, we risk falling back into empiricist characterizations of Memory which would, in turn, return us to the model of recognition and the dogmatic Image of thought. To this end, Deleuze elaborates the properties of memory in a series of paradoxes. As always, we must not understand the Deleuzian use of paradox as arising from a taste for the bizarre, but as a full-fledged methodology for upsetting empiricist assumptions surrounding the model of recognition and uncovering the being of the transcendental. In short, there is a discipline and pedagogy of paradox. Paradox has the form of an encounter. In other words, paradox serves the dual critical roles of critiquing the assumptions of empirical experience or recognition and of allowing us to trace the properties of the transcendental. If such a thing as paradox is possible, this is always from the perspective of empiricism and recognition, and not the transcendental itself.

The first paradox of memory is expressed as follows:

> No present would ever pass were it not past "at the same time" as it is present; no past would ever be constituted unless it were first constituted "at the same time" as the present. This is the first paradox: the contem-

poraneity of the past with the present that it *was*. It gives us the reason for the passing of the present. Every present passes, in favour of a new present, because the past is contemporaneous with itself as present. (*DR* 81)

We have already seen why the past must be contemporaneous with the present. If the past were not contemporaneous with the present, then the present would be unable to pass. As such, time would deteriorate into a collection of disconnected instants forming nothing but an eternal present. The paradox of all this is that the past is both the past *as such* yet present with the present as well. In other words, the past is not past in the sense of being consigned to oblivion, erased for all time, but is actually there with the present in the moment of the present's passing. However, even more remarkably, the past and present constitute themselves at one and the same time. This is one of the signature marks of Deleuze's concept of time. For Deleuze, time does not move in a linear fashion from instant to instant, but progresses by perpetually dividing itself between past and present like a river dividing its flow at a fork between two streams.

Deleuze explains the necessity of this first aspect of memory from the perspective of both the active synthesis of recognition or the ego and the passive synthesis of habit which serves as the condition under which active synthesis is possible.

> The former present cannot be represented in the present one without the present one itself being represented in that representation. It is of the essence of representation not only to represent something but to represent its own representivity. The present and former present are not, therefore, like two successive instants on the line of time; rather, the present one necessarily contains an extra dimension in which it represents the former and also represents itself. The present present is treated not as the future object of a memory but as that which reflects itself at the same time as it forms the memory of the former present. Active synthesis, therefore, has two correlative—albeit non-symmetrical—aspects: reproduction and reflection, remembrance and recognition, memory and understanding . . . As a result, the active synthesis of memory is founded upon the passive synthesis of habit, since the latter constitutes the general possibility of any present. (*DR* 80–81)

If the present, when viewed from the perspective of the active synthesis of recognition, must represent both itself and the former present, this is because it cannot represent its difference from the former present without representing itself at the same time that it represents that former present. Consequently, it is impossible to say, as some would like to, that we are ever *in* a pure present. Even from the perspective of active synthesis, there is a double mediation insofar as (1) we are never just in the present present, but must represent the past present with the present present, and (2) the present present must be represented in its difference from the former present in order to represent itself as the present present. In Deleuze's language, the present present must differenciate itself from the past present in order for the passage of time to be possible. As such, representation, presence, is already pervaded by difference and absence. Presence always already differs from itself.

However, the active synthesis of the present also contains a third mediation, insofar as

> this active synthesis of memory is founded upon the passive synthesis of habit, since the latter constitutes the general possibility of any present. But the two syntheses are profoundly different: the asymmetry here follows from the constant augmentation of dimensions, their infinite proliferation. The passive synthesis of habit constituted time as a *contraction* of instants with respect to a present, but the active synthesis of memory constitutes it as the *embedding* of presents themselves. (*DR* 81)

The first passive synthesis of time contracts differences to form what Deleuze calls a "signal-sign system." In other words, it sets up a system of temporal relations between differences which function as signs of retention and expectation within experience. Unlike the essences discovered in differential topology, the relations belonging to these systems are associative and arbitrary insofar as the relations are external to their terms. Like the miraculous coincidence of being struck by lightning while cursing God, the association fails to establish a relationship of necessity among its terms. In this respect, *habitus* serves as a condition for active synthesis insofar as it delimits the representational possibilities or relations between present presents and former presents. It is necessary for there to be a system of sign relations preceding any act of active representation on the part of consciousness. One might say that there must be a system of "indexicals" upon which active representation is based. However,

> the whole problem is: with respect to what? It is with respect to the pure element of the past, understood as the past in general, as an *a priori* past, that a given former present is reproducible and the present present is able to reflect itself. Far from being derived from the present or from representation, the past is presupposed by every representation. In this

sense, the active synthesis of memory may well be founded upon the (empirical) passive synthesis of habit, but on the other hand it can be grounded only by another (transcendental) passive synthesis which is peculiar to memory itself. Whereas the passive synthesis of habit constitutes the living present in time and makes the past and the future two asymmetrical elements of that present, the passive synthesis of memory constitutes the pure past in time, and makes the former and the present present (thus the present in reproduction and the future in reflection) two asymmetrical elements of this past as such. (*DR* 80)

Both the active synthesis of memory and the passive synthesis of habit refer to the pure past as the ground of the possibility of their own respective syntheses. It is in this respect that we must say the past is contemporaneous with the present. If the past is contemporaneous with the present, if it is present with the present, then this is because it functions as the ground enabling the first passive synthesis and the active synthesis to take place. The past is the third term functioning as the medium of communication in which events unfold. It is the pure past, the past *as such,* which enables the active synthesis to reproduce the former present in the present present, and which allows the first passive synthesis to contract differences in the formation of a living present or duration.

The Second Paradox of Memory: Coexistence

The first paradox of contemporaneity leads to the second paradox of coexistence.

A second paradox emerges: the paradox of coexistence. If each past is contemporaneous with the present that it was, then *all* of the past coexists with the new present in relation to that which it is now past. The past is no more "in" this second present than it is "after" the first—whence the Bergsonian idea that each present present is only the entire past in its most contracted state. The past does not cause the present to pass without calling forth another, but itself neither passes nor comes forth. For this reason the past, far from being a dimension of time, is the synthesis of all time of which the present and the future are only dimensions. We cannot say that it was. It no longer exists, it does not exist, but it insists, it consists, it *is*. It insists with the former present, it consists with the new or present present. It is the in-itself of time as the final ground or the passage of time. In this sense it forms a pure, general, *a priori* element of all time. In effect, when we say that it is contemporaneous with the present that it *was,* we necessarily speak of a past which never *was* present, since it was not formed "after." (*DR* 81–82)

Consequently, in contrast to empirical forgetting, we here encounter a transcendental forgetting in which the ground as pure past effaces itself even as it is actualized. There is a great deal of ambiguity in this second paradox. What does Deleuze mean when he claims that the past is not "in" the second present, or "after" the first present? First, let us suppose a temporal series between the first present and the second present. The first present is the present that comes before the second present, just as the second present is the present which comes after the first present. We can then say that the second present is the present which is now present, while the first present is the one that has passed. Now, from the perspective of the active synthesis of memory or recognition, the past is thought to be in this second present and after the first. According to recognition, the past is constituted after the present in that something must first be present if it is to later be remembered. You can't take a rabbit out of a hat without first putting it in the hat, says the empiricist. In other words, the past is what comes after the first present elapses as a present. When expanded in this way, the nature of Deleuze's claim becomes clear: To treat the past as being in the second present and after the first present is to understand the past entirely in terms of the present, in terms of the actual. But if this is the case, then we have departed from the domain of the being *of* the past, of Memory *as such,* and are treating the past purely in empirical terms. If the past is the condition under which the present passes, then it cannot be constituted *after* the present passes, for in this case time would be powerless to begin.

However, while we can certainly grant this thesis from the perspective of the requirements of articulating a transcendental condition, it is still not immediately clear why this entails that the entirety of the past coexists with the present, that *all* the past is in some sense already there. Does this not effectively undermine the claim that the present passes and that pillar of Deleuze thought: that being is creative? If the entirety of the past is always already there, then how is it possible for anything new to be created at all? Why not simply claim that the past *as such,* as a dimension, as a domain, is already there, but that it is there in such a way that it finds itself as an ever-increasing field?

Not unpredictably, we can once again say that if the entirety of the past did not coexist with the present, if the past were constituted with the present, then we would find ourselves involved in the contradiction of claiming that the past is both what allows the present to pass and that which itself passes. But if this were the case, then we would have to ask what it is that allows the past to pass, which would destroy the role of memory as ground. Once again, this question involves us in the empiricist fallacy of tracing the transcendental from the empirical insofar as we are led to this question by asserting or assuming the privilege of the present and treating the past as that which was once present. Consequently, while we can indeed say that the past is "different" for each present present from the perspective of active synthesis, this is not because the past passes, but because different dimensions of the past are actualized with the emergence of a present. As Deleuze puts it, time does not move from present to past, but from past to present. In and of itself, the past does not pass at all (which is why we say that it *is*). It is also for this reason that Deleuze often claims that we place ourselves directly in the past, that we leap into the past itself, in the act of recollection.

When the past comes to be treated as an ontological dimension, when it is no longer treated as a dimension of the present or that which comes after the passing of a present, we can no longer say that we recollect the past in the present, but rather must say that we jump directly into the past. Such a claim certainly seems bizarre and odd from the perspective of empirical experience, but if it seems such, this is not because it is inherently absurd, but rather because we continue to assume that the past consists of presents that were once present. In short, we think of memory as a representation of the present rather than granting it the ontological autonomy which belongs to it. On the basis of this assumption, we then take Deleuze to be claiming that a leap into the past involves some sort of time travel which returns us to the present which has been lost. This would indeed be a highly suspect and speculative claim. What must forever be kept firmly in mind is that the past is a past that has never been present. It is also for this reason that the past is not said to exist, but to insist and consist. In keeping with the ontological difference between Being and beings, we cannot say that the past exists because that would be to treat it as *a* being. It is the past which renders existence as *ex-stasis* or standing-forth possible insofar as it is the condition under which active synthesis and the first passive synthesis become possible.

It is also because the entirety of the past coexists with the present that it is possible for something new to be created. Because the entirety of the past coexists with the present, it follows that each present must be absolutely new. To say that the entirety of the past coexists with the present is also to say, putting it crudely, that for each present there is no going back, that we have lived it once and for all. It is for this reason that Deleuze says that repetition is never a repetition of the same, but rather it is always a repetition of the different, of the unique, of the new. If repetition is always a repetition of the new, then it is because each iteration differenciates from the others. I am powerless to repeat because each iteration marks itself as an iteration of the others. As such it echoes all the others without being identical to them. For the moment, it is enough to simply note this point. The notion of something being novel simply because it is different or unrepeatable in terms of sameness or identity is a rather minimal and uninteresting notion of novelty, though it nonetheless undermines the notion of identity. While this thesis certainly holds, we seek a more nuanced notion of novelty in keeping with the artistic essences spoken of in Deleuze's reading of Proust.

Before proceeding, it is worthwhile here to address a criticism leveled against Deleuze by Badiou. In characterizing Deleuze's position on the relationship between truth and time, Badiou remarks that

> truth, which begins as disjunctive synthesis, or the experience of the separation of the present, culminates in the memorial injunction to recommence perpetually.
>
> This amounts to saying that there is no commencement, but only an abolished present (undergoing virtualization) and a memory that rises to the surface (undergoing actualization).
>
> And this is what I cannot consent to—for I maintain that every truth is the end of memory, the unfolding of a commencement.[3]

On the issue of Deleuze's concept of truth, Badiou has been one of the most sensitive and careful readers to be found. Where it is generally claimed that Deleuze rejects the notion of truth in favor of fictions and sense, Badiou demonstrates that Deleuze advocates a notion of ontological truth embodied within sense. The alternative between "Truth" and "fiction," along with equating the two with each other, places us in a rather undesirable straitjacket, insofar as the notion of Truth is deeply wedded to the tradition of onto-theology, while the alternative of fictions seems to authorize a subjectively relativistic free-for-all, as can be witnessed in much of the literature parading under the names of constructivism and postmodernsim. If truth is a fiction, it certainly is not a fiction of my own making, or of society's making. Such a perspective provides an initial orientation for navigating the twin perils of onto-theological terror and relativistic postmodern banalities.

This point can be demonstrated both textually and in terms of the logic of Deleuze's arguments against the notion of representational truth, and hence ought to be assented to. The fact that Deleuze's position regarding truth has been generally ignored gives some indication of just how much readings of Deleuze tend to be dominated by his commentary on Nietzsche. However, when Badiou criticizes Deleuze for relegating truth to the domain of memory, he speaks in a misleading way which muddles the issue. While it is certainly true that Truth belongs to the domain of memory, this in no way undermines the novelty of (ontological) truth, nor does it undermine the nature of truth as a commencement. On the one hand, the fact that the past coexists with the present ensures that each new present is precisely that: new. On the other hand, the past, as we shall see, consists of all sorts of levels defined in terms of contractions and relaxations, such that levels of the past are actualized in the present. When Deleuze speaks of the event as that which is eternally about to happen or eternally elapsed but never happen*ing*, he is not describing a state of affairs in which the event of truth is powerless to ever commence, but rather the very nature of what it means to commence. To live within an event is to live within a field in which truth has been actualized in a particular way, making certain truths possible. In this respect Badiou is much closer to Deleuze than he believes. For just as Badiou's concept of the event involves the notion of forgetting or the end of memory, so too does Deleuze's notion of the eternity of the event imply the notion of "that which we affirm once and for all, and for all time" or a forgetting of time (where time is understood as the synthesis of all time involved in memory as such). On the other hand, from a Deleuzian perspective, we can criticize Badiou for rendering the notion of the event incomprehensible insofar as he reduces it to a sort of pure present defined in terms of a spatial multiplicity, which makes the event look like a mysterious entity descending on the state of affairs from nowhere, and also leads us to wonder how it is possible for the present to pass within Badiou's philosophy. This point will be gradually unfolded in the next three chapters as we progressively approach Deleuze's concept of essence and his account of individuation. In this connection, it is impossible to affirm the new as such. For to affirm is to affirm *something*. An affirmation of the new would be an affirmation that committed itself to nothing and which would therefore be for nothing.

The Third Paradox of Memory: The Preexistence of the Past

As might be expected from comments surrounding the second paradox of memory, the third paradox of memory consists in the preexistence of the past.

Its manner of coexisting with the new present is one of being posed in itself, conserving itself in itself and being presupposed by the new present which comes forth only by contracting this past. The paradox of preexistence thus completes the other two: each past is contemporaneous with the present it was, the whole past coexists with the present in relation to which it is past, but the pure element of the past in general preexists the passing present. There is thus a substantial temporal element (the Past which was never present) playing the role of ground. This is not itself represented. It is always the former or present present which is represented. The transcendental passive synthesis bears upon this pure past from the triple point of view of contemporaneity, coexistence and pre-existence. By contrast, the active synthesis is the representation of the present under the dual aspect of the reproduction of the former and the reflection of the new. The latter synthesis is founded upon the former, and if the new present is always endowed with a supplementary dimension, this is because it is reflected *in* the element of the pure past in general, whereas it is only *through* this element that we focus upon the former present as a particular. (*DR* 82)

If the past must preexist any particular present, then this is because the present is pure passing (which is why it *is not*) and thus requires the past in order that it may pass. Once again, it is only from the perspective of recognition, representation, or empirical experience that this preexistence of the past appears to be a paradox. Beginning with the assumption that the present is what is and that the past is a present that once was, the thesis that the past preexists the present necessarily appears paradoxical insofar as it simultaneously claims being for that which is not and attributes non-being to that which allows the past to be constituted. By couching the preexistence of the past in the form of a paradox, we are able to uncover the assumptions of the empiricist position and move beyond them. With respect to the third paradox, we are also reminded of the Bergsonian thesis that duration is substance. To claim that duration is substance is not to claim that it is existence. Rather, to claim that memory is substance (recalling here the other Bergsonian claim that duration is memory) is to claim that the past, Memory, is that which stands beneath, that which supports, that which enables; that it is *hupokeimenon*. Far from claiming that Memory is existence, which can only properly be attributed to the present or that which *is not*, the claim that Memory is substance is nothing other than the claim that Memory is the transcendental condition under which the present is able to pass.

The Fourth Paradox of Memory: The Coexistence of the Past with Itself

The third paradox leads to a fourth and final paradox revolving around the coexistence of the past with itself.

> It must first be the case that this whole past coexists with *itself*, in varying degrees of relaxation . . . and of contraction. The present can be the most contracted degree of the past which coexists with it only if the past first coexists with itself in an infinity of diverse degrees of relaxation and contraction at an infinity of levels (this is the meaning of the famous Bergsonian metaphor of the cone, the fourth paradox in relation to the past). Consider what we call repetition within a life—more precisely, within a spiritual life. Presents succeed, encroaching upon one another. Nevertheless, however strong the incoherence or possible opposition between successive presents, we have the impression that each of them plays out "the same life" at different levels. This is what we call destiny. (*DR* 82–83)

Once again, the paradox of the coexistence of the past with itself is only a paradox from the perspective of an empirical concept of memory. From the perspective of empirical memory, the notion of the past coexisting with itself is incomprehensible because the past is always constituted *after* the present. From this point of view, the past is treated as what follows or succeeds the present insofar as it is thought of as being composed of presents which were once present. It is clear that such a notion of the past will prove unacceptable from the perspective of transcendental memory. In the first place, the past is that which allows the present to pass. If we were to say that the past is constituted after the present, then we would be unable to determine the conditions under which it is possible for the present to pass.

Second, even if we were to suppose that there is a past *as such* or *in itself* which functions as a sort of container for passing presents, we would again find ourselves facing three problems. First, to say that there is a general past which functions as a sort of container that gets filled by various passing presents would still involve us in the difficulty of claiming that the past is constituted *after* the present. In other words, we would still be privileging the temporal dimension of the present in our interpretation of the past. In response to this, we might insist that we have indeed granted the being of the past its due by positing a past in general in the function of a container, a form of the past as it were, but in truth this gets us no further. The mark of the past is precisely that it is past. This holds for each singular memory to the same degree that it holds for memory in general. The past can never be reconstituted out of degraded presents. Second, and perhaps more importantly, speaking of the past in terms of a container implies that it is itself contained within something else, for it is in the nature of containers that they themselves are in turn contained. However, this returns us to all the empiricist assumptions which would claim that memory is in the mind or the brain rather than being a distinct ontological dimension of its own. All things being equal, the brain too must be preserved across its duration of being. Consequently, the strategy of treating memory as being contained in the brain merely defers the issue.

Finally, in speaking of a past in general which comes to contain presents that have become past we are once again returned to the problems of how it is possible for the present to pass.

> We are too accustomed to thinking in terms of the "present." We believe that a present is only past when it is replaced by another present. Nevertheless, let us stop and reflect for a moment: How would a new present come about if the old present did not pass at the same time that it *is* present? How would any present whatsoever pass, if it were not past *at the same time* as present? The past would never be constituted if it *had not been* constituted first of all, at the same time that it was present . . . If the past had to wait in order to be no longer, if it was not immediately and now that it had passed, "past in general," it could never become what it is, it would never be *that* past. (*B* 58–59)

In other words, it's not just that there is a dimension of experience referred to as the past in general functioning in the capacity of a container coming to be filled by various passing presents, but rather the passing present always already has one foot in the door of the past. For Deleuze the movement of time is not a linear movement from past to present, but rather a perpetual dividing like a forked road in which the past is not constituted *by* the present, but *with* the present. Put otherwise, half of the passing present is always already submerged in the past. There is no generality here, but rather the singularity of the event. Consequently, to speak of a past in general is not to say that there is a quality of pastness *as such* which then comes to be filled by particular presents which pass, but is rather to say that the ontological dimension of the past is fully at work in all of our experience. In fact, here we come before one of the most important aspects of memory: unlike kinds, memories are always singular and unique. There is no such thing as a general memory, an abstract memory. Rather, memories always have the character of events. What is general in memory is not memory as such, but the motor diagrams or schemes that come to be formed between memory and habit, between the first synthesis of time and the second synthesis of time. For it is in the dimension of the future as it is found in *habitus* that generality, serving as the foundation of the active synthesis of recognition, comes to characterize our experience.

In light of this singularity of memory, we can now make sense of what Deleuze means when he talks about "contracted degrees of the past" existing in varying degrees of relaxation and contraction. Given the uniqueness of the past, of memory, we can say that

> not only does the past coexist with the present that has been, but, as it preserves itself in itself (while the present passes), it is the whole, integral past; it is *all* our past, which coexists with each present. The famous metaphor of the cone represents this complete state of coexistence. But such a state implies, finally, that in the past itself there appear all kinds of levels of profundity, marking all the possible intervals in this coexistence. The past AB coexists with the present S, but by including in itself all the sections A'B', A"B", etc., that measure the degrees of a purely ideal proximity or distance in relation to S. Each of these sections is itself *virtual*, belonging to the being in itself of the past. Each of these sections or each of these levels includes not particular elements of the past, but always the totality of the past. It includes this totality at a more or less expanded or contracted level. (*B* 59–60)

Consequently, all of our experience is accompanied by an essential unconscious, by a halo of obscurity flickering about its field of clarity, such that each present expresses the totality of the past in a contracted state. It is worth pointing out just how much this notion of memory resembles the Proustian notion of essence I discussed in chapter 2. This should come as no surprise given that Proust, as is well known, was deeply inspired by Bergson. There essence was defined in Leibnizian fashion as a point of view on the world centering around individuating difference. By the same token, each level in the cone of memory could be said to constitute a sort of world or essence. Periods of our lives become contracted together, expressing a general sense of being or essence. The singularity of the levels of the cone does not correspond to individual memories, but rather to a world defined as a set of relations belonging to that world and that world alone. It is in this respect that each level individuates all the way down to the individual, without any gap between the general and the particular. Specific memories, on the other hand, correspond to the actualization of Memory within psychological or empirical experience. The point at which memory converges with the present constitutes the most contracted degree of Memory, while the Whole of Memory constitutes the most relaxed moment of Memory. Each specific level or plane of Memory expresses all of the others, contains all of the others, or coexists with all of the others but in a more or less contracted way.

It is the degrees of contraction and relaxation which ensure the singularity of each level of memory. This point can be elucidated by drawing on an *empirical* example. Here we can only use empirical examples to elucidate the point because (1) memory *as such* is necessarily *forgotten* and is thus unspeakable, and (2) because any discussion of memory constitutes a creative *actualization* of memory which draws it into empirical experience. To say that the Revolutionary War was a war for American independence from England represents a very relaxed degree of the past. This is because it leaves the relations composing the war highly unspecified. A greater contraction of such a memory would consist in claiming that the war was brought about due to a lack of representation with respect to taxes. Finally, the greatest degree of contraction would consist in living through an individual skirmish expressive of the war as an event. In each of these cases the degree or level of the past involved is distinct from the others, yet nonetheless they all express one another in a manner similar to Russian dolls embedded within one another. Each contraction involves a specification of relations moving forward in degrees of ever-greater complexity. It is in this sense that the past coexists with *itself*. Not only do the various levels of memory coexist with one another, but they express or implicate one another as well.

Freedom and Destiny

At this point it is likely that the question of freedom raises itself quite forcibly. This is especially the case with respect to the third paradox of the past, referring to the preexistence of the past. To be sure, Deleuze has managed to explain how it is possible for the present to pass, or how the past functions as the ground. But has he not demonstrated this at the expense of showing that everything has always already transpired or taken place? In Deleuze's view, is not the actualization of events a superfluous addition that makes no real contribution to these events themselves? Is it not the case that for Deleuze all is already accomplished, finished with, done? Our concern only grows when Deleuze refers to this past in terms of Destiny, for in the concept of destiny we get the sense that all is determined and accomplished. As Deleuze puts it elsewhere,

> Bergson saw that memory was a function of the future, that memory and will were but one and the same function, that only a being capable of memory could turn away from its past, detach itself, not repeat it, do something new. In this way the word "difference" designates both *the particular that is* and the *new which is made*. Recollection is defined both in relation to the perception with which it is contemporaneous and the following moment in which it prolongs itself. Reuniting the two senses produces a bizarre impression: that of acting and being "acted" at the same time. ("BCD" 56)

The claim that by virtue of memory we are able to detach ourselves from the past and create something new seems entirely in accord with the notion of freedom. Such a view suggests that the past does not weigh down heavily upon us, determining our actions from the outset, but instead is that which allows us to depart from the past by rendering it present. However, the notion of being "acted," which is directly related to that of destiny, is precisely where the concern with determinism arises. Where can there possibly be freedom when we are acted, when we are implicated in destiny?

In response to these potential difficulties, Deleuze claims that

> destiny never consists in step-by-step deterministic relations between presents which succeed one another according to the order of a present time. Rather, it implies between successive presents non-localisable connections, actions at a distance, systems of replay, resonance and echoes, objective chances, signs, signals and roles which transcend spatial locations and temporal successions. We say of successive presents which express a destiny that they always play out the same thing, the same story, but at different levels: here more or less relaxed, there more or less contracted. This is why destiny accords so badly with determinism but so well with freedom: freedom lies in choosing the levels. The succession of present presents is only the manifestation of something more profound—namely, the manner in which each continues the whole life, but at a different level or degree to the preceding, since all levels and degrees coexist and present themselves for our choice on the basis of a past which was never present. (*DR* 83)

On the one hand, Deleuze associates the thesis of determinism with that of linear relations of causation in space between presents. Determinism is based on the premise of mechanical causality between events. Once again, it is a matter of conceiving being under the model of billiard balls transferring quantities of force to each other. By contrast, the concept of destiny as conceived by Deleuze offers two degrees of freedom with respect to the despotic grip of the present in its determinative capacity. First, insofar as memory involves us in a replaying of the past, in a system of echoes and resonances, it creates a sort of hollow or gap between the ironclad grip of links between causes in the present. This repetition is never a repetition of the same, but a repetition that produces difference as it is unfolded. We might think of it as being similar to a continual variation of a musical theme. Memory, insofar as it is composed of levels or planes, ensures that a purely deterministic relation never obtains between two causes or presents, because it always intervenes between these presents and thus opens the way for a degree of freedom from the present.

Incidentally, we also see here why memory serves as the condition for the possibility of structure. If structural causality must be opposed to mechanical causality, to the causality of the present, this is because structure does not function like billiard balls exchanging force, forever changing their configurations, but perpetually reproduces a pattern within mechanical causality, inhibiting the deterministic relations among objects, allowing for a veritable infinity of variations on a theme.

It is very difficult to grasp this point. The difference between mechanical or efficient causality and structural causality can be expressed as a difference between horizontal and vertical forms of movement. With efficient causality we have a sort of horizontal relation between causes in a series, such that one cause is directly related to the next *and* modifies the relations of all the elements involved. The horizontal knows no preservation of the relation. Structural causality, by contrast, functions by virtue of a sort of vertical leap forth from the structure in such a way that the relations belonging to the structure are maintained. *With respect* to the actualized elements of the structure, the structure remains invariant; while, as we saw in chapter 2, there is nonetheless a specifically structural variation. We might think here of the way in which DNA maintains the relations of which it is composed, standing beneath its actualizations as it were, undergoing a specifically structural variation in the course of its evolution. It is with respect to this structural causality that a sort of hollow or gap is produced between cause and effect that allows for a degree of freedom from the present.

We encounter here one of the crucial differences between mechanical causality and structuralist accounts of causality. A causal account is able to *predict* the form that future events will take, if only in an abstract and general way. By contrast, structural accounts do not predict what form the future configuration of elements will take, but rather *explain* them on the basis of principles that are more simple than those of actualized forms. As Hjelmslev puts it,

> *A priori* it would seem to be a generally valid thesis that for every *process* there is a corresponding *system,* by which the process can be analyzed and described by means of a limited number of premises. It must be assumed that any process can be analyzed into a limited number of elements recurring in various combinations. Then, on the basis of this analysis, it should be possible to order these elements into classes according to their possibilities of combination. And it should be further possible to set up a general and exhaustive calculus of the possible combinations.[4]

A properly structural causality reveals the system accounting for this process in such a way that the system functions as a sort of gap between the linear or horizontal causes characterizing the present.

As Deleuze's account of actualization and his interest in genetic approaches clearly reveal, matters are no different with respect to transcendental empiricism. We can discern this premise at work everywhere in his thought. It manifests itself in the brilliant essay "Coldness and Cruelty," where he returns to the systems generating the surface manifestations of sadism and masochism. It is found again in his elaborate reading of Proust in *Proust and Signs,* where he shows that *Remembrance of Things Past* is organized around four central types of signs defining an apprenticeship in signs. We also find it in his masterful work *Foucault,* and even his brilliant analysis of cinema in *Cinema I* and *Cinema II.* It is always a matter of returning to the system underlying surface manifestations which function as genetic principles. Initially it might seem that mechanical causal accounts are superior when compared to structural causal accounts by virtue of their predictive power. However, as I hope to demonstrate much later in this book, horizontal causal accounts are themselves dependent upon vertical causal accounts. Moreover, at the very least, we are able to see that accounts which admit of no other form of causality but mechanical causality are unable to account for why certain forms of organization persist when they are constantly threatened from without by so many buffeting forces.

The notion of destiny produces a degree of freedom from the present insofar as it allows something new to be introduced into the present, something inherently creative and novel which could not have been anticipated from the relations among causes and effects alone. For instance, by exploiting qualities of the signifiers within various languages, James Joyce is able to produce effects of sense that are entirely novel. From the perspective of the present alone, nothing really new is ever produced. This perhaps seems like an exaggerated claim to make insofar as we are inclined to say that each new present is absolutely new. Materialist ontologies tend to be led inevitably to a sort of atomism where each atom is treated as self-identical and unchanging and only efficient or causal relations are admitted between these atoms. While we can certainly imagine a vast number of possible configurations among the atoms, the types of relations possible are finite and deterministic. On the other hand, with the dimension of memory, something absolutely novel can be introduced into being through the relation between the levels of memory and the first passive synthesis, creating new ways of experiencing the world or of being in the world altogether.

However, despite the fact that Deleuze is able to preserve freedom with respect to the closed despotism of the present, there is nonetheless the disquieting suspicion that Deleuze maintains a determinism in another more profound sense. Here we would have a determinism of the past, weighing down upon us, shackling us to a particular level of the cone of memory. Yet this is a problem only if we think of the past as exerting force, as weighing down upon us, as functioning in the sense of mechanical causality. We must remember that the past itself does not pass, that it does not stand in a causal relation to the present in the way that presents stand in relations of causation with one another. Rather, the past functions as ground. Unlike the present which *is not* because it has always already passed, or is always already passing, the past *is*. Insofar as the past *is*, it both preexists the present and coexists with itself. It is also for this reason that we say that we leap directly into the past, that we place ourselves directly in a level of the past. But if all of this is the case, if all of this holds according to the demands of being a transcendental condition, then we can no longer say that the structural causality effectuated by the past weighs down upon us in a deterministic fashion, abolishing all degrees of freedom. Rather, as Deleuze says, our freedom consists in choosing the level, of passing between levels, in the course of actualizing these levels within our experience. It is true that we perpetually play out themes, refrains, structures, or topological essences, but we choose the level of the past with which to actualize these themes or styles. Consequently, there are indeed restrictions on action, but there are degrees of freedom within the field of these restrictions. Just as chess places restrictions on sanctioned movements while allowing for more unique games than there are particles in the universe, so too does the destiny of structure allow for indefinite creative variations.

It is for this same reason that we cannot treat the past as accomplished, as finished, complete, as if we were subject to some strange illusion in which the past were complete in one great eternity while we were nonetheless doomed to live the past as the unfolding of time. There is indeed a sense in which the past is accomplished and complete. As we have seen, the past *is,* it preexists the present, and it coexists with itself. However, to ask whether this means that all has already happened, that all has already occurred, is to confuse the being *of* the past with the empirical past or history. Between the empirical past and the being of the past there is no resemblance, only a dual serialization related by a disjunctive synthesis. As Deleuze succinctly puts it,

> All is repetition in the temporal series, in relation to this symbolic image. The past itself is repetition by default, and it prepares this other repetition constituted by the metamorphosis in the present. Historians sometimes look for empirical correspondences between the present and the past, but however rich it may be, this network of historical correspondences involves repetition only by analogy or similitude. In truth, the past is in itself repetition as is the present, but they are repetition in two different modes which repeat each other. (*DR* 90)

To say that the past preexists the present and coexists with itself is not to say that all history is accomplished, because history itself belongs to the domain of active synthesis which, while dependent upon the two passive syntheses, is itself distinct from these syntheses.

> What we call the empirical character of the present which makes us up is constituted by the relations of succession and simultaneity between them, their relations of contiguity, causality, resemblance and even opposition. What we call their noumenal character is constituted by the relations of virtual coexistence between the levels of a pure past, each present being no more than the actualisation or representation of one of these levels. In short, what we live empirically as a succession of different presents from the point of view of active synthesis is also *the ever-increasing coexistence of levels of the past within passive synthesis.* (*DR* 83)

In other words, the levels of the first passive synthesis and the active synthesis introduce something new into time which is not found within the pure past.

The past functions as the ground of these two syntheses, but it does not determine them once and for all. This point is driven home later in *Difference and Repetition* when Deleuze criticizes Kant's notion of the aesthetic.

> If this aesthetic [the first passive synthesis] appears more profound to us than that of Kant, it is for the following reasons: Kant defines the passive

self in terms of simple receptivity, thereby assuming sensations already formed, then merely relating these to the *a priori* forms of their representations which are determined as space and time. In this manner, not only does he unify the passive self by ruling out the possibility of composing space step by step, not only does he deprive this passive self of all power of synthesis (synthesis being reserved for activity), but moreover he cuts the Aesthetic into two parts: the objective element of sensation guaranteed by space and the subjective element which is incarnate in pleasure and pain. The aim of the preceding analyses, on the contrary, has been to show that receptivity must be defined in terms of the formation of local selves or egos, in terms of the passive syntheses of contemplation or contraction, thereby accounting simultaneously for the possibility of experiencing sensations, the power of reproducing them and the value that pleasure assumes as a principle. (*DR* 98)

It's worth pointing out that this error is not simply restricted to Kant's transcendental philosophy, but manifests itself in classical empiricism as well. In both cases, impressions or the a posteriori are treated as a ready-made given which our faculties are designed to apprehend in advance. However, in the case of Kant these impressions or sensations are organized by the a priori forms of intuition and categories of the understanding, while for the empiricists they are related to one another through associations based on resemblance and contiguity, and then grouped to form abstract ideas. By contrast, Deleuze conceives of a genesis of sensibility itself within sensibility, which I referred to earlier as the experience of experience producing experience. However, with respect to the point at hand, the significance of this thesis is that the first passive synthesis, which is distinct from the second passive synthesis, and which serves as the basis for the active synthesis, produces something new which cannot simply be attributed to the workings of the pure past. By virtue of this new creation, which serves as the foundation of the active synthesis by forming a system of retentions and expectations, empirical history itself becomes possible at the level of active synthesis. In short, for Deleuze the finite subject of representation is something which is produced, not something assumed on the basis of affects that are held to be given in passive receptivity.

The Force of Memory

The contemporaneity of the past with the present, its coexistence with the present, its preexistence with respect to the present, and the coexistence of the past with respect to itself form the four paradoxes of the pure past. Nonetheless, it seems as if we have strayed far from our initial questions revolving around why the *sentiendum* in turn forces the *memorandum* or the superior exercise of memory, which leads us to pose a problem. In this connection, the first question to ask is that of why the *sentiendum* forces us to pose a problem. What is it about the *sentiendum* which leads us to formulate a problem? On the other hand, we must ask why posing a problem has an essential relation to the being of the past, why it forces us to leap back into the past. In light of the foregoing analysis of Memory, we can now answer these questions with ease.

As we saw in the last chapter, the *sentiendum* is a sign which can only be sensed and which cannot be characterized as either a natural or an artificial sign. Natural signs, it will be recalled, are signs of the present based on the first passive synthesis, while artificial signs are signs of the past or future belonging to the active synthesis of recognition. By contrast, the *sentiendum,* the being *of* the sensible, or sign that can only be sensed, falls outside of both of these categorizations insofar as it *forces* us to think, thereby evading both the present of *habitus* consisting of retention and expectation, and the past-future of active synthesis based on recognition. The *sentiendum* is not a sign belonging to the present because it is not retended or expected, nor is it a sign of the past or future because it forces us to think. Rather, it is a sign of the transcendental (not to be confused with a transcendental signifier) indicating an internal difference. But as a sign of the transcendental evading both *habitus* and recognition, the *sentiendum* also calls into question *habitus* and recognition, introduces a gap into it, or calls forth a hollow within the continuous space of retention and anticipation. The transcendental sign marks the space in which there is something else to be found. The mark of the sign that can only be sensed is precisely that it is the unexpected. It is in this sense that it constitutes a sort of event, a trauma even.

It is this gap, this event, this moment of the unexpected which marks the first moment of problematization. At the very least, the sign which forces us to think, which can only be sensed, calls into question the nature of our experience. To this we can respond either by seeking ways to explain away the sign as some sort of simple error or by rethinking our experience on the basis of the possibility of the sign. However, what must be avoided above all—from the theoretical point of view—is thinking that the sign is itself nothing, that it is a pure negativity, that it is simply opposed to experience. While the sign indeed stands in harsh contrast to experience as it is understood from the perspective of recognition (it literally forces itself to be taken note of), it nonetheless does not stand in a simple dialectical relation consisting of being the absence of recognition or the inverse of recognition. The sign that can only be sensed is not *opposed* to recognition but is *other* than recognition. Nor, when taking up the sign that can only be sensed and seeking to explicate it, do we aim to return to recognition. As Deleuze puts it somewhat dramatically,

> Recognition is a sign of the celebration of monstrous nuptials, in which thought "rediscovers" the State, rediscovers "the Church" and rediscovers all the current values that it subtly presented in the pure form of an eternally blessed unspecified eternal object. Nietzsche's distinction between the creation of new values and the recognition of established values should not be understood in a historically relative manner, as though the established values were new in their time and the new values simply needed time to become established. In fact it concerns a difference which is both formal and in kind. The new, with its power of beginning and beginning again, remains forever new, just as the established was always established from the outset, even if a certain amount of empirical time was necessary for this to be recognised. (*DR* 136)

Once again, the model of recognition is not a passing empirical moment destined to disappear under the force of a new model. Although the model of recognition might commit the error of tracing the transcendental from the empirical, and of treating difference entirely in terms of external difference, the nature of this error is itself constitutive or, in a sense, transcendental. In this respect, the Image of thought is more akin to a transcendental illusion in the Kantian sense of the term than to a simple fallacy or error born of making a mistake, miscalculating, or incorrectly denoting the truth.

If the sign that can only be sensed is perpetually new and does not return to the model of thought, this is because (1) it is unrecognizable by right (it is not governed by the simple relation of subject and object), (2) it is not based on a convergence of the faculties of memory and perception, imagination and sensibility, but approaches each of these faculties in their being *as such*, and (3) it opens up an entirely *other* domain functioning according to principles which depart from the model of recognition. As a result, the sign that can only be sensed inaugurates the way to *other* values which can never be acceptable from the point of view of recognition. If these values "destroy the Image of thought" it is not because the Image of thought ceases to function or exercise itself, but rather because its authority no longer has sway within this *other* domain. We are no longer shackled or dominated by the demands of representation.

Given this, it is clear that the sign which can only be sensed is not merely the absence of recognition but instead refers to an *other* content. Viewed from the perspective of recognition, the sign which forces us to think indeed appears to be a gap or hollow, a space of negativity. Yet when the sign which can only be sensed is taken up in and of itself, it indicates an-*other* content or form that can be explored for its own sake. Here the dialectical relation is abolished for a second time insofar as the explication of the sign that can only be sensed does not refer us back to recognition, but instead to a divergent logic or structure all its own. However, it is precisely here that the sign which can only be sensed forces us to pose a problem. Initially the problem posed itself in terms of recognition: what has gone astray with recognition allowing for such unexpected results? Yet recognition finds that it can only explain this bizarre and contradictory sign if it explains it away or treats it in terms of a failed convergence between the faculties. This, for example, is what Searle does in relation to Derrida when discussing performatives used in performances. It cannot express the sign in and for itself. For this reason, the *sentiendum* violently forces the *memorandum* into action in the form of that which can only be remembered and that which is perpetually forgotten. With respect to recognition, it was found that memory was to no avail. All that could be said was that memory had forgotten something crucial with respect to sensibility, that somehow the desired convergence in expectation had failed to take place. As a result, we find that we must depart from the assumptions of empirical memory, that this memory no longer serves us. But if we depart from empirical memory, to what do we turn? If not empirical memory, then we must turn to memory *as such,* to the being *of* the past. It is precisely in this sense, in this essential forgetting, that the being of the sensible both forces us to pose a problem and forces memory into its transcendental or superior exercise. Memory becomes a memory of the past *as such,* while the posing of the problem becomes a matter of destiny, a matter of choosing the level within the coexistent degrees of relaxation and contraction in the past. Here the gap produced by the *sentiendum* is no longer a gap, but rather the fullness of the past made present, the fullness of a structure informing experience, the splendor of a style, theme, or essence. But with this posing of the problem, we have already moved into the third moment.

6

Third Moment of the Encounter: The *Cogitandum*

The Explication of Problems

The encounter has the effect of forcing us to pose a problem, but in posing the problem we are thereby forced to explicate the problem. Although related, these two moments are distinct. Posing the problem forces us to return to the domain of Memory, to remember that which can only be remembered and which is necessarily forgotten, to select a level of the past as such. This moment has a dual structure. On the one hand, it is negative insofar as it forces us to trace the poorly analyzed composites belonging to recognition. On the other hand, it forces us to jump into memory, to select a level within the cone of the past, to remember that which is *essentially* and necessarily forgotten. With explication, on the other hand, matters are different. No longer do we simply jump back into the past, critiquing the present of recognition. Rather, we now trace the outlines of the problem, follow the lines constituting its structure, develop it in its essentiality. We might say that the *memorandum* forces us to pose a question—for this is precisely what posing a problem consists of—while the moment of explication consists of developing, formulating, or tracing the problem which belongs to the question.

This third moment of explication consists in the transcendental or superior exercise of thought.

> The third characteristic of transcendental memory is that, in turn, it forces thought to grasp that which can only be thought, the *cogitandum* or *noeteon*, the Essence: not the intelligible, for this is still no more than the mode in which we think that which might be something other than thought, but the being of the intelligible as though this were both the final power of thought and the unthinkable. The violence of that which forces thought develops from the *sentiendum* to the *cogitandum*. (*DR* 141)

If the *memorandum* forces thought into its superior exercise, if it forces it to think that which belongs to thought alone, by right, then this is because the faculty of memory no longer converges with the faculty of thought to form the continuity of a recognition characterized by good and common sense. The difference between the two perspectives of thought here can be characterized in terms of Descartes.

> What makes Descartes a philosopher is that he . . . erect[s] an image
> of thought as it is *in principle:* good nature and an affinity with the true
> belong in principle to thought, whatever the difficulty of translating this
> principle into fact or rediscovering it behind the facts. Natural good
> sense or common sense are taken to be determinations of pure thought.
> Sense is able to adjudicate with regard to its own universality, and to
> suppose itself universal and communicable in principle. (*DR* 132–33;
> modified)

Descartes is indeed a philosopher because he attempts to render explicit all subjective presuppositions belonging to thought, he attempts to present an Image of thought without *doxa.* This is what it means to say that thought must be determined by what it is *in principle.* To determine what thought is *in principle* is to determine what belongs to thought by right, *as such,* essentially. As such, we do not seek to determine thought in terms of what thought *ought* to be, or in terms of what we *should* think about, nor to what *purposes* thought should be put to. While these questions are not unimportant, they are all secondary to the question of what belongs to thought as such.

If Descartes' attempt to articulate the being *of* thought ultimately ends up failing, this is because he ends up determining the being of thought in terms of something other than thought. That this is the case comes out clearly insofar as thought is determined naturally by Descartes in terms of good and common sense. What is problematic here is not simply that Descartes assumes that good and common sense belong to thought by right, but rather that determining thought in this way leaves us with no means of determining what belongs to thought as such. In order to see this, we must avoid being swayed by the connotative sense belonging to the terms *good* and *common* sense. Descartes is not to be criticized because he attributes this power to everyone, thus ensuring the most mediocre and conventional form of thought as the model of thought as such. It is not a matter of thought degenerating into the empirical common sense or general wisdom characterizing a historical time period. No, images of thought are to be evaluated by what they claim *in principle,* apart from this or that historical instantiation. Rather, we will recall that *common sense* signifies the convergence of the faculties upon a same object, thus assuming the identity of subject and object; while good sense assumes the distribution of the faculties for each particular case. Given this, it is the presupposition of the convergence of the faculties, along with their distribution, that becomes problematic.

Insofar as thought is treated as a convergence of the faculties, it becomes impossible to say what belongs to it as such. Thought comes to be treated as an effect of this convergence, and the being of thought is glossed over entirely. This point can be clearly discerned in terms of how Descartes defines thought:

> By the term "thought," I understand everything which we are aware of as happening within us, in so far as we have awareness of it. Hence, *thinking* is to be identified here not merely with understanding, willing and imagining, but also with sensory awareness. For if I say "I am seeing, or I am walking, therefore I exist," and take this as applying to vision or walking as bodily activities, then the conclusion is not absolutely certain. This is because, as often happens during sleep, it is closed and I am not moving about; such thoughts might even be possible if I had no body at all. But if I take "seeing" or "walking" to apply to the actual sense or awareness of seeing or walking, then the conclusion is quite certain, since it relates to the mind, which alone has the sensation or thought that it is seeing or walking.[1]

Initially Descartes seems to identify thought with any movement of the soul. In this respect, thought would be the common genus characterizing the species of understanding, willing, imagining, remembering, sensing, and so on, *qua* movements of the soul. The benefit of such a characterization is that it does indeed seem to provide us with a clear distinguishing difference characterizing the being of thought. Thought simply consists in being conscious or aware of movements of the soul. In this respect we are able to claim certainty for anything belonging to our field of awareness. Descartes' strategy thus consists in distinguishing between the *phenomenon* of thought and the *referent* of thought. Movements of the soul or awareness belong to the luminous domain of the phenomenon of thought, while the object represented is the referent of thought. If I can be certain of the phenomenon of thought, then this is because it is characterized by immediacy or auto-affectivity, whereas the referent of thought stands only in a mediated relation to consciousness. Here Descartes, at least, appears to be in agreement with Plato insofar as Plato characterizes thought as that which moves the soul to think, although the two do indeed differ with respect to their conception of the mind or soul.

However, characterizing this movement proves to be more difficult than might first be expected. Where we began by seeking a *real* definition of thought characterizing its essential being, Descartes ends by defining thought in terms of one of its modes or species. By the end of the passage Descartes marks the identifying feature of thought with "sensation." What is characteristic of thought is not simply that it consists in being a movement of the soul, but rather that we sense or feel this movement. But logically we are not entitled to define thought in terms of one of its modes, because thought, insofar as it is supposed to serve in the capacity of a genus, is supposed to characterize all of its modes. In other words, we are led into a contradiction whereby thought is supposed to define the identifying feature of all its modes but is also defined by one of its modes. As a result, we are left without an identifying mark for thought. Thought dissipates as a sort of effect or phantasm haunting all of its different modes, defining all of them and *also* being defined by them.

It is not difficult to identify the assumption lurking behind Descartes' curious gesture. What is it that leads Descartes to define thought in terms of one of its modes? It is the criterion of certainty. No sooner does Descartes define thought as movements of the soul than he proceeds to justify his argument in terms of the criterion of certainty. Thought, according to Descartes, is what we can be certain of. But this is a strange gesture, for why should thought, from the outset, be held up to the standard of certainty rather than being characterized in terms of its own internal being? What need has thought of certainty? We can indeed see that certainty, perhaps, has need of thought, yet there is no essential reason for assuming the reciprocity of this relation. As Deleuze puts it, "The criticism that must be addressed to this image of thought is precisely that it has based its supposed principle upon extrapolation from certain facts, particularly insignificant facts such as Recognition, everyday banality in person; as though thought should not seek its models among stranger and more compromising adventures" (*DR* 135). It is not a taste for the bizarre and the unusual which leads us to seek the model of thought in "stranger and more compromising adventures," but rather that these examples are better able to reveal what belongs to thought by right as opposed to examples that homogenize thought according to a model of "normal functioning."

The situation here is similar to that of psychoanalysis, which discovers more about the subject's unconscious through slips of the tongue and bungled actions than through "normal" well-formed speech. Just as we can be certain that *there is* thought without being certain of *what is* thought in the case of the formations of the unconscious, so too should

we treat the encounter as a sign that thought is taking place without being certain of what is being thought. As Žižek somewhere puts it, it is the
exception which allows the rule to define itself. It is the criterion of certainty—which, I might add, is external and ulterior to thought, and not
internal in principle—which leads Descartes to characterize thought in
terms of sensation or feeling, which, by necessity, cannot be doubted.

But if Descartes is led to hold thought up to the criterion of certainty which in turn leads him to characterize it in terms of sensibility, of
feeling oneself think, then this is because he ultimately seeks a principle
of communicability or good sense for thought. As Descartes says somewhat sarcastically,

> Good sense is mankind's most equitably divided endowment, for ev-
> eryone thinks that he is so abundantly provided with it that even those
> with the most insatiable appetites and most difficult to please in other
> ways do not usually want more than they have of this. As it is not likely
> that everyone is mistaken, this evidence shows that the ability to judge
> correctly, and to distinguish the true from the false—which is really
> what is meant by good sense or reason—is the same by innate nature in
> all men; and that differences of opinion are not due to differences in
> intelligence, but merely to the fact that we use different approaches and
> consider different things.[2]

Again, thought is characterized in terms of an extrinsic feature. First
characterized in terms of the extrinsic determination of sensation, then
characterized in terms of the extrinsic criterion of certainty, it is now to
be characterized in terms of the extrinsic demand of *communicability*.
For the attribution of a universal good sense characterizing all thought
is precisely the claim that thought is in principle communicable. We
say that all of these characterizations are extrinsic not because there
is no sensation, or because there is no certainty, nor again because
communicability is not a fact, but rather because none of these
determinations can be said to belong *necessarily* to thought. In other
words, they are not essential or internal determinations belonging
to thought, but are rather normative conditions imposed upon it
externally.

If good sense is to be treated as characteristic of thought, it is because it can be claimed to be innate for all men by right, thus establishing the possibility of an a priori communicability. Here, then, we find
a reciprocal interpenetration on the part of certainty and good sense.
Good sense is what allows us to claim the universal conditions of certainty, while certainty is what allows us to claim something like good

sense. If Descartes is led to speak somewhat sarcastically about the universal distribution of good sense, this is not because good sense is not in fact universally distributed. In fact, good sense is universally distributed by right. What is not universally distributed is the correct or proper *use* or employment of good sense. Certainty, then, is established upon the ground of good sense. Insofar as good sense is universally distributed it establishes a principle of communicability, for that which is innate and universally distributed is communicable by right. But it is for this reason also that sensibility is chosen as the defining mark of thought. For while we might not be able to agree on the nature of our sensations, while these sensations themselves might differ, we can at least be in agreement that we have these sensations. Sensibility provides the first step toward certainty.

The Moral Image of Thought

The aims of the Cartesian model of thought turn out to be quite different from those of a simple elucidation of the nature of thought. It must be emphasized that this criticism does not amount to a dismissal of the Cartesian model of thought. In our estimation, readings of Deleuze overly influenced by Nietzsche tend to immediately dismiss the objects of Deleuze's criticisms as being "moral," only to go to the opposite extreme. But the opposite extreme which would celebrate the "monstrous," the "anarchic," the "chaotic" prove to be no less moral than the model they attempt to supplant. To choose the anarchic over the State is to make a moral decision or decision of preference. Rather, if the Image of thought must be rejected, it is not to be rejected on the grounds that it is moral (this only characterizes what it is), but on the grounds that it is inadequate for articulating the form of being that it seeks to articulate. What ought to be sought is an amoral Image of thought, capable of accounting for *both* moral *and* immoral images of thought.

If the *memorandum* forces thought to its superior exercise, this is not because it leads to certainty (everywhere Deleuze will claim that thought is by right unconscious and therefore other than conscious certainty), but because it introduces an internal difference into thought. The movement here is complex. Deleuze is in agreement with Descartes' claim that thought is a movement of the soul; but in opposition to Descartes, he seeks to articulate the nature of this movement *as such.* It is true that Deleuze too refers to sensibility in articulating the being of thought, but in a manner which is vastly different. For Deleuze, "feeling ourselves thinking" is not the defining feature of thought, but that which forces thought to think.

> The text of *The Republic* defines that which is essentially encountered, and must be distinguished from all recognition as the object of a "contradictory perception." Whereas a finger always calls for recognition and is never more than a finger, that which is hard is never hard without also being soft, since it is inseparable from a becoming or a relation which includes the opposite within it (the same is true of the large and the small, the one and the many). The sign or point of departure for that which forces thought is thus the coexistence of contraries, the coexistence of more and less in an unlimited qualitative becoming. Recognition, by contrast, measures and limits the quality by relating it to something, thereby interrupting the mad-becoming. (*DR* 141)

It is not thought which the *sentiendum* introduces to us, but rather the being *of* the sensible embodied in the coexistence of contraries in one and the same becoming. Where recognition selects and limits becoming to one of the qualities, the being *of* the sensible shows that both of the qualities belong to the same becoming.

Initially one might think that this concept of becoming is identical to that of Hegel. According to Hegel,

> *Pure being* and *pure nothing* are, therefore, the same. What is truth is neither being nor nothing, but that being—does not pass over but has passed over—into nothing, and nothing into being. But it is equally true that they are not undistinguished from each other, that, on the contrary, they are not the same, that they are absolutely distinct, and yet that they are unseparated and inseparable and that each immediately *vanishes in its opposite*. Their truth is, therefore, this movement of the immediate vanishing of the one in the other: *becoming*, a movement in which both are distinguished, but by a difference which has equally immediately resolved itself.[3]

For Hegel, becoming consists in the "always already" of being having passed over into nothing and nothing having passed over into being. While this might at first appear identical to Deleuze's concept of becoming as the unity of contraries, such cannot be said to be the case. For Deleuze, becoming is the qualitative unity of opposites—or better still, qualitative unity without opposition—while for Hegel (put in empirical rather than logical terms), becoming consists of the unity of a quality with its negation.

> Becoming is in this way in a double determination. In one of them, *nothing* is immediate, that is, the determination starts from nothing which relates itself to being, or in other words changes into it, in the other, *being* is immediate, that is, the determination starts from being which changes into nothing: the former is coming-to-be and the latter is ceasing-to-be.
>
> Both are the same, *becoming,* and although they differ so in direction they interpenetrate and paralyze each other. The one is *ceasing-to-be;* being passes over into nothing, but nothing is equally the opposite of itself, transition into being, coming-to-be. This coming-to-be is the other direction: nothing passes over into being, but being equally sublates itself and is rather transition into nothing, is ceasing-to-be. They are not reciprocally sublated—the one does not sublate the other externally—but each sublates itself in itself and is in its own self the opposite of itself.[4]

In treating becoming in terms of coming-to-be and ceasing-to-be, Hegel selects *one* of the qualities in the qualitative unity of becoming and uses this to define movement. Hence, for example, the becoming-green of a tree in the spring is the coming-to-be of "greenness" from its ceasing-to-be in the fall and winter. Since, in Hegel's estimation, the unity of becoming is always already at work—meaning that there is never a pure encounter with being or nothing, but rather mediation is always already at work—the coming-to-be of the tree greening constitutes a sort of negation of a negation.

However, given this, it is clear that Hegel thinks becoming in terms of the rights of recognition. For what is important in Hegel's conception of becoming is the *identity* of the quality. It is for this reason that the quality is conceived in terms of negation: Red-not-red:red-not-red, and so on. By contrast, the Deleuzian conception of becoming is one of qualitative alteration without negativity. Here qualities cannot be treated as ontologically primitive terms, but as the result of an actualization in which an identity is established. If a quality comes up missing, if negation enters the picture, this is not because the becoming contains negativity, nor is it because sensibility contains negation, but it is because empirical consciousness employs a convergence of the faculties between memory and sensibility according to the identity of *one* quality. In short, empirical consciousness measures the present against the past such that it treats a present that was once present as now absent. Negation emerges from a convergent use of the faculties. Here the being of the past is particularly important because, as Deleuze will argue, something can only be missing if it has a place from which to be missing. In other words, structure or the symbolic which belongs to the domain of memory must be affirmed in such a way as to precede the present in order for something to be missing or negated.

The *sentiendum* is a necessary condition for thought because it calls into question the unity and identity of recognition, but it is not the defining feature of thought. Rather, the *sentiendum* is what *forces* thought. If it forces thought, this is because it awakens us from our "dogmatic slumbers," because it calls into question the reassuring complacency of recognition. As Deleuze puts it in relation to the poet Artaud,

> Artaud said that the problem (for him) was not to orientate his thought, or to perfect the expression of what he thought, or to acquire application and method or to perfect his poems, but simply to manage to think something. For him, this was the only conceivable "work": it presupposes an impulse, a compulsion to think which passes through all sorts of bifurcations, spreading through the nerves and being communicated to the soul in order to arrive at thought. Henceforth, thought is also forced to think its central collapse, its fracture, its own natural "powerless" which is indistinguishable from the greatest power—in other words, from those unformulated forces, the *cogitanda*, as though from so many thefts or trespasses in thought . . . He knows that *difficulty* as such, along with its cortege of problems and questions, is not a *de facto* state of affairs but a *de jure* structure of thought; that there is an acephalism of thought just as there is an amnesia in memory, an aphasia in language and an agnosia in sensibility. He knows that thinking is not innate, but must be engendered in thought. (*DR* 147)

If it is so difficult to think, then this is because we are characterized by recognition, because we develop within or as a result of the first passive synthesis of repetition, which ensures the passage from the particular to the general. We cannot rely on the autonomous will of the self to think because this will inevitably end up willing mere recognition or our gratifying image in the mirror. As a result, difficulty must belong to thought by right. We cannot say that thought is an innate capacity shared universally by all humankind, but must instead say that thought must be engendered within thinking. In this respect, if the *sentiendum* has an essential place within thought, it is not because it is the defining feature of thinking, because we feel ourselves thinking, but because it forces us to think. The *sentiendum* introduces a "hollow" or gap into recognition, an-other space.

The Being of Thought: Essence

The *sentiendum* forces memory to remember that which can only be remembered by virtue of bringing us before an encounter that can no longer be tamed by the convergent use of the faculties in recognition. But the *memorandum* forces thought to think that which can only be thought by virtue of forcing thought to grasp that which can only be thought, or essence. As a result, there is a "discord of the faculties, chain of force and fuse along which each confronts its limits, receiving from (or communicating to) the other only a violence which brings it face to face with its own element, as though with its disappearance or its perfection" (*DR* 141). No longer is there a convergence and harmony of the faculties, but a discord and divergent exercise of each going all the way to its own limit.

Not surprisingly, the *cogitandum* is both that which is unthinkable and that which can only be thought. If the *cogitandum* is that which is unthinkable, then this is because it evades the convergence of the faculties characteristic of recognition. It is for this reason that Deleuze says that it is "not the intelligible, for this is still no more than the mode in which we think that which might be something other than thought" (*DR* 141). Insofar as the intelligible belongs to the domain of recognition, and thus assumes the convergent use of the faculties, it can be excluded from the superior exercise of thought a priori. Thought thinks that which pertains to thought alone, that which can only be thought, and does not assume a convergence of the faculties upon one and the same object for one and the same subject. While it is certainly true that the faculties are related to one another in thought, this relation is one of force and divergence rather than harmony. Each faculty goes to its limit without depending on the others to establish the identity of the quality or the object. Each faculty strives to exercise that which belongs to it alone by right.

But what is it that belongs to thought alone? What is it that thought thinks and which is unthinkable by the empirical exercise of thought? We have said that thought thinks Essence or the *noeteon*, but this answer remains vague and easily confused with the intelligible so long as we do not articulate the being of essence. It is not surprising that the concept of essence has today fallen into disrepute. However, if the notion of essence has today become suspect, this is not for the reasons usually offered. It will be said that there are no essences because being is socially, linguistically, or historically constructed. There is truth in all of this, but not the truth normally thought. In saying that there is no essence, that everything is constructed socially, linguistically, historically, or by power, one would like to say that all is appearances. *What goes unnoticed in this criticism is that it reproduces the very appearance-essence distinction it claims to abolish.* Under views such as these it is not the case that there are no essences, but rather that essence cannot be attributed to that which is *conditioned* by the force in question. In other words, essence does not belong to things or subjects, but rather to the forces conditioning these beings, whether these forces be linguistic, social, historical, or affairs of power.

Language, the social, the historical, or power become the new essences. Peoples, things, time periods, social organizations become the new accidents. All becomes a matter of lifting the veil of maya from our gaze to see the true essences governing our experience. We "de-essentialize" our perspective in order to reach the true essences. But this seems to differ very little from the Platonic notion of confusing the world of appearances with the world of truth. If there is some truth to positions such as these, it is not the banal view that there are no essences, but rather in the latent insight that essence cannot be drawn or traced from the empirical.

Regardless of what Foucault himself thinks he is doing, when he claims that "man" is the construction or a result of a particular historical *episteme,* when he shows that the body is constructed by forces of power, or that there is no sexuality *as such,* he does not thereby abolish essence, but rather shows that such things are unsuitable beings for determining essence. This is the danger of discourses that restrict themselves to mere discourse analysis, thinking that texts are sufficient for settling the issues with which they deal. Foucault, like Judith Butler, suffers from a positivism of the text, believing that discursive constructions define the limits of what is, and thus drawing conclusions that do not follow from their arguments. The fact that things have been talked about differently is not sufficient to establish that they have been different. In other words, what is implicitly discovered is that essences are being traced from the actual, the empirical, the merely nominal, or that which contains only differences in degree. The nature or the force of the critique thereby becomes apparent. In demonstrating that essence is being defined in terms of the actual or the empirical, which is arbitrary and conventional, the next obvious step consists in showing how this practice then becomes blind to itself. Having traced essence from the empirical which is arbitrary and conventional by stint of being founded upon recognition, one then erases this "origin" by universalizing its point of view. This is why genealogies like those offered by Foucault and Nietzsche can be startling and disconcerting. They return us to the contingency of the origins, the arbitrariness of tracing the transcendental from the empirical.

In tracing the essential from what is empirically thinkable, we find ourselves caught in the dead-end alternatives of realism and nominalism. On the one hand, we are led to say that the essential consists of kinds characterizing each individual instance. Thus we say that there is an essence of man characterizing all individual men. But this attempt seems to fail once we recognize the great degree of variations departing from the standard notion of "man," as well as the variability of the articulation of the essence throughout history. For this reason we take, on the other hand, the route of nominalism and claim that only individual entities exist. Each individual is thereby treated as its own essence and the only relation between individuals admitted is that of resemblance. However, how can two things resemble one another in some respect without sharing a property? And how can two things share a property without sharing an identifying difference?

The common postulate in both positions is the primacy of the actualized being. Realism traces essence from the empirical individual, while nominalism claims that there is nothing but individuals. Another way of expressing the difference between these two positions is in terms of their respective accounts of conditioning. On the one hand, realism treats essences as conditioning individuals without being conditioned by them, while on the other hand, nominalism treats individuals as conditioning essences without being conditioned by them. But paradoxically, realism finds itself unable to determine essence without referring to individuals, while nominalism finds itself unable to determine individuals without referring to essence. Insofar as both of these positions are led to problems which are the exact inverse of one another, it is clear that it is this common assumption which is itself problematic. What is needed is (1) an account of essence that no longer draws essence from the empirical or the actualized (which no longer draws essence from something other than thought), and which (2) nonetheless is able to account for the genesis of the actual on the basis of essence.

Difference: The Transcendental Condition of the Diverse Given

If we are to avoid these problems, then we need a concept of essence which is not drawn from the empirical but which instead explains how this empirical is generated. It is this instance which Deleuze identifies in difference. "Difference is not diversity. Diversity is given, but difference is that by which the given is given, that by which the given is given as diverse" (DR 222). It is this difference which gives the given and not the given itself that forms the proper object of thought and transcendental empiricism. In this respect, the surest way to misread Deleuze and distort his position is to confuse the diverse given with difference. Difference is not diversity. Difference is the condition for diversity. There are not only individuals because individuals rely on difference for their production as the given. Nor are there unconditioned essences which merely condition individuals abstractly, because essence is able to produce a plurality of individuals which diverge vastly from one another. But how are we to conceive these essences?

> As we shall see, it will be necessary to reserve the name of Ideas not for pure *cogitanda* but rather for those instances which go from sensibility to thought and from thought to sensibility, capable of engendering in each case, according to their own order, the limit—or transcendent—object of each faculty. Ideas are problems, but problems only furnish the conditions under which the faculties attain their superior exercise. (*DR* 146)

While we cannot strictly identify Ideas or problems with *cogitanda*, we can say that thought thinks problems as problems. It is here that we come to see the nature of the relations characterizing the disharmonious exercise of the faculties. Sensibility or the *sentiendum* senses the problem or Idea as that which can only be sensed. Memory or the *memorandum* recollects the problem as that which can only be remembered. Finally, thought or the *cogitandum* thinks the problem as that which can only be thought. From one faculty to another, the problem takes each faculty to its limit, forcing it to encounter that which belongs to it alone by right.

In going from thought to sensibility and from sensibility to thought, we can now see what it means to say that transcendental empiricism is the experience of experience producing experience. "In going from A to B and B to A, we do not arrive at the point of departure as in a bare repetition; rather, the repetition between A and B and B and A is the progressive tour or description of the whole of a problematic field" (*DR* 210). On the basis of the Idea or Problem, each faculty is made to go to its limit and to force the others to their limit. In passing from one faculty to another and back again the problematic field does not remain unchanged, but changes the nature of experience itself. It is for this reason that we can claim that problems or Ideas and *cogitanda* are identical while nonetheless claiming that they differ. Thus we can claim that problems are essences.

However, no sooner have we made these claims than we find ourselves once again faced with all the problems of recognition, of good and common sense. In claiming that Ideas go from sensibility to thought and from thought to sensibility, that Ideas are the instances circulating throughout the faculties, does not Deleuze in effect return us to the identity of the object upon which the faculties converge? In other words, does he not return us to one of the central postulates of the Image of thought? Such a criticism is indeed suggested by the claim that Ideas are distinct from *cogitanda* (as well as from the *sentiendum* and the *memorandum*), which implicitly indicates not only the *exteriority* of a relation between the faculties and that to which the faculties pertain in the final instance, but also indicates that the Idea is a sort of self-identity, unsullied by the differences among the faculties, upon which all the faculties converge.

The difficulty here is that this criticism assumes that the Idea or problem is something independent of the faculties which treat it as their instance. To criticize essence in this way is to assume either (a) that essence is the correlate of an intention, or (b) that essence is a being rather than that by which being is given. However, from a Deleuzian perspective, intentionality is not itself possible without essence and the given cannot be given without difference. By contrast, it is not that Ideas are independent of the faculties, that they are an existence apart from the faculties which the faculties strive to represent; rather, the Ideas are produced by the disjunctive or disharmonious play of the faculties. In short, ideas are not an object or referent thought by the faculties, but are instead the very *process* the faculties undergo in being problematized. Consequently, we must not think ideas preexist thought. Rather, they only emerge in and through thought, testifying to a power similar to that of divine intuition.

We can already see that this is the case in Deleuze's discussion of essence in *Proust and Signs*. According to Deleuze,

> Each subject expresses the world from a certain viewpoint. But the viewpoint is the different itself, the absolute internal difference. Each subject therefore expresses an absolutely different world. And doubtless the world so expressed does not exist outside the subject expressing it (what we call the external world is only the disappointing projection, the standardizing limit of all these worlds expressed). But the world expressed is not identified with the subject; it is distinguished from the subject precisely as essence is distinguished from existence, even from the subject's own existence. Essence does not exist outside the subject expressing it, but is expressed as the essence not of the subject but of Being, or of the region of Being that is revealed to the subject . . . It is not reducible to a psychological state, nor to a psychological subjectivity, nor even to some form of a higher subjectivity . . . It is not the subject that explains essence, rather it is essence that implicates, envelops, wraps itself up in the subject. Rather, in coiling round itself, it is essence that constitutes subjectivity . . . Essence is not only individual, it *individualizes*. (*PS* 42–43)

Initially this passage seems to confirm all of our worries insofar as it does indeed appear to assert that essence is independent of its medium. However, a moment's reflection is sufficient to demonstrate that matters are much more complicated than they might initially appear. In the first place, while it is true that essence is distinct from the subjects and objects it individuates, it nonetheless does not exist outside of these subjects and objects. Moreover, essence is not independent of its subjects and objects but is the very process in which they unfold. Hence, in a strange way, essence is dependent upon subjects and objects to the same degree that subjects and objects are dependent upon essence. *Another way of putting this would be to say that there is no virtualization without actualization.* Unlike the dimension of the possible which can remain unrealized, the virtual actualizes itself completely at all times. Second, and more importantly, the claim that "essence . . . implicates, envelops, wraps itself in a subject," that it coils around itself constituting a subjectivity, refers us to precisely the sort of activity described by the play of the faculties. Essence is not independent of this play, but is rather that which is produced through the play of the faculties. It is true that we can say that essence is independent of the faculties, but this is not because it represents a substantial existence or is a thing, but rather because it can only be produced in a disharmonious play of the faculties as an *effect*. In order to think essence one must think recursively or iteratively, after the fashion of Mandelbrot, where an operation is repeated upon itself, producing a new effect in the process. It is for precisely this reason that transcendental empiricism is an account of *learning* rather than an *epistemology* or an account of coming to know. Where knowledge assumes the separation between subject and object in a relationship of passive representation, where the object preexists the activity of knowing and is unaffected by it, learning assumes a transformation of oneself and how we relate to the world.

Consequently, we cannot agree with Ronald Bogue's otherwise brilliant account of Deleuze's transcendental empiricism. According to Bogue,

> The experiences that provoke thought are those of contradictory perceptions. Such contradictions lead thought to essences, says Socrates, but according to Deleuze they are evidence of the existence of simulacra, which impinge on thought and force it into its proper activity. It is through such contradictory experiences that a critical examination of the mental faculties is made possible, one which Deleuze describes as a "transcendental empiricism."[5]

Although Bogue correctly recognizes the importance of the encounter and the disharmonic relationship among the faculties, he mistakenly seems to oppose essence to simulacra and to claim that the aim of transcendental empiricism consists in the analysis of the faculties. As Deleuze everywhere argues, the proper opposition in Plato is not between models and copies, but between copies and simulacra. The issue is not one of showing that there are no models, that essences do not exist, but rather of showing that there are no "good" copies, that the notion of the true copy is based on a sort of moral decision, that the model renders both its copies and the simulacra possible. However, it is not that contradictory perceptions indicate that there are simulacra. To claim this would be to fall into a substance ontology and to depart from the domain of the transcendental. Rather, contradictory perceptions call the sensibility into its higher or superior exercise, in turn forcing the other faculties into action, and, as a result, *producing simulacra as effects of this play of difference.*

This is precisely what Deleuze means by a style.

> As the quality of a world, essence is never to be confused with an object but on the contrary brings together two different objects, concerning which we in fact perceive that they have this quality in the revealing medium. At the same time that essence is incarnated in a substance, the ultimate quality constituting it is therefore expressed as the *quality common* to two different objects, kneaded in this luminous substance, plunged into this refracting medium. It is in this that style consists: "One can string out an indefinite succession, in a description, the objects that figured in the described place; the true will begin only when the writer takes two different objects, posits their relation, analogous in the world of art to that of the causal law in the world of science, and envelops them in the necessary rings of a great style." Which is to say that style is essentially metaphor. But the metaphor is essentially metamorphosis and indicates how the two objects exchange their determinations, exchange even the names that designate them, in the new medium that confers the common quality upon them. (*PS* 47–48)

Style is that which confers the common quality upon the subjects and objects which incarnate it. If style is metaphorical, it is not because style as structure is a metamorphosis of beings, but because it is what allows the text to be produced as a metaphor. It is for this reason that the actual is composed of simulacra rather than simple copies. The variations on a style are not copies of that style, but so many simulacra produced as effects of style. It is not that the existence of simulacra must be demonstrated, but rather that we must provide an account of how they are generated.

On the other hand, Bogue's claim that the contradictory perceptions allow us to critically evaluate the mental faculties fares a bit better. If by this Bogue means that they allow us to call into question the model of recognition and determine the nature of the faculties involved in their being as such, then he is entirely correct. However, this task is only a beginning and is really only a first step. Bogue's characterization of transcendental empiricism suffers an additional defect in that it suggests that what is of central concern is the being of these faculties themselves. In this respect, Bogue remains tied to the position that philosophy begins with the transcendental subject, which is precisely what Deleuze attempts to overcome. While it is certainly true that accounting for the being *of* the faculties is of central importance for transcendental empiricism, the true objects of inquiry are the conditions of real experience or essence, which brings us before the rule or principle governing the variation found in diversity. A perspective that limited itself to the analysis of the faculties would remain entirely abstract and thus subject to criticisms of being empiricist. On the other hand, insofar as subjects are not the primary individuating factors, insofar as they must themselves be individuated or explicated as simulacra, we cannot say that faculties are mental, but must instead conceive them ontologically in a manner akin to Bergsonian tendencies. The faculties are tendencies within being, not a subject. Deleuze is thus highly misleading when he evokes the faculties. The tendencies or faculties are conditions for subjects, not the reverse. We shall see more precisely why this is the case, in the full critical sense of the "Copernican revolution," in the next chapter. For the moment it suffices to see that this is the reason why Deleuze is perpetually concerned to determine faculties like sensibility, memory, thought, language, and so on in their *being* rather than their empirical manifestation.

Essence and the Metaphysical Structure of Point of View

Before proceeding to a discussion of why Deleuze equates problems and essences, it is first necessary to clarify what Deleuze means when he claims that essence or difference is a point of view on the world, a perspective. If Deleuze's choice of the terms *point of view* and *perspectivism* in particular contexts (notably *Nietzsche and Philosophy*) is regrettable, this is because of the subjectivist associations surrounding these terms. Matters are only exacerbated by the claim that each subject embodies an entirely different world. With respect to these connotations, perspective, point of view, or essence is treated as the internal domain of a subject independent of every other subject's point of view and unreachable by any other subject's point of view. Under this popular position—which is just another variant of the cult of the individual—matters quickly degenerate into unsupportable and incoherent moral assertions to the effect that "this is my point of view, that is yours," which are supposed to be democratic and tolerant but which in fact prove to be a form of mastery in which one no longer has to hear or engage with the alterity of the other. Moreover, this strategy fails to see that it is itself based on a universalist perspective that aims to transcend any particular point of view. The claim that we ought to be tolerant of the views of others is not simply one point of view, but a regulative principle governing all points of view. In the worst cases, theory is rejected altogether (since theory is supposed to only pertain to universals), and critical engagement degenerates into a banal sort of descriptivism or reporting of "personal experiences." In our opinion, this sort of subjectivism represents a variant of the constitutive ontological yearning for a lost plenitude, presence, or fullness which would like to deny difference and renounce alterity. Far from preserving tolerance and democracy, such views are predicated on the abolition of difference and alterity. Such a view is that of the beautiful soul in that it denies that holding any position involves the affirmation of some principles and the rejection of others. To be is to affirm. To affirm is to select. To select is to exclude.

While there is some merit to reading Deleuze in this way, few things are more challenging to the supposed presence and fullness of the subject than the Deleuzian concept of perspective or point of view. The reason for this is that a point of view or a perspective is not something that *belongs to* a subject, but rather a subject belongs to, occupies, or is occupied by a point of view or perspective. Another way of saying this would be to claim that there is not a relativity of truth, but a truth of relativity. Perspective is indeed a condition for the production of truth because it exercises a selection which allows diversity or beings to show forth, to manifest themselves. In other words, while the entire cone of memory may be expressed, it is not entirely actualized. But this relativity is not a relativity to a subject. Consequently, for Deleuze perspective does not depend on the subject for its being. There is a being proper to perspective as such. Perspectives are not individuated by their inclusion or possession by a subject, but rather subjects and individuals are individuated by perspectives. The perspective precedes the subject such that the subject occupies its perspective like a zebra occupies the plains. It does not exist within the confines of interiority, but is rather an objective structure or style which the subject itself occupies much as one might occupy a field or plane as a medium of movement. Thus,

[if] Leibniz makes of the monad a sort of point of view on the city, must we understand that a certain form corresponds to each point of view? For example, a street of one form or another? In conic sections, there is no separate point of view to which the ellipse would return, and another for the parabola, and another for the circle. The point of view, the summit of the cone, is the condition under which we apprehend the group of varied forms or the series of curves to the second degree. It does not suffice to state that the point of view apprehends a perspective, a profile that would each time offer the entirety of a city in its own fashion. For it also brings forth the connection of all the related profiles, the series of all curvatures or inflections. What can be apprehended from one point of view is therefore neither a determined street nor a relation that might be determined with other streets, which are constants, but the variety of all possible connections between the course of a given street and that of another. The city seems to be a labyrinth that can be ordered. The world is an infinite series of curvatures or inflections, and the entire world is enclosed in the soul from one point of view. (*FLB* 24)

A perspective or point of view does not express my subjective apprehension of the world right now, at this moment, but instead constitutes a sort of system or structure which allows for this subjective apprehension to take place. Here we might think of Einstein's example of the two trains moving with respect to each other, viewed from the perspective of someone standing alongside the tracks and another person on the train. It is not a subjective impression which leads to a differential in speed for the person on the train and the person observing the trains, but an objective feature of the two perspectives themselves. Nonetheless, Deleuze's claim that the world is in the soul still suggests that this "world-structure" is an internal possession of the subject. However, while the world or perspective is in the folds of the soul, it is not there as a possession of the subject, as something that the subject actively produces, but rather as a space or field that the subject occupies. Perspective is the structure wherein the subject unfolds and without which it would not be. In this respect, perspective is similar to Heidegger's being-in-the-world. Perspective is the inseparability of the subject from its world. In other words, the perspective is not in the subject; rather, the subject is in the perspective. Given this, personalistic approaches risk being perpetually blind to perspective insofar as they often implicitly think the subject independently of world. Rather than articulating a perspective, they assume it in their act of articulation while nonetheless effacing the fact that they speak from a perspective.

From one point of view, we can immediately see the benefit of treating essences as problems. Insofar as the deadlock between realism and nominalism arises because both define themselves by reference to the empirical object, an approach beginning with problems or the idea of the problematic proves superior insofar as we tend to think the being of the problem as that which is not yet actualized, and which is thus independent of individual entities. In principle, an account of essence based on problems ought to allow us to go beyond the stale opposition between realism and nominalism. In fact, to some extent we have already seen how Deleuze goes some of the way toward navigating this deadlock in his account of style or essence. Insofar as individuals (whether they be subjects or objects) are not the primary individuating factors of being but must themselves be individuated by the individuating factor of difference or essence, the peril of nominalism is avoided. Insofar as essence or difference does not exist outside of the subjects and objects expressing it, the peril of realism is avoided. In fact, as we will see later, Deleuze reverses the traditional hierarchy between essence and existence. Unlike traditional realisms which treat essence as an abstract universal, Deleuzian essences are absolutely singular and thus completely individuated. It is in the process of actualization, or actualizing essence, that generalities or what Deleuze calls "qualities," "species," and "parts" are produced.

However, from another perspective the equation of essence with problems is deeply perplexing. If the equation of essence with problems is perplexing, then this is because we tend to equate problems with merely negative moments that disappear with their solutions. Similarly, we tend to equate problems with a lack of essence, since if we knew the essence, the problem would not exist. Problems are thus conceived as the absence of knowledge. It is not difficult to discern another empiricist assumption at work in these concerns. In claiming that problems are merely negative instances, that they disappear with their solutions, we shackle problems to their solutions rather than defining problems in terms of their own internal being. In other words, we define problems in terms of what they are not, in terms of something other than problems, rather than articulating the being *of* the problem. Rather than treating problems as genetic instances presiding over the production of solutions, we treat them merely as the absence of a solution. It is clear that we here encounter another variant of the fallacy of tracing the transcendental from the empirical. In this case, solutions serve as the empirical instance and problems are reduced to shadowy doubles of the solutions they bring about.

We can see how this notion of the problem is based upon the model of recognition. As Deleuze puts it,

> We are led to believe that problems are given ready-made, and that they disappear in the responses or the solution . . . We are led to believe that the activity of thinking, along with truth and falsehood in relation to that activity, begins only with the search for solutions, that both of these concern only solutions. This belief probably has the same origin as the other postulates of the dogmatic image: puerile examples taken out of context and arbitrarily erected into models. According to this infantile prejudice, the master sets a problem, our task is to solve it, and the result is accredited true or false by a powerful authority. It is also a social prejudice with the visible interest of maintaining us in an infantile state, which calls upon us to solve problems that come from elsewhere, consoling or distracting us by telling us that we have won simply by being able to respond. (*DR* 158)

In treating problems as ready-made, we restrict them to the model of recognition. By claiming that problems are given—that they have already been set, that they are already there—we restrict them to the rights of the recognized. In other words, we not only decide in advance which solutions we will accept (only the recognizable ones will suffice), but in a way, we act as if we already knew the solutions.

This is more than evident in the manner in which emphasis is placed on the truth or falsity of the solution.

> The dogmatic image of thought supports itself with psychologically puerile and socially reactionary examples (cases of recognition, error, simple propositions and solutions or responses) in order to prejudge what should be the most valued in regard to thought—namely, the genesis of the act of thinking and the *sense* of truth and falsehood. There is, therefore, a seventh postulate to add to the others: the postulate of responses and solutions according to which truth and falsehood only begin with solutions or only qualify responses. (*DR* 158)

In emphasizing the truth and falsity of solutions, we restrict problems to what can be recognized, to the convergence of the faculties, to the identity of the object and the subject. This is what Deleuze means when he claims that the seventh postulate of thought takes examples out of context and erects them as models. Recognition takes the actualized solution and treats it as the destination or truth of the problem. In and of itself the problem is said to have no truth value of its own. Everything is shackled to the solution. When all emphasis is placed on the solution, the problem comes to appear as the negative image of the solution, as its shadowy double, in such a way that it is simply the absence of a solution.

It is precisely this which constitutes the activity of tracing problems from their solutions. For instance, one says that we have thumbs so that we might grasp things. Here, the problem is treated as an absence of being able to grasp things, while the solution consists in the production of thumbs. Such a view assumes that the problem of needing to grasp things was already there, ready-made (which is strange when we think about fish or worms that get along just fine without grasping things), and has the effect of naturalizing their solutions (as if thumbs were the only solution to the problem of grasping). At any rate, understanding problems as the shadowy double of solutions, as the inverse or negation of the solution, has the effect of treating solutions as being there just waiting to be found or discovered rather than as being generated and variable products of problems.

The activity of tracing problems from solutions is yet another variant of conceiving the conditions in terms of the conditioned. As a result, it is subject to all of the circularities involved in assuming a ready-made denotation in order to halt the chain of signification. For this reason, it cannot be said that this conception of problems is truly critical insofar as it fails to restrict itself to the conditions under which experience is possible, but instead bases itself on the dogmatic assertion of a denotation. By contrast, Deleuze attempts to formulate an ontology of the problem or Idea which departs from these difficulties.

> It is then fatal that the ground should itself be no more than a simple external conditioning. A strange leap on the spot or vicious circle by which philosophy, claiming to extend the truth of solutions to problems themselves but remaining imprisoned by the dogmatic image, refers the truth of problems to the possibility of their solution. What is missed is the internal character of the problem as such, the imperative internal element which decides in the first place its truth or falsity and measures its intrinsic genetic power: that is, the very object of the dialectic or combinatory, the "differential." Problems are tests and selections. What is essential is that there occurs at the heart of problems a genesis of truth, a production of the true in thought. Problems are the differential elements in thought, the genetic elements in the true. We can therefore substitute for the simple point of view of conditioning a point of view of effective genesis. (*DR* 161–62)

The aim of this shift is to think problematicity as such, to think the being *of* the problem, which in turn frees a transcendental dialectic from the shackles of noumenal solutions. As a result, we no longer restrict truth and falsity to solutions, but rather (1) apply the test of the true and false to problems themselves, and (2) determine the genesis of the truth of experience in terms of problems. In this respect, it is clear that accounts of Deleuze's thought which claim that he rejects the philosophical category of truth must be rethought. As Deleuze puts it,

> The problem or sense is at once both the site of an originary truth and the genesis of a derived truth. The notions of nonsense, false sense and misconstrual must be related to problems themselves (there are problems which are false through indetermination, others through overdetermination, while stupidity is finally the faculty for false problems; it is evidence of an inability to constitute, comprehend or determine a problem as such). (*DR* 159)

On the one hand there is the truth of denotation, the derived truth of experience, while on the other hand there is the truth of the problem itself. Why is it that problems or Ideas have these characteristics of producing or generating truth? What is the nature of problems such that they produce experience?

Problems and the Dialectical Illusions of *Being*

Surprisingly, Deleuze's inspiration for this concept of problematicity comes not from Bergson per se, nor from Nietzsche, *but rather from Kant.*

> (The Kantian idea of inner illusion, internal to reason, is radically different from the extrinsic mechanism of error. The Hegelian idea of alienation supposes a profound restructuring of the true-false relation. The Schopenhauerian notions of vulgarity and stupidity imply a complete reversal of the will-understanding relation.) What prevents these richer determinations from being developed on their own account, however, is the maintenance, despite everything, of the dogmatic image, along with the postulates of common sense, recognition and representations which comprise its cortege. (*DR* 150)

From the perspective of recognition or the Image of thought, error consists simply in a lack of adequation between a proposition or thought and the object which it is supposed to represent. In this respect, error is treated as an external relation between thought and object, proposition and referent. While philosophy might indeed be interested in determining the conditions under which such a relation is possible, it is also clear that this form of error cannot be the standard by which philosophy measures itself. If error is foreign to philosophy, if it cannot be that which philosophy strives to avoid, this is for no other reason than simply that philosophy is ill equipped to deliver us denotative truths about reality or the world. Philosophy is not an empirical practice, even among those who call themselves empiricists. It is never a matter of making true or false statements about *states of affairs* in the world, but rather a practice of creating and critiquing concepts. Philosophical claims pertain not to referential truths but rather to the medium of basic concepts that free a region of experience so that referential judgments might be made at all. Before one can discourse about the world, the sense of the world must have already announced itself.

In contrast to the notion of error based on recognition or the lack of recognition, philosophy instead conceives of illusions or errors internal to or constitutive of thought itself. The notion of an error or illusion internal to thought itself is not that of a lack of adequation between word and object, between thought and world, but rather is an error which is *inevitably* and *unavoidably* produced by thought itself in the activity of thinking. We see here why Deleuze's reference to dialectic, his thesis that the true dialectic is a dialectic of problems, is not a mistake or an oversight on his part. In opposing dialectic it is Hegelian dialectic which Deleuze rejects, not dialectic as such. It is true that Deleuze levels a trenchant critique against the Hegelian dialectic, yet the dialectic which Deleuze refers to here is not that of Hegel's dialectical movement, but rather that of the second half of Kant's *Critique of Pure Reason*, or even Platonic dialectic. In the latter case, the dialectic always consists in posing problems—"What is knowledge?" "What is justice?"—and progressively freeing it from empiricist assumptions so that the problem might be determined in its being as such. In the Platonic dialogues one speaker always responds to the question by citing an instance. However, Plato quickly quells these responses by responding that the object of inquiry is not this or that instance of Justice, but justice as such.

The illusion internal to thought here consists in being compelled to always refer to the instance, the denotation, rather than ascending to the being of the Idea itself. Here Deleuze shares a profound affinity with Plato. Although Deleuze will ultimately reject Plato's universals (by virtue of its moral distinction between copies and simulacra), he nonetheless accepts the inadequacy of the empirical where determining the being of the problem is concerned.

We then find here one of the reasons why Deleuze refers to problems as "Ideas." Ideas or problems will be seen to be the sufficient reason of instances or the actual. In the case of Kant, these illusions arise when reason goes beyond the limits of experience, attempting to think the pure concepts of the understanding apart from intuition, thus being led into undecidable antinomies, paralogisms, and the Ideal of God. In the case of both Kant and Plato, error is not a matter of failed adequation between the thought and object, but rather is internal to the nature of thought itself, produced in the act of thinking.

The activity of diagnosing and denouncing transcendental illusions or errors that pertain to thought alone is one of the primary activities of philosophy. As Deleuze puts it somewhere in *Nietzsche and Philosophy,* philosophy is at its best and most productive as critique. Deleuze will, of course, reject both Kant's and Plato's understanding of transcendental illusions or errors pertaining to thought alone insofar as both of them in their own ways return to the Image of thought. In the case of Plato, this return of the Image of thought consists in universalization of the Ideas rather than asking "which one?" "how many?" "how much?" Rather than determining the conditions of *real* experience, Plato remains tied to the illusion of recognition that universalizes its own contingent organization. Although these questions might initially appear to pertain to instances, they are in fact questions pertaining to the structure and organization of problems or Ideas: Which Idea or problem of justice? How many dimensions or singularities does it contain? In the case of Kant, the transcendental dialectic of reason is rejected for "respecting the rights of the criticized." By this Deleuze means that Kantian critique does not go far enough insofar as it uncovers the grounds for rejecting the Ideas of the Soul, World (as a totality), and God, only to replace them once again. However, while Deleuze might ultimately reject the Platonic and Kantian conceptions of internal illusions, these positions nonetheless provide us with an excellent way of introducing what Deleuze means by an "Idea" or "problem."

Kant and the Being of Problems

Deleuze cites Kant in particular as having been the first to truly provide a proper ontology of problems.

> In what sense, then, does Kantian reason, in so far as it is the faculty of Ideas, pose or constitute problems? The fact is that it alone is capable of drawing together the procedures of the understanding with regard to a set of objects. The understanding by itself would remain entangled in its separate and divided procedures, a prisoner of partial and empirical enquiries or researches in regard to this or that object, never raising

itself to the level of a "problem" capable of providing a systematic unity for all its operations. The understanding alone would obtain answers or results here and there, but these would never constitute a "solution." For every solution presupposes a problem—in other words, the constitution of a unitary and systematic field which orientates and subsumes the researches or investigations in such a manner that the answers, in turn, form precisely cases of solution. Kant even refers to Ideas as problems to which there is no solution. By that he does not mean that Ideas are necessarily false problems and thus insoluble but, on the contrary, that true problems are Ideas, and that these Ideas do not disappear with "their" solutions, since they are the indispensable condition without which no solution would ever exist. (*DR* 168)

Already it can be seen just how much the "Deleuzo-Kantian" concept of problems differs from the notion of problems belonging to common sense. On the one hand, problems are no longer conceived as negative instances or propositions, as inverted solutions, but rather as organizing structures or systems. On the other hand, *there are no solutions to true problems*. What is it that leads Kant to conceive problems in this curious manner?

It is often assumed that the results of the second half of Kant's first *Critique* are purely negative. Under this reading of Kant, the Transcendental Dialectic shows us the impossibility of metaphysics in the form of rational psychology (the paralogisms), the world as a totality (the antinomies), and proofs for the existence of God (the transcendental Ideal). Kant's critique thus demonstrates only that metaphysics is impossible as a science. However, while Kant rejects these ideas in their *transcendent* usage insofar as they profess to go beyond the limits of experience imposed by intuition, he nonetheless argues that these ideas have a perfectly legitimate and *immanent* regulative employment. What struck Kant about the illusions of reason was the fact that we are inevitably led to produce these illusions.

The outcome of all dialectical attempts of pure reason not only confirms . . . that all the inferences that would carry us out beyond the field of possible experience are deceptive and groundless, but it also simultaneously teaches us this particular lesson: that human reason has a natural propensity to overstep all these boundaries, and that transcendental ideas are just as natural to it as the categories are to the understanding, although with this difference, that just as the categories lead to truth, i.e., to the agreement of our concepts with their objects, the ideas effect a mere, but irresistible, illusion, deception by which one can hardly resist even through the most acute criticism.[6]

On the one hand, the categories of the understanding lead to an adequation between concept and object through the intermediary of the schematism which links category to intuition, while on the other hand, the Ideas of reason seem to lead to no such adequation insofar as there are no objects of experience corresponding to them. Yet, strangely, the illusions of reason carry the same sort of necessity that the categories have . . . We are inevitably, unavoidably, led into these illusions.

But why should reason be inevitably and unavoidably led to produce these sorts of illusions if they are entirely useless and lead us astray? Given the inevitability of the illusions produced by reason, ought not these Ideas have some purpose or use? Or is reason something that we ought to dispense with altogether, restricting ourselves instead to the understanding which delivers us adequation? In response to these questions, Kant presents an argument from nature.

> Everything grounded in the nature of our powers must be purposive and consistent with their correct use, if only we can guard against a certain misunderstanding and find out their proper direction. Thus the transcendental ideas too will presumably have a good and consequently *immanent* use, even though, if their significance is misunderstood and they are taken for concepts of real things, they can be transcendent in their application and for that very reason deceptive. For in regard to the whole of possible experience, it is not the idea itself but only its use that can be either *extravagant* (transcendent) or *indigenous* (immanent), according to whether one directs them straightway to a supposed object corresponding to them, or only to the use of the understanding in general regarding the objects with which it has to do; and all errors of subreption are always to be ascribed to a defect in judgment, never to understanding or to reason.[7]

According to Kant, if the illusions of reason are grounded within our cognition, then they must have some use. Consequently, with respect to the Ideas we cannot say that the critique rejects them outright, but rather finds a particular employment of these ideas objectionable. The error of reason is not internal to the Ideas themselves, but consists in confusing them with concepts, with objects of experience. In confusing the Ideas with concepts, we employ them transcendentally, assuming that we have some sort of experiential relation to beings like the soul, the world as a totality, or God, which are all beyond the scope of our experience. Such is the extravagant usage of the Ideas. But what is their "modest," immanent usage?

The key to Kant's argument lies in the nature of the understanding. For Kant, it is true that the categories of the understanding give unity to what would otherwise be a chaotic flux of fleeting and disconnected sensations, but this unity does not provide a unity of all experience as a totality, but a unity of this experience here and now. In other words, the relationship between the categories and intuition makes my experience of objects possible, it makes it possible for them to stand forth and show themselves, but it does not explain how they unify themselves into a whole or totality. "The understanding does not look to this totality at all, but only to the connection *through which series* of conditions always *come about* according to concepts."[8] In this context, the series Kant is referring to is that belonging to intuition in time and space, while the concepts of the understanding order these series in relations of universality and necessity.

However, while understanding might order these intuited series in relations of universality and necessity, it always does so with respect to the experience I am undergoing here and now, and not with respect to the world as a whole or totality. Since the world as a totality cannot be made the object of an intuition, any application of the categories to totalities is empty. For this reason,

> if we survey the cognitions of our understanding in their entire range, then we find that what reason quite uniquely prescribes and seeks to bring about concerning it is the *systematic* in cognition, i.e., its interconnection based on one principle. This unity of reason always presupposes an idea, namely that of the form of a whole of cognition which precedes the determinate cognition of the parts and contains the conditions for determining *a priori* the place of each part and its relation to the others. Accordingly, this idea postulates complete unity of the understanding's cognition through which this cognition comes to be not merely a contingent aggregate but a system interconnected in accordance with necessary laws. One cannot properly say that this idea is the concept of an object, but only that of the thoroughgoing unity of these concepts, insofar as the idea serves the understanding as a rule. Such concepts of reason are not created by nature, rather we question nature according to these ideas, and we take our cognition to be defective so long as it is not adequate to them.[9]

Experience, by the lights of the understanding, presents us with no global organized systematicity. It presents us with nothing but particulars. The role of reason, its problem, is to bring systematicity to these particulars by organizing and arranging them within a structure.

Insofar as this organization is not itself given in experience, we thus say that it is a problem, that it has a problematic status.

Either the universal is *in itself* certain and given, and only *judgment* is required for subsuming, and the particular is necessarily determined through it. This I call the "apodictic" use of reason. Or the universal is assumed only *problematically*, and it is a mere idea, the particular being certain while the universality of the rule for this consequently is still a problem; then several particular cases, which are all certain, are tested by the rule, to see if they flow from it, and in the case in which it seems that all the particular cases cited follow from it, then the universality of the rule is inferred, including all subsequent cases, even those that are not given in themselves.[10]

By necessity, the Kantian critical project must reject the notion of universals given in themselves because experience is finite and intuition presents nothing but fleeting impressions. It is for this reason that we must say that Ideas or universals are problems, rather than givens of experience. To say that they are problems is not to say that they are passing or negative moments which disappear, but rather that they are conditions under which our experience becomes organized. Experience contains the imperative of organization. Become organized!

Nonetheless, does not Kant suggest that we do come to know these universals transcendentally when he claims that the universality of the rule is inferred through the testing of particular cases? In response to this question, he makes an intriguing claim. According to Kant,

The transcendental ideas are never of constitutive use, so that the concepts of certain objects would thereby be given, and in case one so understands them, they are merely sophistical (dialectical) concepts. On the contrary, however, they have an excellent and indispensably neces-sary regulative use, namely that of directing the understanding to a cer-tain goal respecting which the lines of direction of all its rules converge at one point, which, although it is only an idea (*focus imaginarius*)—i.e., a point from which the concepts of the understanding do not really proceed, since it lies entirely outside the bounds of possible experi-ence—nonetheless still serves to obtain for these concepts the greatest unity alongside the greatest extension.[11]

It is at precisely this moment that Kant departs from the model of recognition. On the one hand, problems, which just are Ideas, are no longer shackled to their solvability, but are themselves unsolvable while nonetheless demanding solution. They are unsolvable insofar as they think the world as a totality or whole which is forever beyond the limits of experience or intuition and can thus never be objects of knowledge. However, they are also solvable in the sense that they impel us to forever perfect our knowledge, to draw closer to that utopian point where the Idea would at last completely determine the concepts of the understanding insofar as they propel us to perpetually determine relations between the concepts of experience in attempts to formulate a systematic whole. Here the problem is no longer an inverted solution, a negative proposition, but instead an imperative organizing experience. (Kant speaks elsewhere in the *Critique* of the turbulence and unrest of reason.) On the other hand, we can say of Kant, following Lacan, that the idea of complete truth or a metalanguage has the structure of a fiction. Insofar as problems or Ideas are not based on the adequation of concept and object, insofar as they are not given in experience, we can no longer say that they are based on truth, as is the case with their solutions. Rather, problems or Ideas have the structure of fictions because they cannot be said to constitute articles of knowledge, even though they are what, in another respect, renders knowledge possible. The principles of organization, of structure, of systematicity are not themselves objects of verification in a denotation.

The Insistence of Problems

On the basis of this characterization of the Kantian concept of problems or Ideas, it now becomes possible to define the relationship between problems and truth and falsity. Truth and falsity no longer pertain to solutions, but are instead applied to problems themselves. Now it is clear that the paralogisms, the antinomies, and the transcendental Ideal are all based on the Ideas or problems of reason, but in each of these cases transcendental illusions arise by treating the Ideas as objects of knowledge, by employing them as constitutive, rather than as regulative principles organizing our knowledge. What enables the *Critique* to function as a critique consists in (1) determining the conditions and limits under which our experience is possible, and then (2) determining the nature and reason for why we seem to be inevitably led into certain deadlocks in our attempt to do metaphysics.

The impact of Kant on Deleuze's thought is not to be underestimated. It is true that Deleuze refers to Kant as a philosophical enemy (*N* 6). However, in *Difference and Repetition* especially, one can everywhere discern a sustained discussion taking place with the three critiques. With the possible exception of Bergson, it is our opinion that reading Deleuze next to Kant is far more rewarding than reading him with Nietzsche, Spinoza, or Hume, if for no other reason than that Kant defines the terrain of post-classical philosophy. What, then, is the relationship between the Deleuzian concept of problems and Kant's? For Kant, problems are (1) transcendent to experience (they are not themselves derived from empirical or a posteriori experience) while having only an immanent employment, such that they are (2) organizational principles, which (3) do not disappear with their solutions, rendering them (4) fictions in that they make no claim to knowledge (in their correct or immanent usage) yet are nonetheless employed to arrive at knowledge, which thus (5) have a true (immanent) and false (transcendent) usage, and (6) such that they do not resemble their solutions. Within the Kantian system, problems stand to concepts as concepts stand to intuitions. That is to say, where concepts give order, necessity, and universality to impressions, reason gives order to concepts of experience.

It is clear that all six of these properties are precisely what Deleuze seeks in the concept of a problem. In treating problems as being transcendent to experience, we avoid the empirical fallacy of treating them as merely passing moments on the way to solutions. In treating them as having only an immanent employment, we ensure problems pertain only to solutions. In treating problems as organizational principles we give them a defining feature of their own, a difference which pertains to problems as such, a feature defining the being *of* problems. In this way we avoid defining problems in terms of their solvability, but instead ask what it is that they do.

The same can be said of the claim that problems do not disappear with their solutions. To say that problems do not disappear with their solutions is also to say that problems are that which allow solutions to have a sense or meaning. To this we might add that the unsolvability of problems is what allows something like truth to appear in the field of solutions at all. It is only with respect to the transcendence, organizationality, and the unsolvability of problems that a genesis of derived truth can take place within the field of experience. For individual propositions always make simultaneous reference to both the state of affairs they denote and a global organization of experience in which these states of affairs cohere. The unsolvability of problems does not mean that they are bad or false problems, but instead signifies the manner in which problems continue *to insist* within their solutions, the manner in which they function as imperatives. To say that problems are unsolvable is not to say that there are no solutions to problems, but rather that there are no final solutions; that inquiry has no end, that experience demands organization or structuration in terms of a point of view.

In claiming that problems are fictions, we ensure that problems are no longer defined by the criteria of knowledge or denotative truth and falsity, but instead must be evaluated in terms of their own intrinsic criteria. If problems are fictions, this is not because they are "made up" or fabricated according to the whim of the beautiful soul, the self-creating individual, the Nietzschean superman, but because they are not to be evaluated by the claims of knowledge. In Deleuze it is being that is creative, that creates, not the individual. For this reason it is perhaps best to dispense with the term *fictions* altogether, insofar as postmodernist secondary literature seems incapable of understanding it in a non-empirical way and is inevitably led to attribute to creation a creator. The term *fiction* seems to inevitably lead to the idea that these fictions are somehow arbitrary or a matter of whim. As Deleuze puts it,

> Philosophy is a discipline that is just as creative and inventive as any other discipline, and it entails creating or even inventing concepts. And concepts do not exist ready-made in the sky waiting for a philosopher to seize them. Concepts must be made. To be sure, they are not made just like that. It's not that one just says one day, "Look, I'm going to invent such and such a concept," no more than a painter says one day "Look, I'm going to make a painting like this," or a filmmaker, "Look, I'm going to make such and such a film!" There must be a necessity, as much in philosophy as elsewhere, for if not there is nothing at all. A creator is not a being who works for pleasure. A creator does only what he or she absolutely needs to do.[12]

Ontologically, the idea that we create problems or Ideas through mere whim, for the sake of whatever catches our fancy, returns us to all the difficulties of the sovereign subject who is reputed to have absolute transparency with respect to the contents of his or her consciousness. As a result, it returns us to all the difficulties of the empirical that would trace difference from external differences between subjects and objects. Practically, this notion of creating Ideas all too easily ends up reinventing the wheel insofar as one wakes up one morning claiming that one is going to create a concept—not any concept in particular, just a concept—and then casts about for a concept to create, only to arrive at an object of recognition.

One often witnesses this activity in debates about the so-called evils of structuralism in contrast to the supposedly more open post-structuralisms and postmodernism. One accuses structuralism of effecting a closure and of shackling everything to the despotic signifier, only to re-create structuralism by formulating a superior concept based on relations. As if the central idea of structuralism were not that of the relation! In cases such as these, it is all too clear that one has treated the notion of structure empirically in terms of signifiers dealt with by *structuralists,* rather than transcendentally in terms of what must belong to the concept of structure by right. There is no reason to assume that signifiers belong to structure *by right;* rather, signifiers are only one empirical manifestation structure can take.

Finally, the notion that problems are created by the whim of the subject, the one with the will to produce fictions, often produces the worst banalities and superficialities insofar as everything (1) quickly degenerates into a sort of free association where all pretensions to rigor evaporate, and (2) one is given the license to ignore all that has come before under the illusory principle that one has the sovereign power to create free of all constraints. But this notion of creation all too readily lends itself to the reproduction of clichés. *Fiction* is a dangerous word. With Nietzsche we can thus say that there is an essential frailty of thought. I am not the origin of my thoughts, but rather thought comes to me like an event. The moral of this story is that the creation of concepts cannot be treated as an ideal or project because we are powerless to think or create. The New is an empty ideal that cannot be willed as such. Rather, what is to be willed is that which comes to us in the event of thought. The specificity of *this* thought should always be affirmed over the new, for the affirmation of the new commits us to nothing, produces nothing, or infinitely defers the new to the future in that one knows not which "new" to produce. By contrast, the affirmation of *this* thought produces the commitment or fidelity and labor through which the new is produced. My authenticity and singularity consist not in the idea of novelty, but in *this* thought which I affirm and pursue regardless of whether it is novel, for without this thought I am nothing.

Finally, the claim that problems do not resemble their solutions ensures that problems not be treated by tracing them from their solutions. Under the empirical concept of problems, the problem is conceived in the inverted image of its solution, as its negation, and is thus conceived as containing all the properties of the solution in an unrealized form. By contrast, the transcendental concept of problems does not assume that the problematicity of problems resembles their solutions, but rather that problems have an immanent organization of their own irreducible to any particular case of solution. In this respect, all solutions are absolutely creative insofar as they represent novel actualizations of the problematic field.

We get a sense of this difference between problems and solutions from Deleuze's discussion of structuralism in his essay "How Do We Recognize Structuralism?" written around the time of *Difference and Repetition* and *The Logic of Sense*. According to Deleuze,

> We can say at least that the corresponding structure has no relationship with a sensible form, nor with a figure of the imagination, nor with an intelligible essence. It has nothing to do with *form:* for structure is not de-

fined by an autonomy of the whole, by a preeminence of the whole over its parts, by Gestalt that would operate in the real and in perception. Structure is defined, on the contrary, by the nature of certain atomic elements that claim to account both for the formation of wholes and for the variation of their parts. It has nothing to do either with *figures* of the imagination, although structuralism is riddled with reflections on rhetoric, metaphor, and metonymy, for these figures themselves imply structural displacements that must account for both the literal and the figurative. It has nothing to do finally with an *essence,* for it is a matter of a combinatory formula supporting formal elements that by themselves have neither form, nor signification, nor representation, nor content, nor given empirical reality, nor hypothetical functional model, nor intelligibility behind appearances. ("HRS" 261)

It is not difficult to recognize Lacan's distribution of the Symbolic, the Imaginary, and the Real in Deleuze's discussion of structure here. Deleuze conceives the Real as the world of objects as they exist apart from mind (a substantial misreading of the Lacanian concept of the Real). The Imaginary corresponds to the domain of identifications. And the Symbolic corresponds to the domain of relations and elements (neither of which exists apart from the other). The point, then, is that structure is irreducible to either the Real or the Imaginary. As we saw in the first chapter of this book, structure is the condition of both denotation and manifestation: it is their genetic principle. Structure, according to Deleuze, is just what a problem is and has the status of being virtual. "The idea is . . . defined as a structure. A structure of an Idea is a 'complex theme,' an internal multiplicity—in other words, a system of multiple, non-localisable connections between differential elements which is incarnated in real relations and actual terms" (*DR* 183). If structures, Ideas, or problems are irreducible to either the Real or the Imaginary, this is because the relations and singularities of which the multiplicity is composed are not actual entities, nor the relations between actual entities. For instance, a structural relation is not a relation of tallness between two individuals. Relations such as tallness are only possible on the basis of structural relations which generate the specific space within which these individuals are actualized.

Structural Essences

We must be careful with respect to Deleuze's claim that structure is at odds with essence. When Deleuze claims that structure is nothing like essence, he is not referring to a specifically structural or problematic essence, but rather to intelligible essences conceived after the manner of forms or wholes existing apart from their actualizations. Problematic essences are concrete in that there is no gap between them and their individuals, while there is always a gap between form and content. Under this view, form is conceived as being identical to its realizations, differing only in the respect that it is unrealized or possible. Given this, it is clear that intelligible essences are traced from the empirical actualizations given by recognition, that they are conceived in terms of resemblance. By contrast, a structural essence shares no resemblance to its actualizations, nor is it formal, insofar as it consists of a multiplicity of relations between elements that do not define a whole. The multiplicity of structure is never actualized in a single being, but undergoes a series of divergent actualizations . . . Hence the reason why very different life forms such as molluscs and humans can resemble each other with respect to parts—the eye—while nonetheless having evolved according to different histories and environments. It is for this reason that Deleuze refers to structures as concrete universals or essences. "The Idea or problem is universal. It is not the solution which lends its generality to the problem, but the problem which lends its universality to the solution" (*DR* 162). If problems are universals, then this is because the solutions are variations of the complex theme or style: they are topological variations.

These universals do not exist over and above their solutions like Platonic forms but go all the way down to the individual. By way of example, Deleuze claims that

> an Idea is an n-dimensional, continuous, defined multiplicity. Colour—or rather, the Idea of colour—is a three-dimensional multiplicity. By dimensions, we mean the variables or co-ordinates upon which a phenomenon depends; by continuity, we mean the set of relations between changes in these variables—for example, a quadratic form of the differentials of the co-ordinates; by definition, we mean the elements reciprocally determined by these relations, elements which cannot change unless the multiplicity changes its order and its metric. (*DR* 182–83)

By dimensions or variables of the color-multiplicity, Deleuze means hue, lightness, and saturation. The colored object does not resemble any of these three singularities, but rather actualizes, envelops, or embodies them. Moreover, the relations of hue, lightness, and saturation do not exist apart from one another, but rather are only together in the multiplicity insofar as they are related to one another. The continuity belonging to the multiplicity is defined on the basis of the variations the multiplicity can undergo in terms of diminution and increase. (We see here just how much Deleuze departs from Bergson, who rejected the notion of intensity as a spatialization of qualities, rather than discerning the continuity of the multiplicity in its variations.)[13]

The consequence of this way of understanding the universal or essence is that we no longer treat each individual color as an essence, but rather as a variation on the style, theme, or multiplicity. Just as we saw earlier in the case of "white light," an essence problematically envelops all its variations. Consequently, structural essences do not trace themselves from the actualized entity, from the form, but instead seek to determine the singularities or positions and relations belonging to the multiplicity.

> What does the symbolic element of the structure consist of? . . . Distinct from the real and the imaginary, it cannot be defined either by preexisting realities to which it would refer and that it would designate, nor by the imaginary or conceptual contents that it would implicate, and which would give to it a signification. The elements of a structure have neither extrinsic designation nor intrinsic signification. Then what is left? As Levi-Strauss recalls rigorously, they have nothing other than a *sense:* a sense that is necessarily and uniquely "positional." It is not a matter of a location [*place*] in real spatial expanse nor of sites of imaginary extensions, but rather places and sites in a properly structural space, that is, a topological space. Space is what is structural, but an unextended, preextensive space, pure *spatium* constituted bit by bit as an order of proximity, in which the notion of proximity first of all has precisely an ordinal sense and not a signification in extension . . . In short, places in a purely structural space are primary in relation to the things and real beings that come to occupy them, primary also in relation to the always somewhat imaginary roles and events that necessarily appear when they are occupied.
>
> The scientific ambition of structuralism is not quantitative, but topological and relational. ("HRS" 262)

To claim that singularities or variables are ordinal (rather than cardinal) is to claim that they define a position rather than a progression in a series. An ordinal position is not a place from which one can move to another place. No, to do so would be to either occupy the structure and thus assume the positions, or to subtract a position from the multiplicity, thus forming another multiplicity. Rather, the ordinality of positions is defined in terms of the other positions belonging to the multiplicity and defines (1) the variations in continuity the multiplicity can undergo, and (2) the determination belonging to the multiplicity as such. Each position does not so much define a space or form, but rather a series of variations going from zero to infinity in a general becoming. It is for this reason that the multiplicity of color is simultaneously "white light" (degree zero) and all the individuated colors found in traversing the positions as they relate to one another.

We tend to associate the term *symbolic* with language. It is true that Deleuze follows the structuralists in this gesture, but he diverges from them in claiming that language cannot be identified with signifiers (we already saw this to a certain degree with his critique of signification in chapter 1). Rather,

> if structuralism then extends into other domains, this occurs henceforth without it being a question of analogy, nor merely in order to establish methods "equivalent" to those that first succeeded for the analysis of language. In truth, language is the only thing that can properly be said to have structure, be it an esoteric or even a nonverbal language. There is a structure of the unconscious only to the extent that the unconscious speaks and is language. There is a structure of bodies only to the extent that bodies are supposed to speak with a language that is one of its symptoms. Even things possess a structure only insofar as they maintain a silent discourse, which is the language of signs. So the question "What is structuralism?" is further transformed—It is better to ask, What do we recognize in those that we call structuralists? And what do they themselves recognize?—since one does not recognize people, in a visible manner, except by the invisible and imperceptible things that they recognize in their own fashion. How do structuralists go about recognizing a language in something, the language proper to a domain? What do they discover in this domain? We thus propose only to discern certain *formal* criteria of recognition, the simplest ones. ("HRS" 259)

If *a* language cannot be identified with signifiers, this is because signifiers are not the formal being of language, but its material instantiation. As Saussure is quick to point out, linguistics is not concerned with sounds, but sound-images. And these images can only be defined relationally as traces, as a kind of mnemonic writing. Language consists of a system of interdependent elements which have only a relational identity and in which no element knows autonomy from the rest. For this reason it is possible to speak of languages which are very different from linguistic forms. For instance, the language of DNA. What we have here is an organizational system which shares no resemblance to its actualizations or which differs in kind from its actualizations.

It is with respect to this concept of problems that we can also understand why the *cogitandum* is both that which can only be thought and that which is unthinkable. If it is unthinkable from the perspective of empirical experience, then this is because the problem is precisely that which is not given in empirical experience, which is forever transcendent to that experience, which is always unrecognizable and beyond the demand for identity. "The problem is at once both transcendent and immanent in relation to solutions. Transcendent, because it consists in a system of ideal liaisons of differential relations between genetic elements. Immanent, because these liaisons or relations are incarnated in the actual relations which do not resemble them and are defined by the field of solutions" (*DR* 163). If problems are that which can only be thought, then this is because, for the same reason, problems are never manifested in empirical experience, but are rather that which belongs to thought *as such*. They define thought in its transcendental functioning, apart from the convergence of the faculties. *Thought is the faculty of problems*.

In light of the foregoing analysis, we can discern just where Deleuze departs from Kant's concept of the problem. It is true that Deleuze's account of problems is deeply inspired by Kant, but nonetheless empiricist problems remain in the Kantian conception. First, for Kant, problems are governed above all by the structure of genus and species. This is to say that the problem of problems is for Kant, like Aristotle and unlike the Sophists, a taxonomical problem.

> That all the manifoldness of individual things does not exclude the identity of *species;* that the several species must be treated only as various determinations of fewer *genera,* and the latter of still higher *families,* etc.; that therefore a certain systematic unity of all possible empirical concepts must be sought insofar as they can be derived from higher and more general ones: this is a scholastic rule or logical principle, without which there could be no use of reason, because we can infer from the universal to the particular only on the ground of the universal properties of things under which the particular properties stand.[14]

Initially, it might seem that Kant takes the structuralist route in articulating the being of problems insofar as genera, species, and families are defined in terms of one another. However, a moment's reflection is enough to show that this is not the case. First, the relations of genera, species, and families are not defined in terms of their ordinal position, but rather in terms of content. Unlike Deleuzian multiplicities or structures which are defined by their variables or dimensions, the Kantian taxonomy consists not of variables, but of a genealogy determined in terms of increasing and decreasing generality. Second, taxonomical trees are defined in terms of representation, insofar as they are based on identity with regard to the genus, oppositions with regard to species, analogy with respect to judgments, and resemblance with respect to objects. Insofar as taxonomical trees are based on these characteristics, it is clear that they tacitly assume the model of recognition as their organizational principle. As a result, Kant's attempt to formulate a concept of problems free of the empiricist activity of tracing problems from solutions ends up falling back into the assumptions of empiricism.

In the second place, the exteriority between concepts and problems in Kant is unacceptable from a Deleuzian perspective. This exteriority is one of the marks of the Kantian system overall and inevitably leads to an account of mere conditioning rather than a true genetic perspective. Hence, from this perspective reason remains untouched by concepts, just as concepts remain untouched by intuitions. We can then say that reason conditions concepts, just as concepts condition intuitions. Without repeating all the arguments of the first chapter, the difficulty with approaches based on conditioning is that they risk renewing all the dogmatic *formal* essences that they originally sought to overcome. In doing so, approaches based on conditioning are only able to account for experience in the most abstract terms, in terms of possibility. What is paradoxical in all of this is that although these conditioning forms are the most abstract of all, they are nonetheless traced from the outlines of the empirical, from the actualized entities that we find in experience. Kant's understanding of reason is still too transcendent, too conditioning, and thereby finds itself unable to articulate the internal being of the problematic in any but formal terms. The two senses of the aesthetic remain external to one another.

In light of the last five chapters, we are now in a position to see both how Deleuze's position diverges from Bergson's and also how he avoids the assumptions of the Image of thought. No longer is Deleuze's "methodology" a matter of carefully distinguishing differences in kind according to a method and showing how they recombine. Rather, it consists in undergoing the force of an encounter which allows each faculty to be pushed to its limit, to its superior and transcendental exercise. It is in this respect that the Deleuzian position consists in an apprenticeship or *learning* rather than *knowing*.

> To learn is to enter into the universal of the relations which constitute the Idea, and into their corresponding singularities. The idea of the sea,

for example, as Leibniz showed, is a system of liaisons or differential relations between particulars and singularities corresponding to the degrees of variation among these relations—the totality of the system being incarnated in the real movement of the waves. To learn to swim is to conjugate the distinctive points of our bodies with the singular points of the objective Idea in order to form a problematic field. This conjugation determines for us a threshold of consciousness at which our real acts are adjusted to our perceptions of the real relations, thereby providing a solution to the problem. (*DR* 165)

No longer is it a question of how we recognize or how we represent a world external to us, but rather it is now a question of what it means to learn, of what takes place in the force of an encounter, of how problems are actualized in solutions.

On the other hand, we can now see how Deleuze's transcendental empiricism avoids the assumptions governing recognition. No longer is it a matter of the convergent use of the faculties, but rather of each faculty being *forced* to its limit under the constraint and necessity of an encounter and by the force of the other faculties. The faculties no longer function together in a convergent and harmonious exercise directed at thinking the identity of a single and same object, but rather function according to a discordant exercise where each faculty encounters not an object, not an intention, but that which pertains to it alone by right.

However, another question forcefully interjects itself here. Although Deleuze has overcome the assumptions of the convergent use of the faculties and the centrality of the object, can it be said that he overcomes recognition's assumption of the primacy of the subject as well? We have already seen that there is some indication that the faculties belong to being and not the subject, that a subject must itself be produced. It might also be said that since the faculties only encounter their superior exercise under the force and violence of an encounter, the transcendental or superior exercise of the faculties cannot be attributed to the subject. However, none of this remains very convincing so long as we are not given reasons for asserting that Deleuze does indeed go beyond the restrictions of the Kantian-Copernican turn.

7

Overcoming Speculative Dogmatism: Time and the Transcendental Field

The Threat of Dogmatic *Schwärmerei*

A very important question interjects itself at this point: can Deleuze's transcendental empiricism be said to be a critical philosophy, or is it a speculative position born of enthusiasm and fanaticism? By "speculative" I understand any position which claims to have knowledge of reality or being through intuition, reason, method, or some other means without accounting for the conditions under which this knowledge is possible and the limits to which it is subject. It is in this respect that a speculative philosophy is subject to enthusiasm and fanaticism. As Kant puts it in the *Critique of Judgment,*

> If enthusiasm is comparable to *madness* [*Wahnwitz*], fanaticism is comparable to *mania* [*Wahnwitz*]. Of these the latter is least of all compatible with the sublime, because it is ridiculous in a somber way; [for] in enthusiasm, an affect, the imagination is unbridled, but in fanaticism, a deepseated and brooding passion, it is ruleless. Madness is a passing accident that presumably strikes even the soundest understanding on occasion; mania is the disease that deranges it.[1]

Enthusiasm is like taking a passing idea and raising it to the status of the secret of the universe, while fanaticism consists in dogmatically and tenaciously holding to such an idea regardless of whether or not one can provide reasons defending it. In contrast, by "critical" I understand a position which takes account of the conditions and limits that knowledge is subject to, thus establishing what can be known and what claims can be considered dogmatic.

In Kant the critical turn revolves around the "Copernican revolution," which involves resolving to see how objects conform to mind, rather than the mind to objects. In this chapter my aim is (1) to determine how Deleuze manages to overcome assuming the primacy of the subject with respect to his transcendental empiricism, and (2) to determine where Deleuze's position falls with respect to critical and speculative philosophy. As we shall see, Deleuze cannot be easily described as *either* a speculative *or* a critical philosopher, but instead blurs this distinction altogether on the basis of a reading of time. In effect, we can say that Deleuze effects a third "Copernican revolution." If such a move is necessary, then this is because Deleuze must demonstrate how it is possible to overcome the premises of representation founded in the supposed passivity of the subject and its finitude.

There is certainly much to lend itself to the claim that Deleuze is a speculative or dogmatic philosopher. In the last four chapters, this accusation perpetually asserted itself in terms of the status Deleuze attributes to the encounter. In giving the encounter this privileged status, a status which overcomes recognition and calls into question the primacy of the subject, Deleuze seems to make of it a sort of sign of the beyond, a sign of a reality or being apart from mind. Moreover, in our view, much of Deleuze's later work, postdating his collaboration with Guattari, *appears* to become entirely dogmatic. For example, in *Dialogues* Deleuze remarks that

> we should distinguish between two planes, two types of planes. On
> the one hand, a plane that could be called one of *organization*. It con-
> cerns both the development of forms and the formation of subjects.
> It is therefore, as much as one wishes, structural *and* genetic. In any
> case, it possesses a supplementary dimension, one dimension more,
> a hidden dimension, since it is not given for itself, but must always be
> concluded, inferred, induced on the basis of what it organizes . . . It is
> therefore a plane of transcendence, a kind of design, in the mind of
> man or in the mind of a god, even when it is accorded a maximum of
> immanence by plunging it into the depths of Nature, or of the Uncon-
> scious. (*D* 91–92)

So far, so good. What we have here is a description of a sort of transcendent viewpoint which Deleuze is right to call into question. Here Kant would be entirely in agreement with Deleuze in that the plane of transcendence must be called into question with respect to its claims to knowledge.

However, Deleuze then goes on to claim that

> there is a completely different plane which does not deal with these
> things: the plane of Consistence. This other plane knows only relations
> of movement and rest, of speed and slowness, between unformed, or rel-
> atively unformed, elements, molecules or particles borne away by fluxes.
> It knows nothing of subjects, but rather what are called "hecceities." In

fact, no individuation takes place in the manner of a subject or even a thing. An hour, a day, a season, a climate, one or several years—a degree of heat, an intensity, very different intensities which combine—have a perfect individuality which should not be confused with that of a thing or of a formed subject . . . A hecceity can last as long as, and even longer than, the time required for the development of a form and the evolution of a subject. But it is not the same kind of time: floating times, the float-ing lines of Aion as distinct from Chronos. Hecceities are simply degrees of power which combine, to which correspond a power to affect and be affected, active or passive affects, intensities. (D 92)

What is it that entitles Deleuze to make these sorts of claims? By all lights, what we have in this description, which is also a description of immanence, is something akin to the fullness of being apart from all the interruptions and discontinuities which the subject introduces into it by virtue of its finitude and limitations. How could this not be a dogmatic position insofar as it seems to assert an unmediated relationship with being foreclosed to human beings? Is this not the height of fanaticism, since it asserts a direct relationship with being apart from our being as subjects? Deleuze would like to claim that we must dispense with the subject and even the individual.

It is hecceities that are being expressed in indefinite, but not indetermi-nate, articles and pronouns; in proper names which do not designate people but mark events, in verbs in the infinitive which are not undiffer-entiated but constitute becomings or processes. (D 92)

Not persons, not subjects, not individuals, not things, just the seamless undifferenciation of a chaotic flux, the purity of being. But Deleuze perpetually vacillates on precisely this point. On the one hand, the purity of being without subjects. On the other hand, the subject's desire to occupy this place. Deleuzians are fond of renouncing figures like Kant or Hegel and theoretical approaches like structuralism and psychoanalysis on the basis of being state philosophies based on the primacy of lack. What really seems to transpire here is a sort of specifically Deleuzian fanaticism born of a fundamental fantasy that would return the person to the lost primordial unity. The joke is that this lost unity is created as a result of the very search for it. It is for this reason that Deleuzians often end up perpetually expressing themselves in oppositions, rather than actually returning to this primordial plane of consistency itself. If they actually approached the object of their desire, then they would have to renounce their fundamental fantasy, which would amount to the death of themselves as a subject. The only way to avoid this problem is through a critical approach to Deleuze's thought.

There is thus a twofold critical problem for Deleuze. On the one hand, Deleuze must reject the primacy of the subject in order to escape the model of recognition which contains a dogmatism of its own sort. The rejection of the subject does not mean that there are no subjects, but that the subject cannot function as the ultimate ground in the form of the supremely individuated world. In other words, the subject is not ontologically primitive, nor is the difference between finitude and infinitude a difference in kind. However, if Deleuze is not to fall into a speculative position, if he is to remain within the critical orbit, then it seems that he must adopt the primacy of the subject as his starting point; for we, at least, begin with the "illusion" that finitude and representation are absolute. This, then, constitutes the first problem: how to remain critical while rejecting the primacy of the subject? On the other hand, consistent with the claims of critical philosophy, Deleuze must somehow find a way to avoid attributing an unmediated relation with reality to the subject. How can Deleuze avoid positing a sort of return to the plenitude of the infantile world, preceding any introduction into language or the symbolic? Surprisingly, Deleuze finds the solution to both of these problems within Kant himself.

The Kantian Split Subject

Deleuze discerns the possibility of a transcendental ground more fundamental than that of mind in Kant's articulation of the manner in which the subject is split or fissured by the form of time. We can trace the trajectory of Deleuze's reasoning here by following Kant's articulation of this split. According to Kant,

> The understanding . . . does not *find* some sort of combination of the manifold already in inner sense, but *produces* it, by *affecting* inner sense. But how the I that I think is to differ from the I that intuits itself (for I can represent other kinds of intuition as at least possible) and yet be identical with the latter as the same subject, how therefore I can say that *I* as intelligence and *thinking* subject cognize my self as an object that is *thought,* insofar as I am also given to myself in intuition, only, like other phenomena, not as I am for the understanding but rather as I appear to myself, this is no more and no less difficult than how I can be an object for myself in general and indeed one of intuition and inner perception . . . Hence we must order the determinations of inner sense as appear-

ances in time in just the same way as we order those of outer sense in space; hence if we admit that by the latter that we cognize objects by means only insofar as we are externally affected, then we must also concede that through inner sense we intuit ourselves only as we are internally affected *by our selves*, i.e., as far as inner intuition is concerned we cognize our own subject only as appearance but not in accordance with what it is in itself.[2]

It goes without saying that Deleuze will reject the transcendental unity of apperception as an empiricist assumption based on the model of recognition. To be sure, he will attribute some unity and identity to the subject, but like all other unities and identities, these will be produced as effects of synthesis, rather than a transcendental unity akin to a categorical operation. Consequently, there will be a transcendental or genetic condition for being a subject, but the subject will not be transcendent to the world.

According to Kant, the empirical self is itself to be treated as yet another appearance among appearances, and thus cannot be granted any privilege in terms of immediacy. Rather than being immediate to itself, rather than being its own *spontaneity,* the self can only *represent* itself as spontaneous or as the origin of its own thoughts. This is similar to the situation in psychoanalysis where it is noted that we do not really know what we're going to say until we say it.[3] The Kantian subject is a split or barred subject. It is split by the intuition of time which runs through all of its self-manifestations, and within which even the subject must appear as a phenomenon. Just as all appearances must occur in time, so too must the self's appearance to itself transpire or unfold in time. As Heidegger famously argued, this already suggests that time is more fundamental, deeper, than the self as transcendental condition for experience.

However, the surprising moment occurs in the paralogisms where Kant claims,

> I do not cognize any object merely by the fact that I think, but rather I can cognize any object only by determining a given intuition with regard to the unity of consciousness, in which all thinking consists. Thus I cognize myself not by being conscious of myself as thinking, but only if I am conscious of myself, of the constitution of myself as determined in regard to the function of thought. All *modi* of self-consciousness in thinking are therefore not yet themselves concepts of the understanding of objects (categories), but mere functions which provide thought with no object at all, and hence do not present my self as an object to be

> cognized. It is not the consciousness of the *determining* self, but only that of the *determinable* self, i.e., of my inner intuition (insofar as its manifold can be combined in accord with the universal condition of the unity of apperception in thinking), that is the *object.*[4]

The Kantian self, in and of itself, does not present itself as an object to be cognized, but instead must be "produced" or results from synthesis. Following Deleuze, we can say that the self is determinable (by the form of time) but not itself determining (by its own spontaneity, insofar as it can only represent this spontaneity to itself). In and of itself, the self is undetermined, and only takes on determination or differenciated form through syntheses effected by temporal relations.

What is surprising in this passage is not the claim that the determinability of self takes place through time, but rather the parentheses at the end of the passage which claim that the "manifold *can* be combined in accord with the universal condition of the unity of apperception in thinking." The fact that the manifold *can* be combined according to these conditions also suggests that it does not have to be combined according to these conditions. But if the manifold always manifests itself in time, then we are warranted in claiming that the manifold of flowing time presents itself *as such*. In fact, if it were not possible for the manifold of flowing time to present itself independently of the transcendental unity of apperception or the categories of the understanding, it would be very difficult to render the question or problems of critical philosophy intelligible at all. For how would we otherwise understand the necessity of the categories of the understanding as a priori conditions unless they were *not* given in the manifold flux of experience? How could the necessity of the categories be understood if it were not possible for experience to present itself as an un-in-formed flux? And how would we understand this if the manifold flux of experience were not given to us *as* a manifold flux of experience?

Kant's analysis of causality in the second analogy readily comes to mind here. Often the problem of causality here seems incomprehensible to readers because it seems so apparent that the position of the boat on the river at one moment follows that of another moment. However, this is an example of thinking according to the complacent model of recognition. If causality is a problem, this is because at the level of the sheer flow of time itself, perceptions become paradoxical such that we can no longer decide which direction becoming moves in. As Alice grows larger she also grows smaller. The causal sequence is not itself given in the intuition.

Two important conclusions follow from the above. First, the subject itself is only ever encountered as an element in the manifold flux of experience, as being *in* this flow as an event among others. (There is no *given* unity of the subject, and I can only *represent the spontaneity of my thinking*.) I only experience the *effects* of my thinking, and not the spontaneity of thought itself. For if the latter, then I would have a relation to things in themselves. Second, the manifold flux of experience *can* be *thought* independently of the concepts of the understanding and the unity of apperception. But if this is the case, then we seem to be before a transcendental dimension more fundamental and deeper than those found in the understanding or the unity of apperception. Where both subject and object become elements in the manifold flux of experience, it becomes impossible to determine whether time is merely inner sense or whether objects are conforming to mind or whether mind and objects are both being generated by time (understood in a very specific sense). Here, time ceases to be treated as inner sense and becomes duration.

Kant's analysis of the manner in which the subject is an appearance within time provides Deleuze with the doorway for jumping out of the critical philosophy, which privileges the categories of the understanding, into an analysis of time as a pure transcendental field independent of both subjects and objects. Although this argument shares some affinity to the one advanced by Heidegger in *Kant and the Problem of Metaphysics,* as we shall see, it differs in that the analysis of duration is not made with reference to the finitude of *Dasein.* Duration is discovered as such and not as the duration *of* the finite subject. In short, the shift to time paves the way for talking about modes of synthesis and forms of relation that are no longer determined by the model of recognition and real relations among objects. Moreover, it also allows us to see the beginnings of how a generative account will be possible. The notion of a transcendental field is thus the idea of time independent of subjects and objects and out of which subjects and objects are generated.

Toward a Third Copernican Revolution

This brings us to the most important difference between Kant and Deleuze: the status of the Copernican revolution. For Kant, a Copernican revolution is effected in philosophy and our thought becomes critical when we cease trying to determine how mind conforms to objects, and instead seek to determine how objects conform to mind. There is no small amount of Cartesianism at work here. If this shift is critical, then this is because mind must somehow have a certain relation to itself, an immanent relationship with its being, a relationship of certainty. For Deleuze, by contrast, the Copernican revolution takes place in and through the eternal return. As he puts it,

> That identity not be first, that it exist as a principle but as a second principle, as a principle *become;* that it revolve around the Different: such would be the nature of a Copernican revolution which opens up the possibility of difference having its own concept, rather than being maintained under the domination of a concept in general already understood as identical. Nietzsche meant nothing more than this by eternal return. Eternal return cannot mean the return of the Identical because it presupposes a world (that of the will to power) in which all previous identities have been abolished and dissolved. Returning is being, but only the being of becoming. The eternal return does not bring back "the same," but returning constitutes the only Same of that which becomes. Returning is the becoming-identical of becoming itself. (*DR* 40–41)

For readers of Deleuze who discern in him the message that "all is different," this passage ought to be enough to dissuade them.[5] It is not that the categories of the Same, Similar, and the Identical disappear from Deleuze's thought; rather, it is that these properties must be produced as *effects,* and primarily as effects of the differential genetic factors.

Nonetheless, in connection with Kant, this passage ought to give us pause. We can very well see how it constitutes a sort of Copernican revolution insofar as it proposes that we treat difference as the condition of identity rather than identity as the condition of difference. In fact, we can almost hear Deleuze saying, "Hitherto we have sought to see how difference arises on the basis of identity in vain; let us see whether we fare better by seeking to determine how identity might arise on the basis of difference." But does this also function as a response to what Kant took the Copernican revolution to be? In other words, is Deleuze simply borrowing a recognizable trope from the history of philosophy for dramatic effect, or is he also responding to the Kantian primacy of the subject as the critical turning point? And if the latter, how does Deleuze respond to the Kantian assertion that we must first interrogate the power of cognition before practicing metaphysics? Does not Deleuze's position fall into a sort of speculative philosophy here? Is he not making a claim which goes beyond the limits of our experience?

On the one hand, we can see how the eternal return as a Copernican revolution constitutes a response to the Kantian Copernican revolution insofar as the primacy of difference contests the identity of the mind which constitutes the beginning of the Kantian critical project.

However, while it may indeed call into question the unity of the Kantian subject, nothing yet explains what, on critical grounds, authorizes Deleuze to make this claim. In other words, asserting does not make it so. *What Deleuze must demonstrate is that the Kantian critical turn itself leads to this conclusion, that critical thought is led to a point where the unity of the subject is dissolved and critical thought becomes indiscernible from speculative thought* (which is not to say that critical thought becomes speculative thought. In short, one must pass through critique to reach the point of *indiscernibility*). It is precisely this point of indiscernibility, this passing over, the "over-Copernicus," which Deleuze discovers in the Kantian split subject. As Deleuze puts it,

> If the eternal return is the highest, most intense thought, this is because its own extreme coherence, at the highest point, excludes the coherence of a thinking subject, of a world which is thought of as a guarantor God. Rather than being concerned with what happens before and after Kant (which amounts to the same thing), we should be concerned with a precise moment within Kantianism, a furtive and explosive moment which is not even continued by Kant, much less by post-Kantianism . . . For when Kant puts rational theology into question, *in the same stroke* he introduces a kind of disequilibrium, a fissure or a crack in the pure Self of the "I think," an alienation in principle, insurmountable in principle: the subject can henceforth represent its own spontaneity only as that of an Other, and in so doing invoke a mysterious coherence in the last instance which excludes its own—namely, that of the world and God. A Cogito for a dissolved Self: the Self of "I think" includes in its essence a receptivity of intuition in relation to which *I* is already other. (*DR* 58)

This is none other than Kant's claim that the subject can only represent its own spontaneity (it does not have an immediate relation to its thought) and that it encounters itself as an appearance in time among other appearances.

What is remarkable in all of this is that Deleuze identifies the Kantian subject with the Nietzschean eternal return. Much later, in the same text, Deleuze goes on to explain the significance of this dissolved Self in the context of Descartes, by discussing the manner in which it introduces a transcendental notion of Difference into thought.

> The entire Kantian critique amounts to objecting against Descartes that it is impossible for determination to bear directly upon the undetermined. The determination ("I think") obviously implies something undetermined ("I am"), but nothing so far tells us how it is that the

undetermined is determinable by the "*I think*": "in the consciousness of myself in the mere thought I am the *being itself,* although nothing in myself is thereby given for thought." Kant therefore adds a third logical value: the determinable, or rather the form in which the undetermined is determinable (by the determination). This third value suffices to make logic a transcendental instance. It amounts to the discovery of Difference—no longer in the form of an empirical difference between two determinations, but in the form of a transcendental difference between the Determination as such and what it determines; no longer in the form of an external difference which separates, but in the form of an internal Difference which establishes an *a priori* relation between thought and being. Kant's answer is well known: the form under which undetermined existence is determinable by the "I think" is that of time . . . The consequences of this are extreme: my undetermined existence can be determined only *within time* as the existence of a phenomenon, of a passive, receptive phenomenal subject *appearing within time.* As a result, the spontaneity of which I am conscious in the "I think" cannot be understood as the attribute of a substantial and spontaneous being, but only as the affection of a passive self which experiences its own thought—its own intelligence, that by virtue of which it can say *I*—being exercised in it and upon it but not by it. (*DR* 85–86)

If the determinable is no longer an empirical difference but a true transcendental difference, this is because it is the condition under which thought is able to determine being. It is not simply the difference between two instances, thought and being, but the internal link, the internal difference, which brings the undetermined and the determined together. The determinable is time. In Deleuze's view, when Kant discovers that the self is itself mediated by time, that it is fissured and cracked by time, that it can only represent itself as thinking and can no longer attribute spontaneity to itself *as such,* a transcendental domain is opened up which takes us beyond the primacy of the conscious knowing subject. This is why he adds emphasis when noting that the subject itself is within time. Where the subject itself manifests itself within time, the subject can no longer be treated as the first term, as the center in the Copernican revolution. We can no longer say whether time is an imposition of the subject or the subject an imposition of time.

It is at precisely this point that critical philosophy becomes indiscernible from speculative philosophy. In that time, as the condition of the subject, comes to render all distinctions between mediacy and immediacy indiscernible, it becomes impossible to draw a rigorous distinction between speculative and critical thought. No longer can we say that the subject's relation to objects is mediated. This is not because the subject now has an immediate relation to objects, but because the subject itself encounters itself in time, because the subject is *in* time. By the same token, we cannot say that the subject entertains a mediate relation to itself, because we cannot determine whether time is the mediate or the immediate. It is precisely this indiscernibility which Deleuze indicates with his emphasis on the subject as being "within" time. It is as if one must pass through the Kantian critical project, with its strict restrictions, in order to encounter a beyond of that critical project.

Time Out of Joint

For Deleuze, then, the transcendental turn, the critical turn, comes when we seek to determine how things and subjects conform to time rather than time to things. However, this way of speaking is not quite accurate. To say things conform to time rather than time to things suggests that time simply conditions beings. However, now what is at stake is determining how things are generated in time, how a properly transcendental genesis takes place. As he puts it elsewhere,

> Time is out of joint, time is unhinged. The hinges are the axis around which the door turns. *Cardo*, in Latin, designates the subordination of time to the cardinal points through which the periodical movements that it measures pass. As long as time remains on its hinges, it is subordinated to movement: It is the measure of movement, interval or number. This was the view of ancient philosophy. But time out of joint signifies the reversal of the movement-time relationship. It is now movement which is subordinate to time. Everything changes, including movement. (*KCP* vii)

Rather than asking how time conforms to movement, to moving things, we instead seek to determine how movement conforms to time, how it is produced by time, how it is rendered possible by time, how it occurs *within* time. This requires a transcendental analysis of the nature of time. We already saw a great deal of this analysis in chapters 2 and 4 of this book. On the one hand, the notion of duration evokes a new concept of time insofar as we no longer place our emphasis on the self-identical moving thing, going from place to place, but rather seek to determine qualitative change as the internal difference belonging to time *as such*. However, from this perspective, time still seems shackled to movement insofar as *a* duration seems to be a variation on the notion of a moving thing.

The crucial shift occurs with the Bergsonian concept of memory. Recalling that duration is itself memory (insofar as a duration is a continuity and not an existence at a point, and thereby must maintain itself in the expanse of its duration), we can then see how movement itself becomes subordinated to time. For, as we saw with the second paradox of memory, the entirety of the past coexists with the present, forming a synthesis of all time. In this respect, each duration becomes an expression of the open whole of time, which thus ensures that a repetition of the same can never take place. As a result,

> time is no longer defined by succession because succession concerns only things and movements which are in time. If time were succession, it would need to succeed in another time, and so on to infinity. Things succeed each other in various times, but they are also simultaneous in the same time, and they remain in an indefinite time . . . Permanence, succession and simultaneity are modes and relationships of time . . . Everything which moves and changes is in time, but time itself does not change, does not move, any more than it is eternal. It is the form of everything that changes and moves, but it is an immutable Form which does not change. It is not an eternal form, but in fact, the form of that which is *not* eternal, the immutable form of change and movement. (*KCP* vii–viii)

Once again we witnessed this property of time with respect to the third paradox of memory, or the preexistence of the past with respect to the present. Insofar as the past must preexist the present, insofar as it is not constituted by passing presents, there is a sense in which it is immutable. Rather than approaching time cardinally in terms of succession, we instead seek to determine its *ordinal* structure (the Past, Present, and Future as *originary positions* of time) as the immutable form of change conditioning movement.

This conception of time is what Deleuze refers to as the "eternal return" insofar as the eternal return is the immutable form of change, the only same in that which is different, and which is arrived at by recognizing the manner in which the subject is split or fissured.

> Time itself unfolds (that is, apparently ceases to be a circle) instead of things unfolding within it (following the overly simple circular figure). It ceases to be cardinal and becomes ordinal, a pure *order* of time. Hölderlin said that it is no longer "rhymed," because it was distributed unequally on both sides of a "caesura," as a result of which beginning and end can no longer coincide. We may define the order of time as this

purely formal distribution of the unequal in the function of a caesura. We can then distinguish a more or less extensive past and a future in inverse proportion, but the future and the past here are not empirical and dynamic determinations of time: they are formal and fixed characteristics which follow *a priori* from the order of time, as though they comprised a static synthesis of time. The synthesis is necessarily static, since time is no longer subordinated to movement; time is the most radical form of change, but the form of change does not change. The caesura, along with the before and after which it ordains once and for all, constitutes the fracture in the I (the caesura is exactly the point at which the fracture appears). (*DR* 88–89)

Initially, it might seem that Deleuze is reverting back to the pre-critical position of defining time in terms of a simple succession of instants, but his point is more nuanced than that. It is not that time is conceived as a series of instants, but rather that we can only conceive something like succession on the basis of a structural notion of time in which past, present, and future are *ordinal.* Put alternatively, conceived transcendentally, the past is that which *was never* present, the present is that which *is only ever present,* and the future is that which *will never* arrive. It is only insofar as time is ordinal, that it is composed of these three originary dimensions in their own right, that instants can manifest themselves in a succession as one instant coming *after* another and being *preceded* by another. As Deleuze explains rather dramatically,

What does this mean: the empty form of time or the third synthesis? The Northern Prince says "time is out of joint." Can it be that the Northern philosopher says the same thing: that he should be Hamletian because he is Oedipal? The joint, *cardo,* is what ensures the subordination of time to those properly cardinal points through which pass the periodic movements which it measures (time, number of the movement, for the soul as much as for the world). By contrast, time is out of joint means demented time or time outside the curve which gave it a god, liberated from its overly simple circular figure, freed from the events which made up its content, its relation to movement overturned; in short, time presenting itself as an empty and pure form. (*DR* 88)

If the ordinal notion of time is Oedipal, this is because Oedipus is the one who encounters the event in such a way that it is just about to happen and has already happened. It is no longer one event simply following another, but a point at which events have already taken place and are just about to take place. The dimensionality of time, its ordinality, thus becomes a constitutive feature of time as such, a true transcendental difference. The future is no longer that which will eventually come to be, nor is the past that which once was. Rather, we now find ourselves enmeshed within these dimensions in such a way that the future can only unfold and the past can only be completed. The future is always coming without ever arriving, while the past is always finished without having been present.

We can therefore see why Deleuze equates the Kantian conception of the split subject with the eternal return. Where past and future become originary, constitutive, dimensions of time, where they become the immutable form of change, the returning of past, present, and future can only bring the different rather than the same. This is because time, under such an account, can never achieve the requisite closure, the requisite circularity, necessary for making repetition a repetition of the identical. Rather, time calls all identities into question by abolishing all circular return between past and future.

Deleuze expresses this point with unparalleled clarity in *Cinema II: The Time-Image*.

> If we take the history of thought, we see that time has always put the notion of truth into crisis. Not that truth varies depending on the epoch. It is not the simple empirical content, it is the form or rather the pure force of time which puts truth into crisis. Since antiquity this crisis has burst out in the paradox of "contingent futures." If it is *true* that a naval battle *may* take place tomorrow, how are we to avoid one of the true following consequences: either the impossible proceeds from the possible (since, if the battle takes place, it is no longer possible that it may not take place), or the past is not necessarily true (since the battle could not have taken place). It is easy to regard this paradox as a sophism. It none the less shows the difficulty of conceiving a direct relation between truth and the form of time, and obliges us to keep the true away from the existent, in the eternal or in what imitates the eternal. (*TI* 130)

Once again, it must be emphasized that Deleuze is not talking here about a merely empirical notion of truth. As Deleuze clearly states,

> A new status of narration follows from this: narration ceases to be truthful, that is, to claim to be true, and becomes fundamentally falsifying. This is not at all a case of "each has its own truth," a variability of content. It is a power of the false which replaces and supersedes the form of the true, because it poses the simultaneity of incompossible presents, or the coexistence of not-necessarily true pasts. (*TI* 131)

It is not that each person fabricates their own truth, or that truth is historically or socially constructed. These are empirical theses and thus, while not unimportant, are philosophically uninteresting. Rather, the power of the false, the variability of the true, is a constitutive feature of truth arising from the ordinal structure of time. Insofar as time, in its transcendental constitution, contains a future that is always coming toward us without ever arriving and a past which has never been present, all propositions claiming truth are inherently upset.

"The battle may happen." Let us imagine time composed of two series, one transcendental and composed of three ordinal dimensions, the other empirical in which the present passes. Initially we treat Deleuze's claim as a sophism, because we assume that the truth value of the proposition remains a constant by virtue of being fixed at the origin. However, the problem here is that where these two series of time cross one another, the truth value of the proposition undergoes mutation and variation in time, abolishing the determinacy of its claim to truth. It is in this respect that possibility yields an impossibility. The proposition begins by expressing a possibility, but with the arrival of the battle the next day the proposition becomes the expression of an impossibility. Namely, it is impossible that the battle not occur. The condition for the possibility of the proposition also becomes the condition for its impossibility.

It may appear here that Deleuze is confusing transcendental and empirical determinations of time. The arrival of the battle is an empirical determination—the passing of the present—while the relationship of the proposition to past, present, and future is a transcendental determination. However, this objection misses the crucial point that all three of the ordinal determinations insist *together* (after the manner of a multiplicity in which each variable only has value with respect to the other variables) within the proposition itself. As a result of this co-insistence of the dimensions of time in the proposition, all determinations of truth must be attributed to the proposition. It is not that the value of truth changes with the passing of time, but that the truth value of the proposition is already "abolished," that it is already indeterminate.

It is only when we restrict the proposition to one temporal dimension, the present, ignoring the constitutive role of the other ordinal dimensions, that we are able to restrict the truth value of the proposition. For this reason, Deleuze refers to the transcendental dimension of the proposition as sense and claims that it is no longer determined in terms of truth and falsity, but rather sense and nonsense. Moreover, we see here why Deleuze equates the Kantian conception of the split or fissured subject with the eternal return of the different. Where the *form* of time itself remains immutable, the passing of duration can only bring the different. No longer is it possible to assume a circularity, a repetition of the same, between past and future, for the future is necessarily indeterminate while the past is always already determinate. The only same of the eternal return is constituted through the *becoming*-identical of the different. Identity is an effect, a synthesis, a production of difference. The domain of the Idea or sense becomes the question of how these constitutive dimensions come to be linked.

The Becoming-Identical of the Different: The Event of Time and the Subject of Difference

It is at this point that we become able to see why the eternal return abolishes the coherence of the subject and contests the nature of the Kantian critical turn. Once again, it must be emphasized that one must pass through Kantian critique in order to reach this point. It is only on the basis of Kant's transcendental analysis that the fact that we must treat the subject as an *appearance* comes to light. Through Kant we are able to see that the subject is a representation to itself, that it is mediated with respect to itself, in much the same way that Peirce claims "man" is a sign. It is only insofar as we resolve to view the experience as giving us nothing but phenomena, nothing but appearances, that it becomes possible to arrive at this point of view. In short, the very concept of appearance must be abolished because it no longer stands opposed to reality. Appearance is on the side of reality.

Pre-critical philosophies are inherently blind to such a thesis insofar as they ignore the question of the conditions under which experience is possible, thus leading them to inevitably privilege the temporal dimension of the present and to substantialize, to hypostatize, the subject. This trend is everywhere apparent in naive readings of Nietzsche, Foucault, and Deleuze. Inevitably these discussions degenerate into a vulgar distinction between power, the State, or *ressentiment* and the true self just waiting to get out to enjoy its bodies and pleasures while joyfully creating itself. In short, power is seen as external, rather than as the very thing that produces the subject. These readings are not unmotivated by the texts in question. But it is all too clear that these positions are based on empiricist assumptions about the primacy of the present and the fullness of the self. If the eternal return abolishes the coherence of the self, if it abolishes its claim to full self-presence and mastery, this is because the self is like a proposition with respect to the ordinal dimensions of time, such that the self is always already what it *was* and always already just about to be what it will be. Never, however, is the self first what it is in the sense of presence. In Derridean terms, we could say that the subject is always caught in a play of *différance* producing a simulacrum of identity through difference as an effect. The possibility of the self is its own impossibility.

> Having abjured its empirical content, having overturned its own ground, time is defined not only by a formal and empty order but also by a totality and a series. In the first place, the idea of a totality of time must be understood as follows: the caesura, of whatever kind, must be determined in the image of a unique and tremendous event, an act which is adequate to time as a whole. This image itself is divided, torn into two unequal parts. Nevertheless, it thereby draws together the totality of time . . . This symbolic image constitutes the totality of time to the extent that it draws together the caesura, the before and the after. However, in so far as it carries out their distribution within inequality, it creates the possibility of a temporal series. In effect, there is always a time at which the imagined act is supposed "too big for me." This defines *a priori* the past or the before. It matters little whether or not the event itself occurs, or whether the act has been performed or not: past, present and future are not distributed according to this empirical criterion . . . The second time, which relates to the caesura itself, is thus the present of metamorphosis, a becoming-equal to the act and a doubling of the self, and the projection of an *ideal* self in the image of the act (this is marked by Hamlet's sea voyage and by the outcome of Oedipus's enquiry: the hero becomes "capable" of the act). As for the third time in which the future appears, this signifies that the event and the act possess a secret coherence which excludes that of the self; that they turn back against the self which has become their equal and smash it to pieces, as though the bearer of the new world were carried away and dispersed by the shock of the multiplicity to which it gives birth: what the self has become equal to is the unequal in itself. (*DR* 89–90)

At the outset, we can ask whether or not Deleuze has in fact descended back into the empirical. In treating the distribution of past, present, and future in terms of an event, this seems to be precisely what he has done. After all, past, present, and future are supposed to be transcendental determinations of time, while events are generally thought to be that which transpire in time. This point is suggested all the more by the manner in which Deleuze seems to equate the distribution of past, present, and future with the power of a symbol; which, as we saw in chapter 3, is associated with the first passive synthesis of time or *habitus*. Do we not encounter a sort of transcendental-empirical doublet here?

It is not easy to see how Deleuze can navigate this difficulty. On the one hand, Deleuze claims that it matters not whether or not the distributive event actually occurs because past, present, and future are not distributed according to empirical criteria. In other words, the distribution of the dimensions of time is not dependent upon whether the event has *actually* passed or is *actually* yet to come. Rather, the event distributing time is similar to Kant's transcendental unity of apperception that we inevitably posit without actually experiencing it. The subject inevitably posits an event distributing the before and after of its being. The event need not transpire in actuality at all for it to function as an event and to fulfill this function. However, it is difficult to see how this approach can succeed since, while Deleuze indeed rescues the distributive event from the Real, it might nonetheless remain within the Imaginary. Insofar as the dimension of the Imaginary, not to be confused or equated with the virtual (since the imaginary too has virtual conditions), is no less empirical than that of the Real, Deleuze seems unable to give the determinations of time a truly transcendental articulation.

The source of these criticisms lies in placing too much emphasis on the event itself. Indeed, the event itself makes *manifest* the transcendental determinations of time, but in and of itself it is only the ever-receding synthesis of time. What is important with respect to the event is what transpires between event and act. And this relation transpiring between event and act is dependent upon the transcendental determinations of time. The transcendental structure of time is the condition for the possibility of the disparity between event and act.

> The narcissistic ego is inseparable not only from a constitutive wound but from the disguises and displacements which are woven from one side to the other, and constitute its modification . . . The importance of the reorganisation which takes place at this level in opposition to the preceding stage of the second synthesis cannot be overstated. For while the passive ego becomes narcissistic, the activity must be *thought*. This can occur only in the form of an affection, in the form of the very modification that the narcissistic ego passively *experiences* on its own account. Thereafter, the narcissistic ego is related to the form of an I which operates upon it as an "Other." This active but fractured I is not only the basis of the superego but the correlate of the passive and wounded narcissistic ego, thereby forming a complex whole that Paul Ricoeur aptly named an "aborted cogito" . . . We saw above that the fracture of the I was no more than the pure and empty form of time separated from its content . . . The whole of time is gathered in the image of the formidable action as this is simultaneously presented, forbidden and predicted by the su-

perego: the action = x . . . The narcissistic ego repeats once in the form
of the before or lack, in the form of the *Id* (this action is too big for me);
a second time in the form of an infinite becoming-equal appropriate to
the *ego ideal;* a third time in the form of the after which realises the pre-
diction of the *superego* (the id and the ego, the condition and the agent,
will themselves be annihilated)! (*DR* 110–11)

We see here that a transcendental distribution of time is a necessary
condition for the relation between past, present, and future belonging
to the subject. The action that is too big for me is dependent upon
the past that has never been present. It is an event which has never
itself transpired in the present. If the subject is dependent upon such
an event, this is because the subject must necessarily occupy a level
of the past in order for the present to pass. It is for this reason that
Deleuze says, "We do not repeat because we repress, we repress because
we repeat" (*DR* 105). If we do not repeat because we repress, this is
because repression is based on this primordial relationship with the past
that repeats itself throughout present experience (by the coexistence
of the past with the present). Repression thus takes place as a result of
the dual serialization between the past that has never been present and
the passing present repeating the past endlessly with potentially infinite
variation like a refrain. What is important here is that the narcissistic
ego must experience the relationship between the pure past and the
present *passively.* This is precisely what Kant indicates when he claims
that the understanding does not find itself as a given in the unity of
the manifold, but must produce this unity by affecting itself by itself in
time.

To say that this affection must take place passively rather than actively is to say that even in the case of the self time must unfold. As Deleuze puts it in *Kant's Critical Philosophy,*

> Kant explains that the ego itself is in time, and thus constantly chang-
> ing: it is a passive, or rather receptive, Ego, which experience changes
> in time. But, on the other hand, the I is an act which constantly carries
> out a synthesis of time, and of that which happens in time, by dividing
> up the present, the past and the future at every instant. The I and the
> Ego are thus separated by the line of time which relates them to each
> other, but under the condition of a fundamental difference. So that my
> existence can never be determined as that of an active and spontaneous
> being . . . I cannot therefore constitute myself as a unique and active
> subject, but as a passive ego which represents to itself only the activity
> of its own thought; that is to say, the *I,* as an Other which affects it. I am

> separated from myself by the form of time, and nevertheless I am one, because the *I* necessarily affects this form by carrying out its synthesis and because the Ego is necessarily affected as content in this form. The form of the determinable means that the determined ego represents determination as an Other. (*KCP* viii–ix)

Returning to Maïmon's attempt to rethink the active-passive opposition, this point is important in that it undermines the notion of an active thinking subject opposed to a passive receptive subject. In this way, it becomes possible to think a productive intuition without having recourse to concepts in that the sensibility of the subject is itself the result of a differential synthesis. It is precisely here that we find the coherence of the self called into question. For insofar as the self must unfold itself in time, we can no longer treat the identity of the self as a given, but must instead treat it as produced.

Insofar as the future functions as the yet to come, insofar as it cannot be anticipated, and insofar as this holds for the subject as well as the object, the coherence of the subject is abolished.

> Eternal return, in its esoteric truth, concerns—and can concern—only the third time of the series. Only there is it determined. That is why it is properly called a belief of the future, a belief in the future. Eternal return affects only the new, what is produced under the condition of default and by the intermediary of metamorphosis. However, it causes neither the *condition* nor the *agent* to return: on the contrary, it repudiates these and expels them with all its centrifugal force. It constitutes the autonomy of the product, the independence of the work. It is repetition by excess which leaves intact nothing of the default or the becoming-equal. It is itself the new, complete novelty. It is by itself the third time in the series, the future as such. (*DR* 90)

If the product is autonomous with respect to the condition and the agent, then this is because the product must itself unfold, because it cannot be anticipated. Since the future as ordinal cannot be reduced to the present, that which is produced in the approach of the future presents itself as absolutely new. Here the condition is the past, the agent is the present, while the future is the product abolishing both condition and agent. This abolition of the condition and agent occurs by virtue of the agent having to passively experience itself in its effects, as an other, as decentered from itself. The same produced in this repetition is not the repetition of an Identity, but rather the perpetual return of this decentering of the self, of this experience of oneself as Other.

When the future becomes a constitutive dimension, when it becomes that which is always arriving without ever arriving, the subject becomes irreducibly split and must experience itself as an Other. This future is not the projection of a project characterizing one's finitude but is the open-ended futurity of that which evades and abolishes all anticipation. The situation here is precisely analogous to that of the proposition's truth value that simultaneously generates its own possibility and impossibility. Event and act come to exclude the coherence of the subject.

Beyond the Subject: Deleuze's Hyper-Critical Turn

What, then, is the significance of the fissured subject with respect to the Kantian project? How does it call into question the primacy of mind involved in Kant's Copernican revolution? On the one hand, we can critique Kant at the outset for tracing the transcendental from the empirical in his assumption of the transcendental unity of apperception. This constitutes a sort of tracing the transcendental from the empirical insofar as we begin with the supposed unity of the subject given in empirical experience and account for it on the basis of a formal possibility. The condition here remains completely external to the conditioned, and contains no content of its own. By contrast, Deleuze is able to provide a genetic account of the subject through his three syntheses of time. However, this criticism remains unsatisfying insofar as it still seems to restrict ontology to the subject, returning us to the whole discourse of mediation and lack. By contrast, lurking in Deleuze's discussion of the Kantian split subject and the eternal return is a "hyper-transcendental" turn which takes us beyond the primacy of the subject and establishes a critical discourse freed of empiricist assumptions. In order to see how this is the case, we must determine how Deleuze transforms the concepts of *conditions* and *limits*.

As Heidegger demonstrates in *Kant and the Problem of Metaphysics*, the mark of the Kantian project consists in a shift to a discourse of finitude. It is in this respect that the notions of conditions and limits become all-important. On the one hand, it is necessary to characterize the conditions characterizing the subject's finite experience in the world. On the other hand, we must determine where these conditions leave off, where we depart from the finitude of our experience and enter a domain where manifestness can no longer take place, where experience can no longer be confirmed. Here it is the passivity of the receptivity that establishes the finitude of the subject. It is because I cannot produce my own sensations that I must be finite. The limits of experience are found in the illegitimate use of concepts independent of intuitions. Deleuze accepts the necessity of characterizing experience in terms of both conditions and limits, but rejects the discourse of finitude belonging to this discourse. This does not mean that Deleuze holds that we have an unmediated experience of the infinite and unconditioned, but that he rejects the manner in which finitude is inevitably traced back to a subject. Rather, the notion of a limit comes to inherently characterize time and the differential itself. In short, Deleuze is under the burden of demonstrating that something like a productive intuition is possible without falling into the absurdity of claiming that we are able to create whatever we will.

What is it about time that functions as a limit? We have already seen how time calls into question the truth value of the proposition along with the coherence of the subject by virtue of the eternal return of the different. This property is not to be restricted simply to propositions of consciousness and the subject, but rather to time as a totality itself. Deleuze refers to this conception of time as the "Whole." As he explains,

> Not only is the instant an immobile section of movement, but movement is a mobile section of duration, that is, of the Whole, or of a whole. Which implies that movement expresses something more profound, which is the change in duration or in the whole. To say that duration is change is part of its definition: it changes and does not stop changing. For example, matter moves, but does not change. Now movement expresses a change in duration or in the whole. What *is* a problem is on the one hand this expression, and on the other, this whole-duration identification. (*MI* 8)

As we saw previously, the past functions as the synthesis of the totality of time. Because of this, we are able to identify it with the Whole that Deleuze speaks of here. By contrast, we can identify these transformations in the Whole with the dimension of the future. Initially, we might be led to think that Deleuze is once again subordinating time to movement, but this is clearly not the case. While it is true that each movement effectuates a change in the whole, it is no less true that each movement is an *expression* of the whole. By way of example, Deleuze refers to Bergson's discussion of sugar melting in a glass of water.

> Putting some sugar in a glass of water, he says that "I must, willy-nilly, wait until the sugar melts." This is slightly strange since Bergson seems

to have forgotten that stirring with a spoon can help it dissolve. But what is his main point? That the movement of translation which detaches the sugar particles and suspends them in the water itself expresses a change in the whole, that is, in the content of the glass; a qualitative transition from water which contains a sugar lump to the state of sugared water. If I stir with the spoon, I speed up the movement, but I also change the whole, which now encompasses the spoon, and the accelerated movement continues to express the change of the whole. (*MI* 9)

In other words, the movement is not the stirring of the spoon or the placing of the sugar in the water. No, this is only movement from an empirical perspective. Rather, the movement is the qualitative transformation taking place in the system itself.

Deleuze identifies this transformation of the whole with the openness of all systems. Insofar as each movement brings about a transformation of the whole, expresses a transformation of the whole, the whole itself must always be open. In other words, we cannot identify the whole with a totality or a closed system.

Why does this spiritual duration bear witness, not only for me who waits, but for a whole which changes? According to Bergson the whole is neither given nor giveable (and the error of modern science, like that of ancient science, lay in taking the whole as given, in two different ways). Many philosophers had already said that the whole was neither given nor giveable: they simply concluded from this that the whole was a meaningless notion. Bergson's conclusion is very different: if the whole is not giveable, it is because it is the Open, and because its nature is to change constantly, or to give rise to something new, in short, to endure. (*MI* 9)

What we find in the notion of the Whole—which is to be identified with time as a totality—is a properly ontological limit. There is indeed some resemblance to Kant here, for in Kant transcendental illusions arise from trying to speak about the totality of being apart from intuition. In other words, for Deleuze, as for Kant, transcendental illusions are illusory precisely because we are subject to the intuitions of space and time which contain this constitutive limit internally and necessarily. However, with Deleuze this limit is no longer to be identified with the finitude of a subject, but rather time and being themselves become equated with one another. Time produces its own limit. The reason for this is that the subject is in time as much as objects are. To be sure, the glimmerings of this insight were already there in Kant, they would be unthinkable without Kant, yet Kant betrays them by assuming both the transcendental unity of apperception and the categories . . . Both of which, for all intents and purposes, take on all the appearances of being atemporal forms of being.

The Limits of Recognition

The consequences of Deleuze's account of the Open Whole are profound. In effect, the Open Whole as the never-given totality of time gives us a priori grounds for critique, the secret skeleton key for Deleuze's animosity toward empiricist accounts, the criticism of the practice of tracing the transcendental from the empirical, as well as the reason why conditioning accounts are to be rejected in favor of genetic accounts. Once again, we find the critical criteria in Deleuze's discussion of Kant.

> Everything which moves and changes is in time, but time itself does not change, does not move, any more than it is eternal. It is the form of everything that changes and moves, but it is an immutable Form which does not change. It is not an eternal form, but in fact the form of that which is *not* eternal, the immutable form of change and movement. (*KCP* viii)

Time is the immutable form of change. As such, time becomes the critical criterion for determining whether or not a position is speculative or dogmatic. A position will be said to be speculative and dogmatic when it rejects the immutability of change in favor of formal essences, or any form of Identity and Sameness that is not produced. If approaches which trace the transcendental from the empirical and which limit themselves to conditioning are to be rejected, this is because they inevitably end up essentializing the empirical, rather than discerning the manner in which the Whole is perpetually open. The same problem arises with respect to external conceptions of difference insofar as they leave one of the terms unconditioned in hopes of thereby capturing a little bit of eternity. Empiricism always amounts to recognition, to the attempt to essentialize and detemporalize that which is contingent and inevitably passing.

We can see just how different this critical criterion is from the Kantian critical criterion. For Kant, one becomes speculative when one goes beyond the intuitional limits of experience through an illegitimate employment of the categories. Despite the fact that these illusions arise by employing the categories apart from intuition, critical experience is nonetheless shackled to the forms of the categories and the transcendental unity of apperception. As a result, the categories and the transcendental unity of apperception themselves take on the appearance of being eternal and immutable forms, with the only exception being that they must be employed with respect to intuition. Consequently, this notion of critique ends up valorizing the model of recognition. Such a view is dependent upon the inference that experience will present more of the same. By contrast, the Deleuzian ground of critique is not based on an illegitimate employment of the categories, but rather on an illegitimate closure of experience in terms of the model of recognition. If a genetic approach is to be preferred, this is because it allows us to see how experience is generated within time, rather than assuming the form of experience at the outset (and thus its closure), and thereby freeing it from the immutable form of change.

The Genetic Conditions of Experience: The Three Moments of Ideas

Deleuze's reworking of the Kantian conception of the split subject and his account of the transcendental structure of time allow us to determine an a priori limit belonging to being, but how do they allow us to determine the conditions under which experience is possible? In other words, what is a condition according to Deleuze? At the outset, we can assume that we can no longer treat the conditions of experience as immutable forms because change itself has become the one law. Nor can we identify these conditions with the transcendental subject because the subject itself is produced as an effect *within* time. Rather, it now becomes necessary to conceive of a transcendental field, irreducible to either subjects or objects. As we shall see, in order to properly conceive this field it becomes necessary to affirm the *necessity of chance*. In this connection, Deleuze retains the criterion of necessity belonging to the concept of a transcendental condition, while rejecting the criterion of universality. A transcendental condition is necessary without being universal. How are we to conceive this sort of a condition?

According to Deleuze, the Whole is to be defined in terms of Relation. In other words, it will be Relation which is the condition under which experience is possible.

> If one had to define the whole, it would be defined by Relation. Relation is not a property of objects, it is always external to its terms. It is also in-

separable from the open, and displays a spiritual or mental existence. Relations do not belong to objects, but to the whole, on the condition that this whole is not confused with a closed set of objects. By movement in space, the objects of a set change their respective positions. But, through relations, the whole is transformed or changes qualitatively. We can say of duration itself or of time, that it is the whole of relations. (*MI* 10)

It is not difficult to discern the Deleuzian concept of multiplicity or structure in this definition of the whole. If relations are external to their terms, this is not because relations are between terms (Deleuze is not talking here about relations such as "being-taller-than"), but because relations preside over the genesis of the terms. Consequently, relations are external to their terms in the sense that "movements" can take place among the terms which do not themselves effectuate a qualitative transformation of the whole. Such a point can be seen with respect to speech and language, where speech acts do not necessarily effect the linguistic Idea itself. As we saw in the last chapter, a multiplicity is just a set of relations and singularities defining a theme, style, or differential essence. We must not confuse Deleuze's claim that relations are external to their terms with the claim that relations are external to singularities. A *term* is not a singularity, but rather an *actualized object*. As we shall see, if relations are external to their terms, this is because relations and the singularities they emit are a necessary condition for the possibility of the actualization of an object and thus cannot themselves be dependent upon the object. For instance, a speech act is dependent upon the linguistic relations and phonemic singularities it actualizes in its enunciation.

In contrast to the spatial relations we find in empirical experience, the relations belonging to the whole are *differential relations*. Unlike spatial relations which are premised on negation and contradiction, differential relations are not born of oppositions, but rather constitute a properly internal difference. "Just as we oppose difference in itself to negativity, so we oppose *dx* to not-A, the symbol of difference to that of contradiction" (*DR* 170). Where relations of contradiction and opposition are defined by oppositions between terms, differential relations only have value by virtue of a reciprocal synthesis or determination.

The symbol *dx* appears as simultaneously undetermined, determinable and determination. Three principles which together form a sufficient reason correspond to these three aspects: a principle of determinability corresponds to the undetermined as such (*dx*, *dy*); a principle of reciprocal determination corresponds to the really determinable (*dx/dy*); a principle of complete determination corresponds to the effectively determined values (dy/dx). In short, dx is the Idea—the Platonic, Leibnizian or Kantian Idea, the "problem" and its being. (*DR* 171)

Initially, we might be inclined to relate this concept of the differential to the Hegelian account of difference given in the *Science of Logic*. There difference is defined in terms of what something is not, or by a contradiction between difference and identity. The differential identity of a thing thus consists in its relation to all things which it is not. Such a reading certainly seems suggested by the fact that in the first moment of sufficient reason Deleuzian differentials are completely undetermined, while they become determinable when related to one another. However, what must be kept in mind is that (1) the moment of the undetermined does not consist of terms which are yet to be determined (as in the case of Hegel's discussion of diversity), and (2) the relation the two relations enter into is not one of contradiction or opposition, but of synthesis. "Dx is strictly nothing in relation to x, as dy is in relation to y" (*DR* 171). If the relations are strictly nothing taken apart from one another, then it strictly follows that there is nothing there through which a contradiction could take place.

It will be recognized that the tripartite relationship between the undetermined, the determinable, and the complete determination is also a feature that follows necessarily from the transcendental structure of time. As such, we are to think sufficient reason dynamically as an unfolding movement rather than as the description of a static thing subsumed under a form. If Ideas must necessarily begin as being undetermined, this is because time itself is open, because it never effects closure, because experience undergoes mutations. As Deleuze puts it with respect to the Kantian conception of problems,

> Ideas have legitimate uses only in relations to concepts of the understanding; but conversely, the concepts of the understanding find the ground of their (maximum) full experimental use only in the degree to which they are related to problematic Ideas: either by being arranged upon lines which converge upon an ideal *focus* which lies outside the bounds of experience, or by being conceived on the basis of a common *horizon* which embraces them all. Such focal points or horizons are Ideas—in other words, problems as such—whose nature is at once both immanent and transcendent. (*DR* 168–69)

Deleuze will accept this characterization of Ideas, while rejecting Kant's treatment of Ideas in terms of the concepts of the understanding. Ideas serve as focal points, as unifying horizons of experience which are immanent by virtue of pulling elements of experience together, while they are transcendent insofar as they are "unsolvable" problems.

In contrast to Kant, Deleuze, following Maïmon, will attempt to show how Ideas are generated within the sensibility itself, and in fact function as the genetic condition of sensibility. Deleuze thus offers a new aesthetic and critique of the given. Rather than treating sensibility in terms of irreducible atomic sensations or what can be sensed, Deleuze instead attempts to account for the very production of sensibility in the sense that a biologist might conceive an evolution of aesthetics in the animal world. For the moment, what is important is the relationship between Ideas, the cogito, and time. If Ideas have an essential relationship to time, it is by virtue of the openness they maintain.

> Ideas, therefore, present three moments: undetermined with regard to their object, determinable with regard to objects of experience, and bearing the ideal of an infinite determination with regard to concepts of the understanding. It is apparent that Ideas here repeat the three aspects of the Cogito: the *I am* as an indeterminate existence, *time* as the form under which this existence is determinable, and the *I think*, as a determination. Ideas are exactly the thoughts of the Cogito, the differentials of thought. Moreover, in so far as the Cogito refers to a fractured I, an I split from end to end by the form of time which runs through it, it must be said that Ideas swarm in the fracture, constantly emerging on its edges, ceaselessly coming out and going back, being composed in a thousand different manners. (*DR* 169)

Within the structure of the Idea we also find the structural progression between past, present, and future as the Idea progressively takes on increasing determination. The past becomes the moment of the undetermined insofar as it is not yet actualized (recalling that the transcendental past is a past that has never been present), the present functions as the moment of determinability insofar as differentials are brought together, while the future represents the ideal of complete determination. While it is indeed true that these are ideas of the cogito, it cannot be said that Ideas are actively formed by the cogito. Rather, *cogito* is the name of that which lives its Ideas as affects. As Deleuze will say later, "The Cogito incorporates all the power of a differential unconscious, an unconscious of pure thought which internalizes the difference between the determinable Self and the determining I, and injects into thought as such something unthought, without which its operation would always remain impossible and empty" (*DR* 174). In a profound reversal, Ideas no longer belong to consciousness, but rather consciousness is produced in and through unconscious differential Ideas. Time itself becomes the "subject." Ideas do not belong to the subject; rather, the subject belongs to its Ideas.

In contrast to Kantian Ideas which provide us with a structure of genus and species for organizing the concepts of experience, Deleuzian Ideas provide an ideal continuity belonging to sensibility. This continuity is the unfolding movement of the differential as it traces its variations. Hence,

> the Idea of fire subsumes fire in the form of a single continuous mass capable of increase. The Idea of silver subsumes its object in the form of a liquid continuity of fine metal. However, while it is true that continuousness must be related to Ideas and to their problematic use, this is on condition that it be no longer defined by characteristics borrowed from sensible or even geometric intuition, as it still is when one speaks of the interpolation of intermediaries, of infinite intercalary series or parts which are never the smallest possible. Continuousness truly belongs to the realm of Ideas only to the extent that an ideal cause of continuity is determined. Taken together with its cause, continuity forms the pure element of quantitabilitiy, which must be distinguished both from the fixed quantities of intuition [*quantum*] and from variable quantities in the form of concepts of the understanding [*quantitas*]. (*DR* 171)

Deleuze's prohibitions against thinking continuousness in terms of geometric and sensible intuition must be taken very seriously here. In this connection, Deleuze conceives Ideas topologically as sets of variations or deformations in which one form can pass into another while maintaining a structural identity, rather than as fixed forms to which individuals more or less correspond. If continuousness cannot be identified with form (geometrical intuition) or fixed qualities, this is because Ideas are the condition under which form and quality are themselves possible. In short, the difference between form and content is a difference in degree rather than kind. To identify continuousness with form or quality would be to trace the transcendental from the empirical or to assume the model of recognition. By contrast, what Ideas define is an ideal topological or differential essence characterizing a field of variations or permutations. In other words, there is no Idea of redness or squareness, but rather redness and squareness are permutations belonging to an Idea.

Deleuze follows Maïmon's example in referring to the property of the "shortest."

> "Shortest" may be understood in two ways: from the point of view of conditioning, as a schema of the imagination which determines space in accordance with the concept (the straight line defined as that which in all parts may be superimposed upon itself)—in this case the difference remains external, incarnated in a rule of construction which is established "between" the concept and intuition. Alternatively, from the genetic point of view, the shortest may be understood as an Idea which overcomes the duality of concept and intuition, interiorises the difference between straight and curved, and expresses this internal difference in the form of a reciprocal determination and in the minimal conditions of an integral. The shortest is not a schema but an Idea; or it is an ideal schema and no longer the schema of a concept. In this sense . . . the shortest distance was not a Euclidean notion at all, but an Archimedean one, more physical than mathematical; that it was inseparable from a method of exhaustion, and that it served less to determine the straight line than to determine the length of a curve by means of the straight line. (*DR* 174)

If the shortest is not a quality, this is because it is not a self-identical property defined by an external relation between a concept and an intuition. For the same reason, it cannot be said to be a quantity. Rather, the shortest defines a series of variations between curved lines and straight lines arrived at in terms of exhaustion . . . literally in terms of becoming exhausted or the degree of exhaustion with respect to movement contrasted between the straight and the curved. The straight is the idea of a continuous approach to the limit of the curved, producing a difference in intuition. It will thus be seen that the Idea of the shortest contains three variables or singularities: the straight, the curved, and the process of exhaustion. These singularities can themselves be Ideas when treated on their own.

Chance and Necessity: The Eternal Return

We have seen how Ideas share a relationship to time through the tripartite relation between the undetermined, the determinable, and the ideal of complete determination. Moreover, we can see how Ideas remain critical in the Deleuzian sense insofar as (1) they are unconscious and thus not reducible to the primacy of the conscious and self-identical subject characterized by recognition, and insofar as (2) they only bear the *ideal* of complete determination. Such a determination is never given once and for all in empirical experience, but is the perpetually vanishing mediator which never comes to fruition and which, for that very reason, perpetually drives us on and serves to produce intuition or sensibility. In fact, these two critical requirements are only arrived at by way of a third, which is a property of time as such.

We encounter here one of the most disturbing and troubling aspects of Deleuze's ontology: the doctrine of chance and necessity. It is natural to ask, with respect to the Ideas, where they come from. To be sure, this question can easily be answered by pointing out that Ideas are the result of syntheses; however, we are still entitled to ask where the "matter" of these syntheses comes from. Now, from the point of view of philosophies of reflection, this question need not arise at all. On the one hand, there is the transcendental structure of mind which is simply treated as the a priori set of conditions governing experience for beings such as ourselves. On the other hand, there is the a posteriori given which is arrived at through experience. With Deleuze matters are different. Where before we relied on the transcendental structure of time, we now find that we can no longer assume such a structure, but must instead account for the conditions under which various temporal fields are generated. Similarly, we can no longer refer to the primacy of the given in experience insofar as experience is composed of qualities which are not themselves the ground of experience, but which are produced through the Ideas. We thus arrive at a strange effect of experience producing the structure of experience. The ground becomes groundless.

It is precisely this affirmation of groundlessness that constitutes Deleuze's transformation of the Kantian critical project. In light of Deleuze's reworking of the Kantian account of time with respect to the subject, it now becomes necessary to rethink the notion of a condition in terms of chance and necessity. For Kant,

> necessity and universality are the criteria of the *a priori*. The *a priori* is defined as being independent of experience, precisely because experience never "gives" us anything which is universal and necessary. The words "all," "always," "necessarily" or even "tomorrow" do not refer to something in experience; they do not derive from experience even if they are applicable to it. Now when we "know," we employ these words; we say *more* than is given to us, we *go beyond* what is given in experience. (*KCP* 11)

In light of Deleuze's reworking of the Kantian conception of time and the subject, it is clear that the criterion of universality can no longer be adequate insofar as we are unable to rely on the immanence of the subject to itself in the active conditioning of experience. In other words, while differential fields will be characterized by a necessity and rigor proper to their idea, we cannot count on a shared or interpersonal transcendental subject in which these differential fields will be universally present. The immutable form of time has riddled experience with chance. However, it is also clear that we are no less in need of a concept of necessity insofar as we find ourselves produced by the differential Ideas of the unconscious. In other words, the Ideas function as a necessary condition under which this particular form of life is possible (in such a way that it can no longer be universalized for all creatures at all times and places).

The problem then is as follows: how do we reconcile the chance belonging to time with the necessity belonging to the Ideas? In order to solve this problem, Deleuze draws upon Nietzsche's concepts of the eternal return and the dice throw. Adopting Nietzsche's metaphor of a throw of the dice, Deleuze claims that

> the dice which are thrown once are the affirmation of *chance*, the combination which they form on falling is the affirmation of *necessity*. Necessity is affirmed of chance in exactly the sense that being is affirmed of becoming and unity is affirmed of multiplicity. It will be replied, in vain, that thrown to chance, the dice do not necessarily produce the winning combination, the double six which brings back the dicethrow. This is true, but only insofar as the player did not know how to *affirm* chance from the outset. For, just as unity does not suppress or deny multiplicity, necessity does not suppress or abolish chance . . . What Nietzsche calls *necessity* (destiny) is thus never the abolition but rather the combination of chance itself. Necessity is affirmed of chance in as much as chance itself is affirmed. For there is only a single combination of chance as such, a single way of combining all the parts of chance, a way which is like the unity of multiplicity, that is to say number or necessity. (*NP* 26)

We can immediately see how the Nietzschean dice throw accords with Deleuze's reworking of the Kantian conception of time. If chance is necessity, then this is because the Ideas are the sufficient reason behind experience. Insofar as the Ideas are the sufficient reason of experience, there can be no reason beyond them. They *are* the reason of experience. They are the groundless grounds of experience, which are themselves the result of a throw of the dice or chance.

If it is difficult to comprehend this point of view, it is because we either shackle chance to a desired outcome or rely on a number of different throws of the dice to achieve the desired outcome. "The bad player counts on several throws of the dice, on a great number of throws. In this way he makes use of causality and probability to produce a combination he sees as desirable. He posits this combination itself as an end to be obtained, hidden behind causality" (*NP* 26–27). This is not a moral shortcoming, but a logico-empiricist fallacy. If the player who counts on a number of throws of the dice constitutes a bad player, this is not because he lacks the proper taste, but because the necessity of chance is already the condition under which he can have the desire for a particular outcome. In short, the bad player suffers from bad faith in that he effaces the manner in which his own decision is based on chance or a contingent choice. It is only insofar as the player already incarnates an Idea that he can desire a particular outcome. To count on a number of different throws would thus plunge us into a circularity. If the throw of the dice constitutes a necessity out of chance, this is because the outcome is the one that came to be. The throw of the dice is thus a stoic affirmation of one's thrownness, similar to Heidegger's resolute embrace of thrownness.

How then is the throw of the dice related to the Ideas? In the first place, the eternal return or the throw of the dice functions as a principle of synthesis.

> We misinterpret the expression "eternal return" if we understand it as "return of the same." It is not being that returns but rather the returning itself that constitutes being insofar as it is affirmed of becoming and of that which passes. It is not some one thing which returns but rather returning itself as the one thing which is affirmed of diversity or multiplicity. In other words, identity in the eternal return does not describe the nature of that which returns but, on the contrary, the fact of returning for that which differs. This is why the eternal return must be thought of as a synthesis; a synthesis of time and its dimensions, a synthesis of diversity and its reproduction, a synthesis of becoming and the being which is affirmed of becoming, a synthesis of double affirmation. (*NP* 48)

Already we recognize Deleuze's reworking of the Kantian conception of time within this account of the eternal return. If the eternal return is not the return of the same, this is because it is itself the immutable form of change, the perpetual openness of time. However, more importantly, within the eternal return we can discern the structure of the Idea insofar as it is a principle of synthesis. Namely, what we find here is the relationship between the undetermined, the determinable, and the ideal of complete determination as a synthesis of that which differs. As Deleuze often claims, not only do Ideas differ from each other, but they differ in themselves.

We can render this relationship between Idea and the eternal return in terms of the dice throw itself. According to Deleuze,

> Problems or Ideas emanate from imperatives of adventure or from events which appear in the form of questions. This is why problems are inseparable from a power of decision, a *fiat* which, when they are infused by it, makes us semi-divine beings . . . It is grounded in the nature of the problems to be resolved, since it is always in relation to an ideal field added by the mathematician that an equation turns out to be reducible or not. The infinite power to add an arbitrary quantity: it is no longer a question of a game after the manner of Leibniz, where the moral imperative of predetermined rules combines with the condition of a given space which must be filled *ex hypothesi*. It is rather a question of a throw of the dice, of the whole sky as open space and of throwing as the only rule. The singular points are on the die; the questions are the dice themselves; the imperative is to throw. Ideas are the problematic combinations which result from throws. (*DR* 197–98)

The question belongs to the undetermined past. It is an imperative of the past with respect to the present, thus mirroring the manner in which the past coexists with the present. The present is the time in which the dice land, revealing the configuration of the differential relations and the singularities that result from them. Finally, the solutions correspond to the future generated on the basis of the problem as an ideal of complete determination. Moreover, each one of these moments differs from the others while nonetheless standing in a synthetic relation to them. The conditions of experience are no longer imposed by a subject in a relation of mere conditioning, but rather the subject itself is implicated in these conditions as one of their solutions and is the result of a genesis. Chance becomes necessity both in the sense that there necessarily is chance and in the sense that chance generates necessity in the form of questions and problems which *demand* answers.

Beyond Individuation and Chaos: The Singular

In light of the foregoing, we can now see how Deleuze evades the false alternative between a supremely individuated being in the form of the Person or Self and an undifferenciated groundlessness offered by metaphysics and transcendental philosophies of reflection. It will be recalled that philosophies of reflection and metaphysics are both led into this alternative insofar as they hypostatize the model of recognition and adopt a purely external concept of difference. Insofar as an undifferenciated and groundless conception of being is in principle unjustifiable, we are led to the alternative of either a being which is completely individuated through the agency of some sort of God (Plato, Aristotle), or a Self which is completely individuated and imposes this individuation upon the matter of experience. The problem is that both alternatives lack the grip of necessity. They both end up valorizing and hypostatizing the contingent. Everything changes when time becomes the groundless ground and we shift from a supremely individuated being to an individua*ting* being in time which becomes the transcendental condition under which experience is possible. As Deleuze puts it with respect to Nietzsche,

> Nietzsche's discovery lies elsewhere when, having liberated himself from Schopenhauer and Wagner, he explored a world of impersonal and preindividual singularities, a world he then called Dionysian or of the will to power, a free and unbound energy. These are nomadic singularities which are no longer imprisoned within the fixed individuality of the infinite Being (the notorious immutability of God), nor inside the sedentary boundaries of the finite subject (the notorious limits of knowledge). This is something neither individual nor personal, but rather singular. Being not an undifferentiated abyss, it leaps from one singularity to another, casting always the dice belonging to the same cast, always fragmented and formed again in each throw. It is a Dionysian sense-producing machine, in which nonsense and sense are no longer found in simple opposition, but are rather co-present to one another within a new discourse. The new discourse is no longer that of the form, but neither is it that of the formless: it is rather that of the pure unformed. (*LS* 107)

It is true that a discourse based on the formless would find itself at a loss to even begin. Where formless chaos reigns supreme, we are powerless to explain how a single form or individual can ever be constituted insofar as any hint of order and organization is immediately carried away by the ever-moving flux of chaos the moment it suggests itself. But in fact (*quid facti*) there are forms and organizations giving order to experience, which means that we must be able to account for the conditions under which such order is possible by right (*quid juris*). Deleuze, following Bergson, instead argues that the question of how something can come from nothing or how order can emerge from chaos is a specious problem.

> In the idea of nonbeing there is in fact the idea of being, plus the logical operation of generalized negation, plus the particular psychological motive for that operation (such as when a being does not correspond to our expectation and we grasp it purely as the lack, the absence of what interests us). In the idea of disorder there is already the idea of order,

plus its negation, plus the motive for that negation (when we encounter an order that is not the one we expected). (*B* 17)

It is precisely this reasoning which leads us into the alternative between a purely undifferentiated groundlessness and a supremely individuated being. But in the case of both metaphysics and philosophies of reflection, the alternative between chaos and order, individuated being and undifferentiated flux, is premised on the expectation of a subject (encountering an order it did not expect) and thus the synthesis of *habitus*.

The unformed is not the formless but the *formable* or determinable. No longer tied to a metaphysics of forms or the individuating factors of a transcendental subject, we now encounter the nomadic singularities resulting from a throw of the dice within the empty form of time. If these nomadic singularities are unformed without being formless, it is because they are durational tendency-subjects constituting a novel creation in the course of their unfolding. If this unfolding, which is both unformed and formable, is a novel creation, it is because the duration of duration maintains itself in a perpetual synthesis with the past as such, with memory as such, which ensures that each event is the expression of the entirety of the past, thus establishing that it must always be a repetition of the different rather than the same. Rather than unconditioned conditions after the manner of Kant, we instead encounter a domain independent of both subjects and objects (but nonetheless immanent to them), which is populated by ideal events as tendency-subjects presiding over the genesis of subjects and objects.

> Problems are of the order of events—not only because cases of solution emerge like real events, but because the conditions of a problem themselves imply events such as sections, ablations, adjunctions. In a sense, it is correct to represent a double series of events which develop on two planes echoing without resembling each other: real events on the level of the engendered solutions, and ideal events embedded in the conditions of the problem, like the acts—or, rather, the dreams—of the gods who double our history. The ideal series enjoys the double property of transcendence and immanence in relation to the real. (*DR* 188–89)

It will be observed that Deleuze is perfectly consistent here. If it is necessary that problems or Ideas, as the genetic conditions of experience, be conceived as events rather than as formal conditions, then this is because the subject itself is within a time that is both whole and perpetually open, such that we can no longer rely on the old formal essences or unconditioned conditions in order to maintain the perpetuation of the same in experience. The necessity of treating conditions as genetic fields rather than unconditioned formal conditions follows immediately from the primacy of an open form of time which has been unwound and must now unfold.

The Transcendental Field and Deleuze's Speculative Turn

In close connection to this thesis, we must ask what entitles Deleuze to grant the singularities populating the field of the unformed as tendency-subjects a status which is neither individual nor personal. It is clear that an argument by definition will be unacceptable in the context of this question. No matter how alluring, exciting, and seductive Deleuze's concept of singularity might prove to be, it should only be accepted on the condition that he can demonstrate why such a process of being is critically necessary. It is precisely with respect to the notion of a transcendental field that the question of singularity arises.

> We seek to determine an impersonal and pre-individual transcendental field, which does not resemble the corresponding empirical fields, and which nevertheless is not confused with an undifferentiated depth. This field can not be determined as that of a consciousness . . . A consciousness is nothing without a synthesis of unification, but there is no synthesis of unification of consciousness without the form of the I, or the point of view of the Self. What is neither individual nor personal are, on the contrary, emissions of singularities insofar as they occur on an unconscious surface and possess a mobile, immanent principle of auto-unification through a *nomadic distribution,* radically distinct from fixed and sedentary distributions as conditions of the syntheses of consciousness. Singularities are the true transcendental events, and Ferlinghetti calls them "the fourth person singular." Far from being individual or personal, singularities preside over the genesis of individuals and persons; they are distributed in a "potential" which admits neither Self nor I, but which produces them by actualizing or realizing itself, although the figures of this actualization do not at all resemble the realized potential. (*LS* 102–3)

Nonetheless, *we are individuals, persons, and selves.* Given that we are individuals, persons, and selves, we are entitled to ask what warrants the assertion of such beings. For if we are consciousnesses, then we seem irredeemably determined by a synthesis of unification (which all too closely resembles a principle of "auto-unification"!) which would seem to forever render such a transcendental field infinitely distant from us and even noumenal and therefore unreachable. Our perplexity only increases when Deleuze articulates the properties of these events or singularities in terms of Kant's table of categories.

> In relation to propositional modes in general, the neutrality of sense appears from several different perspectives. From the point of view of quantity, sense is neither particular nor general, neither universal nor personal. From the point of view of quality, it is entirely independent of both affirmation and negation. From the point of view of modality, it is neither assertoric, nor apodeictic, nor even interrogative (the mode of subjective uncertainty or objective possibility). From the point of view of relation, it is not confused within the proposition which expresses it, either with denotation, or with manifestation, or with signification. Finally, from the point of view of the type, it is not confused with any of the intuitions, or any of the "positions" of consciousness that we could empirically determine thanks to the play of the preceding propositional traits: intuitions or positions of empirical perception, imagination, memory, understanding, volition, etc. (*LS* 101)

Once again, insofar as we are consciousnesses, these dimensions of the proposition would seem to be the only ones open to us. As a result, the postulation of another domain, such as that of sense or singularity, of a transcendental field would seem to be entirely speculative and thus dogmatic. In other words, there seems to be no way in which Deleuze can demonstrate that he is entitled to claim the be-ing of singularity.

Before proceeding to answer these questions, it is first necessary to clarify what Deleuze understands by a transcendental field. In his final essay Deleuze asks:

> What is a transcendental field? It is distinct from experience in that it neither refers to an object nor belongs to a subject (empirical representation). It therefore appears as a pure a-subjective current of consciousness. An impersonal, pre-reflexive consciousness, a qualitative duration of consciousness without self . . . This is clearly not the element of sensation (simple empiricism) since sensation is only a break in the current of absolute consciousness: it is rather, however close together two sensations might be, the passage from one to the other as becoming, as increase or reduction of power (virtual quantity). ("IL." 3)

From this passage we can identify three distinguishing features characterizing a transcendental field. First, a transcendental field is to be identified with duration as such. It is for this reason that Deleuze is quick to claim that the transcendental field is independent of subjects and objects. As we saw in the second chapter, duration is not the time of a moving object, but rather the flow of qualitative change. By contrast, subjects and objects are "habitudes," syntheses of brute repetition which cover over qualitative difference and tend to equalize it. For this reason, second, a transcendental field is not to be identified with qualities themselves, but rather with the passage from one sensation to another defining a becoming. Where the concept of quality implies that of identity, that of singularity, for Deleuze, implies a heterogeneous duration. Where duration is concerned, it is not the qualities that count, for there are no qualities that persist, but rather the transformations that the qualities undergo. We can thus provisionally say that these thresholds (note the resemblance to the limits encountered by the three faculties!) are precisely what Deleuze means by singularities. This adequation appears in a number of places throughout Deleuze's thought. First and foremost it appears in his account of events given in *The Logic of Sense,* where we must think verbs in their infinitive form so as to capture the manner in which they are always already just about to happen and have already happened. We can also see how such a notion of singularity works with respect to the Deleuzian account of the shortest, where the singularity is defined in terms of the threshold between the straight and the curved. Finally, third, we can identify the transcendental field with the domain of qualitative alteration insofar as these thresholds define a perpetual alteration belonging to duration.

Does Deleuze then identify the transcendental field with consciousness? Here we find yet another point at which Deleuze diverges from Bergson. It is true that consciousness is the condition under which we are able to encounter something like the transcendental field, but the transcendental field is not itself identical to consciousness.

> The relation of the transcendental field to consciousness is only *de jure.* Consciousness becomes a fact only if a subject is produced at the same time as its object, all three of them being outside the field and appearing as "transcendentals" . . . It expresses itself as fact only by reflecting itself onto a subject which refers it to objects. This is why the transcendental field cannot be defined by its consciousness which is nonetheless coextensive with it, but withdraws from all revelation. ("IL" 3)

In other words, there is a sense in which we can only infer that there is a transcendental field such that we can only infer duration without actually experiencing it. No one occupies the transcendental field, nor *can* anyone occupy it. Rather, we only ever encounter the effects of the transcendental field. It is simultaneously immanent and transcendent. It is precisely at this point that Deleuze comes closest to falling into a speculative or dogmatic metaphysics. Nor does this peril go unrecognized by him.

> It is incomprehensible only from the point of view of a common sense or that of an exercise traced from the empirical that, for example, thought should find within itself something which it *cannot* think, something which is both unthinkable and that which must be thought. According to an objection often made against Maïmon, Ideas, understood as the differentials of thought, themselves introduce a minimum of "given" which cannot be thought; they restore the duality of infinite and finite understanding, which function respectively as the conditions of existence and the conditions of knowledge, and which the entire Kantian Critique nonetheless proposed to eliminate. This objection, however, applies only to the extent that the faculty of Ideas according to Maïmon is the understanding, just as it was reason according to Kant; that is, in either case, a faculty which constitutes a common sense and cannot tolerate the presence within itself of a kernel on which the empirical exercise of the conjoint faculties would break. It is only under these conditions that the unthought in thought, the unconscious of a pure thought, must be realised in an infinite understanding which serves as the ideal of *knowledge*, and that the differentials are condemned to the status of mere *fictions* unless they acquire the status of a fully *actual* reality in that finite understanding. Once again, however, the alternative is false. We might as well say that the specificity of the problematic and the presence of the unconscious in finite thought remains misunderstood. This is no longer so when Ideas are related to the transcendent exercise of a particular faculty liberated from any common sense. (*DR* 192–93)

By referring to a domain which is no longer the domain of experience, Deleuze seems to claim knowledge of that which cannot be known. This is what Deleuze means to indicate by evoking the criticism of Maïmon with respect to Kant's alternative between infinite and finite knowledge. If man is forever bound by the limits of finite intuition, then he has no right to appeal to the differentials underlying the given as grounds for a knowledge of being insofar as such knowledge, in principle, requires an infinite intuition. However, everything changes once the subject itself is seen to be within time. It is for this reason that Deleuze claims that the alternative between infinite and finite intuition is a false alternative. We have no word for this third alternative which Deleuze offers here.

Where the subject is within time rather than time in the subject, we can no longer decide between infinitude and finitude. The difference between the two is a difference in degree rather than kind. The whole is given, but is given as open and unfolding. Moreover, where the subject finds itself within time, it can no longer encounter itself as bound by its own immanence, as limited to its own immanence. Where the subject is itself split by the form of time, it becomes necessarily opaque to itself. The paradox of this line of argument consists in a critical reversal whereby a position is found to be critical insofar as it is able to introduce a minimum of the given into thought in the form of the unthought, rather than rejecting any such given. Such an approach is said to be critical insofar as it bases itself on the ability of a faculty to be taken to its limit, to encounter its limit such that it belongs to it alone, rather than shackling the faculties to one another under the form of recognition.

If consciousness necessarily belongs to the transcendental field but is not itself identical to it, how then are we to think the transcendental field? What is proper to the transcendental field? According to Deleuze,

> The transcendent is not the transcendental. Without consciousness the transcendental field would be defined as a pure plane of immanence since it escapes every transcendence of the subject as well as of the object. Absolute immanence is in itself: it is not in something, not *to* something: it does not depend on an object and does not belong to a subject. In Spinoza immanence is not immanence *to* substance, but substance and modes are in immanence. When the subject and the object, being outside the plane of immanence, are taken as universal subject or object in general *to* which immanence itself is attributed, then the transcendental is completely denatured and merely reduplicates the empirical (as in Kant) while immanence is deformed and ends up being contained in the transcendent. Immanence does not relate to a Something that is a unity superior to everything, nor to a Subject that is an act operating the synthesis of things: it is when immanence is no longer immanence to anything other than itself that we can talk of a plane of immanence. ("IL" 3–5)

The transcendental field is thus immanence. It is not immanence to you, nor is it immanence to me, but rather to all of the qualitative flows of duration or alteration which occupy it or are within it. If Deleuze is entitled to this claim, then it is because time itself is a Whole, because time gives itself as a Whole both in the eternal return and in Memory. As such, Deleuze is entitled to claim that time is immanent to itself.

If there is a critical point to be discerned in all of this, it is tragic rather than triumphant. Deleuzians often speak as if we, who are subjects, somehow come to occupy the transcendental field or plane of immanence or stand to it in a relation of immediacy. This amounts to the claim that we know the plane of immanence. It is in light of this claim that Deleuzians often seem so naive, speculative, and dogmatic. Here one speaks as if one were not split, as if one exists in a relation of immediacy with oneself. However, *we are subjects, and as subjects we are split.* To claim that we occupy the transcendental field, that we know it, would be tantamount to claiming that immanence is immanence *to* us. It is true that we are within time, that we are split by time, and that we are thus in immanence. But it is no less true that we are transcendent to immanence. The critical point that Deleuze invites us to recognize is not that forms of transcendence are mistaken because immanence is immanent *to* us, but rather that views based on transcendence are mistaken because they fail to take into account this constitutive split in our subjectivity which perpetually renders experience open. To claim that we somehow occupy immanence, that we stand in an immediate relationship with it, is no less dogmatic than positions based on transcendence.

In light of the foregoing discussion of the transcendental field, we can now return to the status of singularity in Deleuze's thought. What is it that entitles Deleuze to the notion of singularity when, in fact, we are subjects defined by all of the characteristics of representation which he seeks to avoid? As Deleuze puts it, it is not being that is equivocal, but we who are equivocal (*DR* 39). As we saw in the first chapter, Deleuze presents an argument which already takes us part of the way toward establishing the being of singularity. The problem with approaches that begin with the structure of the proposition (whether linguistically or as "propositions" of consciousness) is that they inevitably end up tracing the transcendental from the empirical, and thus involve themselves in a circularity. The ground comes to be grounded upon that which was supposed to be grounded. But it is clear that this is not sufficient to establish the domain of a transcendental field insofar as it only demonstrates either (1) that a mistake has been made somewhere in our transcendental thinking and is thus in need of correction, or (2) that transcendental projects are in fact impossible.

In either case, we are not entitled to move entirely in the opposite direction, rejecting the claims of consciousness and asserting a domain of be-ing independent of all of that which characterizes conscious experience. Demonstrating the impossibility of approaches based on conditioning would constitute a critical gesture. Positing the domain of a transcendental field on the basis of this demonstration would prove no less dogmatic than that which transcendental thought seeks to critique and a transcendental operation which seeks to trace the transcendental from the model of recognition. At most, this argument seems to establish the impossibility of tracing the transcendental from what is recognized while nonetheless asserting the necessity of recognition. However, while this argument does not establish the necessity of a transcendental field, it does open the door to something like a transcendental field. The second stage of the argument occurs with respect to the empty form of time or the eternal return. Where the subject itself ends up being split or fissured by time, where its coherence is called into question, it becomes possible to posit a field that is no longer in the circle or sphere of the subject, but belongs to the domain of time and events themselves. In other words, where the coherence of the subject is called into question, all the dimensions or categories characterizing the subject are problematized.

Individuation and the Being of Singularity

How is it that time problematizes the dimensions of the subject? More precisely, how is it that the temporality of singularity calls into question the modalities of propositions? *A singularity is not a point.* So long as we conceive singularity after the fashion of a point, we remain unable to understand the different properties which Deleuze attributes to them. Rather, we must treat singularities as being a sort of thread, flow, distension, or "smear." A singularity is a thread or expanse of becoming. It is a duration. "Singularities-events correspond to heterogeneous series which are organized into a system which is neither stable nor unstable, but rather 'metastable,' endowed with a potential energy wherein the differences between series are distributed. (Potential energy is the energy of the pure event, whereas forms of actualization correspond to the realization of the event)" (*LS* 103). Deleuze borrows this idea of "metastability" from the philosopher Gilbert Simondon. According to Simondon,

> Individuation has resisted thought and description until now because we have recognized the existence of only one form of equilibrium. The idea of "metastable equilibrium" had not been recognized. A being was implicitly presumed to be in a state of stable equilibrium at all times. Stable equilibrium excludes the idea because it corresponds to the lowest level of potential energy possible; it is the sort of equilibrium that is attained in a system when all possible transformations have been achieved and no

other force remains to enact any further changes. With all the potentials actualized, and the system having reached its lowest energy level, it can no longer go through any more transformations. The ancients recognized only the states of instability and stability, movement and rest, but they had no clear and objective idea of metastability. In order to define metastability, it is necessary to introduce the notion of potential energy residing in a given system, the notion of order and that of an increase in entropy.[6]

Initially, one is inclined to reject Deleuze-Simondon's discussion of stable equilibrium and potential energy insofar as these concepts seem to be highly empirical and thus beyond the scope of transcendental philosophy. Insofar as concepts like energy require measurement, observation, and calculation they seem to be beyond the tools open to philosophy. However, it is not difficult to discern in this notion of potential energy or metastability the Bergsonian concept of a tendency or flow of duration. To claim that singularities are metastable or contain a potential energy is to claim that they unfold in time as a qualitative alteration.

If we are warranted in claiming that singularities possess a metastability or potential energy, this is because as the transition between sensations they (1) unfold a domain of experience that is unique and new, and (2) are unanticipatable in their resulting evolution. Moreover, it will be observed that this point is entirely in keeping with the Deleuzian conception of time both with respect to its openness, the coexistence of the entirety of the past with the present, and the synthesis of the entirety of the past with the present. Simondon claims that

> it is fair to assume that the process of individuation does not exhaust everything that came before (the preindividual), and that a metastable regime is not only maintained by the individual, but is actually borne by it, to such an extent that the finally constituted individual carries with it a certain inheritance associated with its preindividual reality, one animated by all the potentials that characterize it. Individuation, then, is a relative phenomenon, like an alteration in the structure of a physical system. There is a certain level of potential that remains, meaning that further individuations are still possible. The preindividual nature, which remains associated with the individual, is a source of future metastable states from which new individuations could eventuate.[7]

Unlike nominalism and realism, which view either the individual (the entity) or the principle of individuation (the form/essence) as the absolute and final principle of individuation, the principle of metastability indicates that the individual is merely a relative moment, a passing phase within the *process* of individuation. To claim that the metastable regime is both maintained and borne by the individual, that it is always possible for new individuations to arise out of the current individuation, is to refer to none other than (1) the preservation involved in transcendental memory, and (2) the perpetual openness of time, the immutable form of change.

If Deleuze is entitled to claim the be-ing of singularity even from the perspective of actualized and individuated subjects, then this is precisely because we are split and fissured by the form of time. Recalling that the thinking subject is undetermined with respect to the past (insofar as the past has not yet been actualized), determinable with respect to the present, and bears the ideal of complete determination with respect to the future, we can see that the subject experiences this fissure within itself as the perpetual unfolding of itself. As we saw earlier, the consequence of Kant's critique of the Cartesian subject with respect to determinability was that the subject does not stand in a relationship of immediacy between its being and thinking, but must instead undergo the effects of itself thinking itself. These effects are experienced as affections of the self by the self. It is precisely here that we see why Deleuze is warranted in positing the be-ing of singularity from the perspective of the subject. Where the subject itself is fissured by time, where it can only experience its thoughts *within* time, the subject discovers itself as something undergoing actualization and individuation in time. Here the transcendental unity of apperception is no longer the condition under which experience is possible, but rather *formable* singularities which produce both subjects and objects become the condition of experience.

Thus we encounter the second mark of a critical philosophy. Deleuze's transcendental empiricism is qualified as a critical philosophy first because it was able to posit a precise limit to experience which allows us to distinguish between critical and dogmatic thought. Insofar as time is whole, open, and not dependent upon subjects, any thought founding itself on the form of identity or the same with respect to subjects or essences shows itself to be dogmatic. Second, Deleuze's transcendental empiricism shows itself to be critical insofar as these singularities or flowing tendencies in duration prove to be the conditions under which experience is possible. Not only do they preside over the genesis of subjects and objects, but they are not dependent on either subjects or objects. But how is it that this genesis takes place? How do we make the transition from the pre-individual to the individual?

8

Individuation: The Genesis of Extensities and the Other-Structure

Three Problems Pertaining to the Process of Actualization

Three problems remain. First, how does the movement from the virtual to the actual take place? How is it that entities are actualized or individuated? Thus far, all that has been said has pertained to the virtual or time in its transcendental determination alone. If Deleuze is to be successful in his project of reconciling the two senses of the aesthetic and articulating the conditions of real rather than all possible experience, then it is necessary that he be able to give an account of individuation or actualization which goes all the way to the individual.

Second, how are we to account for the Image of thought or the model of recognition which Deleuze identifies as the site of "transcendental illusion"? This question is especially pressing and seems to have gone unnoticed within the secondary literature on Deleuze. The mark of a truly critical philosophy consists in being able to anticipate, predict, and account for a set of illusions that are internal to thought itself. To say that these illusions or errors are internal to thought itself is to claim that they are in a way constitutive of thought, that they do not arise from a failed adequation between word and thing, that they are not simply contingent, but are effects of thinking itself. Those interested in "overcoming" the Image of thought and conceiving it as being merely contingent as an institutional imposition forced upon subjects who would otherwise be entirely free if they could just destroy this image, completely fail to recognize this nuance in Deleuze's thinking. Overcoming the Image of thought makes this image no less inevitable, it just means that an *other* set of values becomes possible. But if these illusions are inevitable—which they must be insofar as Deleuze refers to what the Image of thought claims *in principle,* rather than this or that empirical instance—then it is necessary that we be able to account for why and how these illusions are produced through thought.

Finally, third, it is necessary to account for Deleuze's perpetual claims that the Image of thought is moral in character. From one end of his career to another, Deleuze will denounce the Image of thought for being conservative and moral. "We may call this image of thought a dogmatic, orthodox or moral image" (*DR* 131). "When Nietzsche questions the most general presuppositions of philosophy, he says that these are essentially moral, since Morality alone is capable of persuading us that thought has a good nature and the thinker a good will, and that only the good can ground the supposed affinity between thought and the True" (*DR* 132). Thus far I have purposefully avoided pitching Deleuze's critique of the Image of thought in moral terms. In part, this is because Deleuze's arguments in this regard seem particularly weak and prone to degenerate into anti-moralistic reactivity, rather than rigorously accounting for the grounds under which something like an Image of thought is possible. In other words, the connotative dimension of the word *moral* allows Deleuze to present what appears to be a convincing argument without laying all of his premises bare. Those already critical of what is thought to be conservative in morality and those influenced by Nietzsche who have turned the term *moral* into the very antithesis of affirmation and life, will be all the more inclined to reject the Image of thought if they believe that it is moral in character. Consequently, a whole set of relations virtually hang about the term *moral* that allow Deleuze to advance a position without perhaps supporting it in an honest and rigorous manner. Of course, those who endorse this sort of argumentation will be prone to reject these criticisms anyway, citing that the "labor of thought" which calls for strong argumentation and conceptual precision is also a form of negativity and reaction against life. In that case, I see no reason to continue discussion and walk away.

On the other hand, it has seemed to me that Deleuze is much more able to account for the illusions he wishes to overcome by referring to problems surrounding empirical and external difference rather than internal difference. In response to this, one might be inclined to cite Deleuze's reading of Nietzsche in *Nietzsche and Philosophy,* where he carefully traces the genesis of the Image of thought in terms of a play of active and reactive forces. But the metaphysics of forces developed in *Nietzsche and Philosophy* appears nowhere else in his thought, while the Image of thought does. If Deleuze accounts for the Image of thought very differently elsewhere, supporting it not with reference to *ressentiment* and reaction, but by reference to the Other-structure, then why ought we to privilege the account given in the Nietzsche book? One might admire Deleuze's acumen in transforming Nietzsche into a systematic philosopher, but this is no reason to attribute all of the positions that he develops there to his own mature thought. In truth, this exercise of accounting for the Image of thought on the basis of active and passive forces is entirely suspect with respect to Deleuze's own project. In the first place, we find nothing resembling active and reactive forces throughout *Difference and Repetition* or *The Logic of Sense*. This claim can be made equally of *Anti-Oedipus: Capitalism and Schizophrenia, A Thousand Plateaus,* and *What Is Philosophy?* written with Guattari. Regardless of what readers such as Massumi or Hardt might wish to claim, Deleuze simply does not adhere to an ontology of forces.

One might object that the relationship between differentials in the symbol dy/dx indeed resembles an ontology of forces. However, this response inevitably falls short insofar as the relation between the differentials dx and dy is one of *reciprocal* determination, whereas the relationship between a Nietzschean play of forces always involves one force overpowering another, overdetermining it. In short, the relation between forces is external, while that of the differential is internal. For Deleuze's Nietzsche, active forces are entirely indifferent to reactive forces. This is not so in the case of the differential which appears throughout Deleuze's work—including *Nietzsche and Philosophy*—and which is characterized by reciprocal determination. It is indeed true that Deleuze evokes the differential with respect to Nietzsche (*NP* 51), but such an evocation nonetheless remains indefensible from the perspective of reciprocal determination. The choice to underplay Deleuze's Nietzsche arises out of an attempt to avoid the romanticism that has emerged around transcendental empiricism.

If, on the other hand, it can be shown that Deleuze does endorse the position developed in *Nietzsche and Philosophy,* then no damage will have been done, for what a thinker says once need not be shown to be said in all other possible contexts. If Deleuze develops an account of the Image of thought in *Difference and Repetition* that shows how this image is grounded, then it would be redundant to show how he also develops an account in *Nietzsche and Philosophy.* Deleuze's position in *Difference and Repetition* should be privileged over that in *Nietzsche and Philosophy* in that the goal of this book is to determine Deleuze's position, not his position on Nietzsche. Deleuze's position on Nietzsche or any other thinker is, in this context, only relevant insofar as it sheds light on Deleuze's position. Otherwise, discussion of these other texts is just for the sake of idle curiosity. In our view, the only reason so much emphasis is placed on these other texts has been due to the great difficulty of the texts Deleuze wrote explicating his own philosophy. In a curious manner, this has given rise to a tendency to transform Deleuze into his histories rather than to see how Deleuze departs from these histories.

Secondly, throughout *Difference and Repetition* and *The Logic of Sense* we find no reference to the moral terms employed by Nietzsche (*ressentiment,* bad conscience, the ascetic ideal), which ought to come as no surprise given the lack of an ontology of forces within his own independent works. No, if Deleuze is nonetheless inclined to claim that the Image of thought is moral, then we must search for reasons other than those of forces to substantiate this claim. If the truth be told, given the inevitability of the process of actualization and its tendency (as we shall see) to cancel difference through the production of diversity, Deleuze's renunciation of the Image of thought as being moral has the appearance of being a judgment of taste rather than pointing out something which is in itself objectionable. If recognition is to be placed in question, it is because of its tendency to naturalize or essentialize itself, rather than through any insidious moral machinations. Deleuze shows himself to be less than "affirmative" in these moments.

Indi-Different/ciation and the Genesis of Extensities

In fact, all three of these problems are intimately related and are solved together. If there is one defining feature of Deleuze's account of individuation or actualization, it is not simply that Deleuze provides an account of genesis which goes all the way to the individual (which in fact shows how the individual precedes general species), but rather that the process of actualization presides over the formation of extensities which cancel or cover over the differences serving as their condition of possibility. Put alternatively, in his account of actualization or "indi-different/ciation" Deleuze demonstrates how extensities emerge from intensities. Or again, the process of indi-different/ciation shows how extensive, external differences arise from intensive (temporal), internal differences.

This aspect of Deleuze's account of actualization is of tremendous importance in understanding the nature of Deleuze's critique of the Image of thought. If we recall the opposition between extensive and intensive multiplicities from chapter 1, then it will be seen that Deleuze's account of the genesis of extensities explains why we tend to reduce differences in kind (durational differences) to differences in degree or external differences. Insofar as the central error of the model of recognition consists in tracing the transcendental from the empirical, and insofar as this activity is based on a sort of blindness to difference, the genesis of extensity is the first step toward understanding how these errors come about. As Bergson puts it,

> It is this covering that we must grasp to tear it off. But we shall grasp
> it only if we consider first its aspect and its structure, if in addition, we

understand its intended purpose. It is spatial by nature and has a social utility. Spatiality therefore, and in this quite special sense, sociability, are in this case the real causes of the relativity of our knowledge.[1]

By the term "covering" Bergson is referring to space insofar as it covers duration or intensive difference. By the "relativity of knowledge" Bergson is referring to the manner in which empirical or extensive differences can only yield us differences in degree (as we saw in the case of accounts of the sado-masochistic entity governed by the pleasure principle) rather than internal and essential differences.

Here Deleuze, in fact, shows an advance over Bergson by seeking to center his account in terms of extensity rather than spatiality. To refer to these illusions, coverings, or cancellations in terms of spatiality implies a homogeneity belonging to the illusion *as such*. In other words, it becomes difficult to see how we can simultaneously maintain the relativity of spatialized knowledge and the homogeneity of space. By contrast, situating the illusion belonging to the Image of thought in terms of extensi*ties* has the advantage of underlining the manner in which the illusion arises out of a specific individuation. Phrased more precisely, it is not the extensity itself which constitutes the illusion of the Image of thought, since extensities are an inevitable result of the process of individuation. Rather, *it is the spatialization of the extensity which constitutes the illusion specific to the Image of thought.* In other words, the homogenization of extensity, the universalization of *an* extensity as characterizing and defining all extensi*ties* constitutes the illusion of the Image of thought. In this case, a threefold illusion occurs. First, internal and intensive difference is canceled insofar as the extensity in question fails to observe the singular conditions of its own genesis or individuation in and through the Idea. This is similar to the situation in which something is so close, so proximal, so evident that it becomes invisible. The extensity here treats itself as a space rather than an extensity. Here we also see a critique of Kant implicitly unfolding. Rather than treating space as a homogeneous field of a priori intuition, Deleuze seeks to account for the genesis of *spaces* or extensities that are discontinuous with one another. Second, intensive and internal difference is canceled insofar as the extensity treats itself as a medium of homogeneity rather than an intensive multiplicity populated by ordinal singularities and their relations. In other words, all entities populating the extensity are seen to be composed of only varying degrees of the same elements (sugar is composed of smaller amounts of sugar, etc.), rather than as complex multiplicities defined by tendencies or potentials. And third, difference is canceled insofar as any possibility of other extensities is excluded a priori. A case of individuation is here generalized for all individua-tions. We find here the reason for Deleuze's opposition to transcenden-tal accounts which would theorize *all possible* experience rather than real experience. These three cancellations function like so many affir-mations of external difference or the model of the same.

If, according to Bergson, we are inclined to spatialize, then this is because of utility. We already sense here one way in which the Image of thought is moral in character. A judgment of utility is not based on a de-sire to determine internal difference, but rather is a judgment of *value*. In this case, what is valuable is what is useful. If the valuable turns out to be what is extensive, then this is because space is that which can most readily be acted upon, calculated, and manipulated. In close connec-tion to this Bergsonian thesis is the claim to sociability revolving around extensities. Not only is the extensive that which can be most readily acted upon, it is also that which can be most easily communicated (how is it possible to exchange a flow of time?).

In this respect, extensity and language, according to Bergson, con-tain an internal link to one another.

> What is the significance of words? One must not think that social life is
> a habit acquired and transmitted. Man is organized for the life of the
> state as the ant is for the ant-hill, but with this difference, that the ant
> possesses ready-made means of attaining its end, while we bring what is
> necessary to reinvent them and vary their form. Even though each word
> of our speech is conventional, language is not therefore a convention,
> and it is as natural for man to speak as to walk. Now, what is the original
> function of language? It is to establish a communication with a view to
> cooperation. Language transmits orders or warnings. It prescribes or de-
> scribes. In the first case, it is the call to immediate action; in the second,
> it is the description of the thing or some one of its properties, with a
> view to action. But in either case the function is industrial, commercial,
> military, always social.[2]

It is not difficult to discern the first presupposition of Deleuze's Image of thought in this claim. Above all the Image of thought begins with the assumption that "everybody knows." If something like communication is to take place, then it must begin with this assumption insofar as communication requires the transmission of a message from a sender to a receiver, based on a code, in which the message retains its identity from one pole to another. We can also recognize here the importance of the assumptions of good and common sense. Common sense asserts an abstract identity for the subject and the object, a form of subjective identity and a form of objective identity. As such, it claims in principle the communicability of that which fills in the form. Good sense asserts a distribution pertaining to subjects and objects which moves from the particular (the past) to the general (the future), which establishes communicability insofar as the future shall bring more of the same, insofar as extensity will continue to persist in a particular way. It is in light of this claim of communicability, of sociability, that the moral dimension of the Image of thought truly shows itself.

The question is, how do we get from the domain of the temporal populated by nothing but intensive differences to the formation of these extensities and their accompanying social morality? If it is true that Deleuze indeed presents a genetic account of real experience, then he is obligated to provide an account of the genesis of the Image of thought itself. Any account which would treat the Image of thought as being a merely "external" attribution, as an imposed ideology coming from without, would fall into the same empiricist fallacy Deleuze seeks to overcome. Hence we must avoid all naturalistic treatments of the Image of thought which treat it merely as a result of some external social conditioning or State power. If Deleuze is inclined to speak of a State ideology, this cannot be because the state is an external force preventing us from reaching true being, but rather because there is a sense in which the State is produced internal to thought itself.

The Principle of Sufficient Reason:
Indi-Different/ciation

Deleuze's account of (indi)differen*t*/*c*iation or actualization is not an account of what *causes* something to be, but rather a variant of the principle of sufficient reason. It is true that this is also an account which seeks to reconcile *genesis* and structure, that seeks to account for the formation or the morphogenesis of individuals, species, and parts; but this account does not explain how a cause is linked to an effect, but rather articulates the necessary conditions under which individuation is possible. How are we to understand this difference? What is it that the principle of sufficient reason aims for? Deleuze expresses the principle of sufficient reason with unparalleled clarity in his unpublished lectures on Leibniz.

> *Everything must surely have a reason.* The principle of sufficient reason can be expressed as follows: whatever happens to a subject, be it determinations of space and time, of relation, event, whatever happens to a

subject, what happens, that is what one says of it with truth, everything that is said of the subject must be contained in the notion of the subject. ("DLS," 15/04/80)

We must proceed with caution. Deleuze is as deeply indebted to Leibniz as he is to Spinoza, Hume, Kant, Nietzsche, and Bergson, but nonetheless he is not a Leibnizian. This point can be established immediately by the use he makes of the Leibnizian concept of incompossibility, and his rejection of any Leibnizian claim to the best of all possible words.

We can see why the principle of sufficient reason would hold special interest for Deleuze. Where metaphysics based on genus and species conceive matters in terms of a relation between the general and particular such that the particular is merely an instance of the general and all individuating differences are treated as secondary, the principle of sufficient reason seeks to determine instead the conditions for the inclusion of "predicates" within the individual. Granting the principle of identity and indiscernibles in connection with the principle of sufficient reason, it is clear that such an approach is inherently at odds with accounts based on categories, forms, or hierarchies between genus and species. We can also see how the aims of the principle of sufficient reason differ from those of the principle of causality. The principle of sufficient reason seeks to determine conditions of inclusion or the conditions for containment within the notion of the individual. By contrast, the principle of causality seeks to determine *why* or *how* something comes about through a chain of efficient causes. As Deleuze puts it,

> What difference is there between sufficient reason and cause? We understand very well. Cause is never sufficient. One must say that the causality principle poses a necessary cause but never a sufficient one. We must distinguish between necessary cause and sufficient reason. What distinguishes them evidently is that the cause of a thing is always something else. The cause of A is B, the cause of B is C, etc. . . . An indefinite series of causes. Sufficient reason is not at all something other than the thing. The sufficient reason of a thing is the notion of the thing. This sufficient reason expresses the relation of the thing with its own notion whereas cause expresses the relations of the thing with something else. ("DLS," 14/04/80)

Alternatively, we might say that the sufficient reason of a thing accounts for the internal differences composing the thing in its individuality. Here it is not a matter of rejecting causality. No, causality and sufficient reason are certainly interconnected. Rather, it is a question of different domains, different problematics. If the principle of causality proves inadequate in determining the being of the individual, then this is because accounts from causes always refer to something besides the individual in question.

However, we must also be on guard against thinking that the principle of sufficient reason returns us to the old world of *formal* essences.

> The *ratio* corresponding to the principle of sufficient reason is no longer the *ratio essendi,* the reason of essences or the reason for being, it is now the *ratio existendi,* the reason for existing. It is no longer the question: why something rather than nothing, since the principle of identity assured us that there was something, namely the identical. It is no longer: why something rather than nothing, but rather it is why this rather than that? What would its vulgar formulation be? We saw that every thing has a reason. Indeed, every thing must have a reason. What would the scholarly formulation be? You see that we apparently are completely outside the principle of identity. Why? Because the principle of identity concerns the identity of the thing and what it is, but it does not state whether the thing exists. The fact that the thing exists or does not exist is completely different from what it is. I can always define what a thing is independently of the question of knowing if it exists or not. For example, I know that the unicorn does not exist, but I can state what a unicorn is. Thus, a principle is indeed necessary that makes us think of the existent. So just how does a principle, that appears to us as vague as "everything has a reason," make us think of the existent? It is precisely the scholarly formulation that will explain it to us. We find this scholarly formulation in Leibniz's works in the following statement: every predication (predication means the activity of judgment that attributes something to a subject; when I say "the sky is blue," I attribute blue to sky, and I operate a predication), *every predication has a basis in the nature of things.* ("DLS," 06/04/80)

A number of threads come together here which shed a great deal of light on Deleuze's project. First, we see right away that such an account is necessary on the basis of the original task of reunifying the two halves of the aesthetic, of providing an account of the conditions for the possibility of real experience. The former follows from the latter. If we are to provide an account for the conditions of real experience, then we cannot rest content with what *can* be intuited but must provide an account of the genesis of intuition from within intuition. But we also see that a position which would be audacious enough to claim that it had articulated the conditions of real experience can no longer rest content with genus, species, categories, and the most general *forms* of intuition, but must go all the way to the individual, to the singular, to a something, to that which exists.

In this connection, we can also see why Deleuze centers his attention on events from one end of his thought to the other. It is precisely events which pertain to the existent, which define or are predicated of the existent. The existent is an event. It is also for this reason that Deleuze is always so careful to distinguish causes and effects (events) from one another insofar as causes form the chain of necessity while events form the chain of sufficiency. Finally, we see why Deleuze's position must paradoxically proceed by virtue of a critique and renunciation of empiricism and an affirmation of empiricism. If Deleuze must begin with a firm and far-reaching renunciation of empiricism, this is only so that he might return to empiricism in the end. The critique of empiricism is necessitated insofar as the actualized individual (which is not identical to its sufficient reason or the conditions of its individuation) tends to universalize its own actualization, covering over all the divergent actualizations born out of the transcendental field. It tends to erase differences in the course of its actualization. But such a position can only be an empiricism insofar as the individual, the existent, cannot be anticipated a priori, but can only be *encountered* in and through experience. We witness here a strange blurring of the a priori and the a posteriori such that the a priori becomes the a posteriori and the a posteriori becomes the a priori. The conditions are still conditions, they are still a priori, but they are no longer a priori in the sense of being universal. Rather, the a priori has been whittled down to the necessary and sufficient. It is an a posteriori a priori.

What, then, does Deleuze understand by the principle of sufficient reason? How does he conceptualize and unfold it? Moreover, what is the problem or question with which the principle of sufficient reason grapples? We already have a clue for answering this question from Deleuze's adoption of Kant's term "Idea" in his account of the being of problems. On the one hand, Ideas are the site of illusions internal to thought itself . . . illusions which are no longer a matter of error or failures of adequation, but rather in the sense of optical illusions or distortions. On the other hand, the reason why reason produces these Ideas consists in the problem of unity or organization pertaining to experience. Experience itself presents nothing but disconnected and partial representations. The Kantian Idea represents the problem of how to unify these disconnected and partial representations into an ordered and organized system which can be said to properly constitute knowledge.

Nonetheless, if this can be said to be a problem, if the organization of experience is a problem, then this is because the organization of experience is an ideal rather than something that can be brought about in experience. Deleuze will follow Kant in this articulation of the Idea, but will transform it significantly. Like Kant, for Deleuze the problem of the Idea is one of organization. However, unlike Kant, this organization no longer belongs to the conceptual order, but rather belongs to the sensible order and is a question of continuity, of how the continuity we find in actualized experience is possible given the undetermined (and in principle, unknowable/unintuitable) nature of the differentials underlying experience. We find here a "critique of pure sensibility."

> While it is true that continuousness must be related to Ideas and to their problematic use, this is on condition that it be no longer defined by characteristics borrowed from sensible or even geometric intuition, as it still is when one speaks of the interpolation of intermediaries, of infinite intercalary series or parts which are never the smallest possible. Continuousness truly belongs to the realm of Ideas only to the extent that an ideal cause of continuity is determined. Taken together with its cause, continuity forms the pure element of quantitability, which must be distinguished both from the fixed quantities of intuition [*quantum*] and from variable quantities in the form of concepts of the understanding [*quantitas*]. (*DR* 171)

Continuity is what pertains to the individual. Individuals, whether they be subjects or objects, find themselves in a world characterized by systematicity, organization, predictable relations, habits. Only in the dark moments of the encounter does chaos seem to flood in and our world is called into question. The problem of sufficient reason is one of how to account for this continuousness, this order, this organization. We can already discern the question of extensities slowly approaching us.

With respect to the problem of continuity, Deleuze identifies three characteristics or genetic conditions to be accounted for by the principle of sufficient reason, (indi)differen*t*/*c*iation, or actualization.

> The dialectical Idea is doubly determined by the variety of differential relations and the distribution of correlative singularities (differen*tia*-tion). Aesthetic actualisation is doubly determined by the determination of species and by composition (differen*ci*ation). The determination of species incarnates the relations, just as composition does the singularities. The actual qualities and parts, species and numbers, correspond to the element of qualitability and the elements of quantitability in the Idea. However, what carries out the third aspect of sufficient reason—namely,

the element of potentiality in the Idea? No doubt the pre-quantitative and pre-qualitative dramatisation. It is this, in effect, which determines or unleashes, which differenciates the differenciation of the actual in its correspondence with the differentiation of the Idea. (*DR* 221)

We thus see that there are two stages in Deleuze's account of actualization or sufficient reason. First, the formation of the Idea through differential relations and the singularities these relations precipitate. It is this which Deleuze refers to as "differen*t*iation," and which he justifies on the basis of an auto-synthesis. If it is necessary to postulate such an auto-synthesis, then this is because there is an essential groundlessness pertaining to be-ing. This was the meaning of the affirmation of chance. To provide a reason deeper than this auto-synthesis would be to posit a ground beneath the groundless. Beyond the throw of the dice, this essential chance which generates necessity, there we cannot go. The Idea thus represents the true transcendental moment in Deleuze's thought; but it is a "transcendence" which is also immanent and which has only an immanent application. As always, we must firmly keep in mind that the Idea is the result of a passive synthesis—as opposed to an active synthesis—and is thus not based on a decision of consciousness. In fact, the Idea is not even accessible to consciousness in its efficacy. As a passive synthesis it is essentially unconscious.

In the second moment of actualization, the moment of the actualized proper, species and parts are generated corresponding respectively to the relations and singularities belonging to the Idea. It is this moment which Deleuze refers to as "differenciation." Hence, in a strange twist, species and the parts characterizing the species are that which must be generated. In other words, they cannot be assumed from the outset. We get a sense of what Deleuze means by this when he remarks that

> Ideas are objectively made and unmade according to the conditions which determine their fluent synthesis. This is because they combine the greatest power of being differen*t*iated with an inability to be differenciated. Ideas are varieties which include in themselves sub-varieties. We can distinguish three dimensions of variety. In the first, vertical dimension we can distinguish *ordinal varieties* according to the nature of the elements and the differential relations: for example, mathematical, mathematico-physical, chemical, biological, physical, sociological and linguistic Ideas . . . Each level implies differentials of a different dialectical "order," but the elements of one order can pass over into those of another under new relations, either by being dissolved in the larger

superior order or by being reflected in the inferior order. In the second, horizontal dimension we can distinguish characteristic varieties corresponding to the degrees of a differential relation within a given order, and to the distribution of singular points for each degree (such as the equation for conic sections which gives according to the case an ellipse, a hyperbola, a parabola or a straight line; or the varieties of animal ordered from the point of view of unity of composition; or the varieties of language ordered from the point of view of their phonological system). Finally, in depth we can distinguish axiomatic varieties which determine a common axiom for differential relations of a different order, on condition that this axiom itself coincides with a third-order differential relation. (*DR* 187)

The first level or vertical level, that of differentiation, defines the types of relations and singularities belonging to the idea. We can also call this the structural level. The second level or horizontal level refers to differenciation, or the divergent actualizations which the Idea undergoes. Hence, the various species are so many differenciations, so many variations of the differentiated Idea of life. Between differentiation and differenciation lies potentiality, which is the energetic or actualizing factor belonging to the Idea. We already saw in the last chapter why Deleuze is entitled to refer to a notion of potentiality or metastability with respect to singularities. Somewhere in this maze we shall have to locate the place of the individual.

The Static Time of Actualization

The foregoing provides us with a rough outline of Deleuze's account of actualization, but does not yet explain how actualization takes place. It only provides the map. Yet the map is not the territory. Now, the first point to keep in mind is that actualization is not dynamic, but rather static. To claim that actualization, the principle of sufficient reason, is dynamic would be tantamount to offering a causal account of actualization. But, as we saw, causality can only provide necessary reasons for something, never sufficient reasons. Moreover, we have already seen that the principle of causality is dependent upon the first passive synthesis of *habitus*, which sets up a system of retentions and expectations.

Consequently, it follows that the notion of causality is itself necessarily dependent upon the process of actualization and not the reverse. *There is* causality only to the degree that there is actualization. As a result, it is sufficient to understand that the genesis takes place in time not between one actual term, however small, and another actual term, but between the virtual and its actualization—in other words, it goes from the structure to its incarnation, from the conditions of a problem to the cases of solution, from the differential elements and their ideal connections to actual terms and diverse real relations which constitute at each moment the actuality of time. This is a genesis without dynamism, evolving necessarily in the element of a supra-historicity, a *static-genesis* which may be understood as the correlate of the notion of *passive synthesis,* which in turn illuminates that notion. (*DR* 183)

There is certainly something strange in the notion of a "static genesis." The term *genesis* generally denotes movement, change, process, emergence. On the other hand, the term *stasis* generally indicates a lack of movement, standing still, stagnation, self-identity. However, the issue here is not one of an opposition between movement and rest—Deleuze recognizes actualization or static genesis as the only form of "true" movement—but rather of the difference between "horizontal" modes of movement and "vertical" modes of movement.

If it is necessary for static genesis to be static, then this is because genesis must account for the constitution or donation of the extensities within which horizontal or dynamic movements take place. We can think of the difference between the horizontal and the vertical, the dynamic and the static, as the difference between syntagm and paradigm where the syntagm is the plane of combination and the paradigm is the plane or reservoir of selection. To clarify matters further, we might think of the game of chess where the movements throughout the game (the dynamic instances) are first dependent upon the constitution of the space of the game (the board, the configuration, the opposing sides, the values of the pieces, etc.). In other words, a static genesis is a *positional* genesis in the full symbolic sense, defining the ordinality of a system which allows something like a play of presence and absence to take place at the level of actualized experience (something can only be missing insofar as it has a place). If such a notion of genesis is necessary, then this is because only a static genesis of individuals can account for the sufficient reason of the individual without perpetually deferring such an account to something other than the individual.

For this reason Deleuze will claim that every object contains two halves, one virtual and one actual. We can see why such a duality is necessary insofar as the virtual determines the conditions under which the actual is possible. The virtual constitutes the sufficient reason of the actual and thus is necessarily linked to the actual. However, while it is true that the virtual is necessarily linked to the actual, we cannot say that the virtual resembles the actual. The virtual is analogous to a code, and like all codes or combinatorial systems, there is no resemblance to the message.

> The reality of the virtual consists of the differential elements and relations along with the singular points which correspond to them. The reality of the virtual is structure. We must avoid giving the elements and relations which form structure an actuality which they do not have, and withdrawing from them a reality which they have. We have seen a double process of reciprocal determination and complete determination defined that reality: far from being undetermined, the virtual is completely determined . . . The elements, varieties of relations and singular points coexist in the work or the object, in the virtual part of the work or object, without it being possible to designate a point of view privileged over others, a centre which would unify the other centres. How, then, can we speak simultaneously of both complete determination of the object and only a part of the object . . . We must carefully distinguish the object in so far as it is complete and the object in so far as it is whole. What is complete is only the ideal part of the object, which participates with other parts of objects in the Idea (other relations, other singular points), but never constitutes an integral whole as such. What the complete determination lacks is the whole set of relations belonging to actual existence. (DR 209)

It is the virtual which allows the actual, the work, to emerge, to manifest itself, to show itself, to appear. Unlike the actual which undergoes continuous transformations through its relationship to other actualities in time and thus lacks completeness, the virtual is completely determined. The claim that the virtual Idea is completely determined is necessitated by virtue of the nature of intensive multiplicities wherein all of the elements reciprocally determine one another.

These multiplicities are on the order of combinatorial systems. But if the multiplicity or Idea is only half or part of the whole, then how is it possible to say that it functions as the sufficient reason of the object? If the virtual functions as the sufficient reason of the actualized term, then this is because the actual is one of the combinatorial possibilities belonging to the system. Not only do we see here how the relationship between virtual and actual is one of static genesis, but we also see the beginnings of an account of how individuation is carried all the way to the individual . . . To real experience.

The Time of Sufficient Reason

As the term suggests, static genesis involves a special relationship to time. This is no longer the time of succession and simultaneity, but is rather a sort of internal temporality belonging to the process of actualization in its various manifestations. This is the time of sufficient reason, the time of problem solving, the time of determination.

> On the one hand, complete determination carries out the differentiation of singularities, but it bears only on their existence and their distribution. The nature of these singular points is specified only by the form of the neighboring integral curves—in other words, by virtue of the actual or differenciated species and spaces. On the other hand, the essential aspects of sufficient reason—determinability, reciprocal determination, complete determination—find their systematic unity in progressive determination. In effect, the reciprocity of determination does not signify a regression, or a marking of time, but a veritable progression in which the reciprocal terms must be secured step by step, and the relations themselves established between them. The completeness of the determination also implies the progressivity of adjunct fields. In going from A to B and then B to A, we do not arrive back at the point of departure as in a bare repetition; rather the repetition between A and B and B and A is the progressive tour or description of the whole of a problematic field. (DR 210)

What we find here is the phenomenon of iteration in which difference is produced in the process of the field tracing itself. The process here resembles that of Peirce's dimension of the interpretant belonging to signs, where the interpretant can in turn become the semiotic object for another interpretant, thus engendering a series.

How, then, does this constitute a properly structural time?

> In this sense, by virtue of this progressivity, every structure has a purely logical, ideal or dialectical time. However, this virtual time determines a time of differenciation, or rather rhythms of different times of actualisation which correspond to the relations and singularities of the structure and, for their part, measure the passage from the virtual to the actual. In this regard, four terms are synonymous: actualise, differenciate, integrate, and solve . . . Each differenciation is a local integration or a local solution which connects with others in the overall solution of the global integration. (DR 210–11)

The movement from A to B and from B to A is the time of unfolding, a solution which constitutes not a time of passage or succession, but rather an internal temporality belonging to the actualization itself. We might think here of the modes of time found in games, or the development of organisms, or the social codes surrounding the different stages of life between childhood, adulthood, and old age.

The Spatialization of Intensive Time

This internal time or temporality presiding over the actualization of the Idea is rendered possible by the potentiality of the Idea, spatiotemporal dynamisms, or intensities. According to Deleuze, this process of actualization also corresponds to the formation of extensities or spaces pertaining to the actualization.

> With contracted or extended times and according to the reasons for acceleration or delay, other spaces are created. Even the stoppage assumes the aspects of a creative actualisation in the case of neoteny. In principle, the temporal factor allows the transformation of dynamisms, even though these may be asymmetrical, spatially irreducible and completely differenciated—or rather, differenciating. (*DR* 216)

As a first approximation, then, we can say that spatialization, extensialization, takes place as a result of the variable relaxation or contraction of time. A highly contracted time is one containing maximum difference, while a relatively relaxed time is one characterized by relatively little difference, by differences in degree.

This process of actualization and the genesis of extensities it involves contains an essential relationship to singularity. In his lectures on Leibniz, Deleuze attempts to elucidate this relationship by discussing the continuity between the world in which Adam sinned and the seduction of Eve, which are two events defining two singularities.

> What does it mean that there is continuity between the seduction of Eve and Adam's sin? It's that the difference between the two is a difference that tends to disappear. I would say therefore that *truths of essence are governed by the principle of identity, truths of existence are governed by the law of continuity, or evanescent differences, and that comes to the same.* ("DLS," 22/04/80)

If actualized truths of existence tend to disappear, this is because singularities extend into one another. Thus, for example, take a square.

The square is composed of four singularities belonging to each of its corners. Now,

> You take a singularity, it's a point; you take it as the center of a circle. Which circle? All the way into the neighborhood of the other singularity. In other words, in the square *abcd*, you take *a* as center of a circle that stops or whose periphery is in the neighborhood of singularity *b*. You do the same thing with *b*: you trace a circle that stops in the neighborhood of the singularity *a* and you trace another circle that stops in the neighborhood of singularity *c*. These circles intersect. You go on like that constructing, from one singularity to the next, what you will be able to call a continuity. The simplest case of continuity is a straight line, but there is also precisely a continuity of non-straight lines. With your system of circles that intersect, you will say that there is continuity when the values of two ordinary series, those of *ab*, those of *ba*, coincide. When there is a coincidence of values of two ordinary series encompassed in the two circles, you have a continuity . . . If the series of ordinaries that derive from singularities diverge, then you have a discontinuity. ("DLS," 29/04/80)

What we get here is a distribution of singular and ordinary points which shows how the two are interrelated and interdependent. We also find here the significance of the concept of reciprocal determination. If relations must be reciprocally determined, if they are nothing in relation to themselves, this is because singularity can only be defined by its relation to the vicinity of another singularity. It is this passage from one singularity to another which constitutes the being of extensity.

The Intensive Factors of Actualization

In this rudimentary articulation of Deleuze's discussion of the formation of continuities or extensities, we thus discover a paradoxical situation in which singularity, intensity, or the being *of* the sensible is what allows the sensible to be sensed while nonetheless canceling itself as difference. As Deleuze claims, "Difference is not diversity. Diversity is given, but difference is that by which the given is given, that by which the given is given as diverse. Difference is not the phenomenon but the noumenon closest to the phenomenon" (*DR* 222). How are we to understand this paradoxical relationship? As opposed to actual differences presented in the manifold of sensibility which are in fact continuities or extensities, the being of the sensible is referred to by Deleuze as intensive or asymmetrical difference. These asymmetrical differences are none other than the spatiotemporal dynamisms presiding over the actualization of the Idea. According to Deleuze,

> The world can be regarded as a "remainder," and the real in the world understood in terms of fractional or even incommensurable numbers. Every phenomenon refers to an inequality by which it is conditioned diversity and every change refers to a difference which is its sufficient reason. Everything which happens and everything which appears is correlated with orders of differences: differences of level, temperature, pressure, tension, potential, *differences of intensity*. (*DR* 222)

Unlike qualitative and extensive differences that are understood to differ from one another only in terms of degree rather than kind—for instance, a sugar cube that can be thought as being made up of smaller portions of sugar—intensive difference marks an asymmetry or disparity that cannot be thought of as being made up of other differences. In other words, it is these intensive differences, these singular differences, which allow things to stand forth and show themselves, or which are that by which diversity is given. In the case of differences in degree or numerical multiplicities, any division only yields varying quantities of what was already there. We see this in the case of the square where the singularities are drawn into one another such that the ordinary points only differ in degree from one another. However, whenever I divide an intensity or an intensive multiplicity, I am yielded other intensive asymmetries.

Deleuze's examples above are illuminating. A temperature, say the point at which water boils, cannot be thought of as being made up of other temperatures, but instead marks a threshold that is absolutely affirmative and positive in its being. It is an ordinal difference, a position, a place. The case is similar with respect to speeds, sounds, and different pressures and tensions. In all of these cases, certain things are only possible in terms of these differences. Consequently, Deleuze's transcendental empiricism does not offer a relativity of truth that would be relative to a particular subject's or community's perspective, but instead articulates the truth of relativity or of perspective, wherein certain phenomena are only possible in terms of the asymmetrical scale of differences they involve (i.e., the world looks very different when viewed at five miles an hour than it does at fifty miles an hour). Moreover, intensive differences are not themselves sensible because things like temperature, pressure, and so on can only be sensed in terms of their effects rather than their sensible positivity. On the other hand, intensive differences can only be sensed because we must undergo these thresholds of transformation or variation in order to arrive at them. It is in this respect that intensities can be said to be individuating differences belonging to a static genesis. They are not identical to the individual, but they do preside over the manner in which the individual individuates itself.

Deleuze attributes three properties to intensive difference which distinguish it from extensive difference. First, as we have seen, intensive differences include the unequal in itself, or that which cannot be canceled through differences in quantity. As the unequal in itself, intensive differences ought to be thought in terms of ordination or dimensions. Here Deleuze offers examples from mathematics in which number systems are constructed on the basis of inequalities. As he puts it, "We see that every systematic type is constructed on the basis of an essential inequality, and retains that inequality in relation to the next-lowest type: thus, fractions involve the impossibility of reducing the relation between two quantities to a whole number" (DR 232). In short, these inequalities which are positive in character mark domains of different number types that allow for specific mathematical operations. Ordinality thus precedes cardinality (as the example of the square demonstrates) within mathematics. Second, Deleuze contends that intensity affirms difference. Here difference does not indicate negative relations or oppositions between terms (opposition is more an effect of the relation than the reverse), but instead indicates a difference that must be acknowledged as an object of affirmation in that it is a condition for the given of the sensible manifold. As a result, negativity cannot be understood to have an ontological status as in Hegel, but must instead be seen as the inverted image of difference when seen from the perspective of actualized phenomena that are then compared with one another. This does not mean that all talk of negation, negativity, lack, and absence is to be abolished—for instance, Deleuze pays exacting attention to the modes of negation involved in sadism and masochism in his essay "Coldness and Cruelty"—but is rather a call to pay attention to the conditions under which such absence is possible: namely, the positional or symbolic. In short, a structural position is an affirmation which renders lack and absence possible. This situates Deleuze's later criticisms of psychoanalysis in a slightly different light. Psychoanalysis does not begin with the notion of lack in its analysis of the subject, but traces the effects of structuration on the subject insofar as the subject has been subjected to structure such that lack is rendered possible in the first place. To say that lack is never to be discussed, that it is not a real feature of experience and subjects, is to cripple oneself intellectually and to be cruel at the level of actual praxis. Third, and most importantly, intensive difference is implicated or "embryonized" quantity. That is, it is a spatiotemporal dynamism presiding over actualization, generating its internal temporality. In other words, intensive difference is implicated or enveloped within matter in such a way that it allows matter to take on form and be actualized in a perfectly singular way. This takes place through a convergence of singularities extended into one another, as we saw in the case of the square.

Implication and Explication

With this third characteristic, we are returned to the process of individuation and the question of the relationship between the virtual and the actual. As we have seen, intensive difference is the being of the sensible or that through which the given is given. The question to ask is: how does intensive difference enable actualization? Deleuze describes this process as the movement from the implicate to the explicate or the intensive to the extensive. We can also equate this movement with the movement from the singular to the ordinary. Roughly, the movement from intensive difference to extensive difference is the movement from an "energetic" difference caught up in a movement of becoming to an extensive or spatial difference in which differences tend to be annulled and covered over by homogeneous species and parts. As Deleuze puts it,

> A living being is not only defined genetically, by the dynamisms which determine its internal milieu, but also ecologically, by the external move- ments which preside over its distribution within an extensity. A kinetics of population adjoins, without resembling the kinetics of the egg: a geo- graphic process of isolation may be no less formative of species than in- ternal genetic variations, and sometimes precedes the latter. Everything is even more complicated when we consider that the internal space is itself made up of multiple spaces which must be locally integrated and connected, and that this connection, which may be achieved in many ways, pushes the object or living being to its own limits, all in contact with the exterior; and that this relation with the exterior, and with other things and living beings, implies in turn connections and global integra- tions which differ in kind from the preceding. Everywhere staging at several levels. (*DR* 216–17)

It is singularity which presides over the genesis of these parts, extensities, spaces by marking the limits between one extensity and another. For this reason, Deleuze elsewhere refers to the reciprocally determined relation dy/dx as a change of sign. "In what way is the singularity linked to differential calculus? It's that the singular point is the point in the neighborhood of which the differential relation dy/dx changes its sign" ("DLS," 29/04/80). It is in this way that extensities are apportioned. They are defined by the neighborhood of a singularity all the way up to another singularity, thus simultaneously defining a continuity and a threshold.

In an illuminating passage, Deleuze describes this movement in terms of energetics. "Energetics defined a particular energy by the combination of two factors, one *intensive* and one *extensive* (for example, force and distance for linear energy, surface tension and surface area for surface energy, pressure and volume for volume energy, height and weight for gravitational energy, temperature and entropy for thermal energy)" (*DR* 223). In light of this passage, it becomes clear that the relation between intensive and extensive difference is to be thought in terms of a dynamic relation between forces which produce qualities.

Simondon, who was one of the principal inspirations of Deleuze's account of individuation, expresses this process well when he claims that "at the same time that a quantity of potential energy (the necessary condition for a higher order of magnitude) is actualized, a portion of matter is organized and distributed (the necessary condition for a lower order of magnitude) into structured individuals of a *middle* order of magnitude, developing by a mediate process of amplification."[3] Thus, for example, when water (the lower order of magnitude) implicates a particular temperature (the higher order of magnitude), it begins to boil, thus producing particular qualities and parts in the form of rapidly bubbling water and steam (the middle order of magnitude).

What, then, is the relationship between time and space, between duration and extensity? In order to determine this it is necessary to articulate Deleuze's concept of intensity more precisely. Deleuze does not choose the term *intensity* to describe the actualizing factor between Ideas and species and parts casually. *Intensity* does not denote a particularly vibrant or lively sensation or quality, but instead denotes a precise temporal relation pertaining to increase and diminution. In fact, Deleuze borrows his concept of intensity from Kant. According to Kant,

> Perception is empirical consciousness, i.e., one in which there is at the same time sensation. Appearances, as objects of perception, are not pure (merely formal) intuitions, like space and time (for these cannot be perceived in themselves). They therefore also contain in addition to the intuition the materials for some object in general (through which something existing in space or time is represented), i.e., the real of the

sensation, as merely subjective representation, by which one can only be conscious that the subject is affected, and which one relates to an object in general. Now from the empirical consciousness to the pure consciousness a gradual alteration is possible, where the real in the former entirely disappears, and a merely formal (*a priori*) consciousness of the manifold in space and time remains; thus there is also possible a synthesis of the generation of the magnitude of a sensation from its beginning, the pure intuition = 0, to any arbitrary magnitude. Now since sensation in itself is not an objective representation, and in it neither the intuition of space nor that of time is to be encountered, it has, to be sure, no extensive magnitude, but yet it still has a magnitude (and indeed through its apprehension, in which the empirical consciousness can grow in a certain time from nothing = 0 to its given measure), thus it has an *intensive magnitude,* corresponding to which all objects of perception, insofar as they contain sensation, must be ascribed an *intensive magnitude,* i.e., a degree of influence on sense.[4]

The concept of an intensive magnitude is not simply the notion that an intensive magnitude has a degree of influence on the senses. No, if this were the case the intensive magnitude would simply be empirical and would contain no a priori dimension to it. One might object by claiming that it is at least true a priori that the magnitude has a degree. But this is only a priori in the analytic sense, not in the synthetic sense. Rather, the notion of an intensive magnitude pertains to the increase and decrease of a sensation, such that, given any sensation, we can imagine its diminution to 0 and its increase to infinity. If intensity has an a priori dimension, this is because the synthesis involved in intensity is what allows me to claim that for any given sensation I can imagine a sensation smaller or greater than that sensation. Similarly, for any two sensations pertaining to the same intensity, I can imagine varying degrees of the sensation between these two sensations. Although Deleuze rejects Kant's account of intensive magnitude because of its categorical dimension (it will be observed that the notion of the differential as presented by Maïmon is able to account for the same phenomenon without assuming a priori categories), he nonetheless accepts Kant's basic definition of intensive magnitude (*DR* 230).

It is with respect to the role of intensity that Deleuze diverges most markedly from Bergson. For Bergson, internal difference is qualitative difference, and true change or alteration is qualitative change. On this basis, whenever I divide a durational multiplicity I am yielded a qualitative difference which differs in kind from the preceding quality. Consequently, in *Time and Free Will* Bergson argues at length that the concept of intensity is based on a spatialization of duration which fails to take account of qualitative change and the difference in kind that it involves. In opposition to this, Deleuze argues that the

> Bergsonian critique of intensity seems unconvincing . . . [because] it assumes qualities ready-made and extensities already constituted. It distributes differences in kind in the case of qualities and differences in degree in the case of extensity. From this point of view, intensity necessarily appears as no more than an impure mixture, no longer sensible or perceptible. However, Bergson has thereby already attributed to quality everything that belongs to intensive quantities. He wanted to free quality from the superficial movement which ties it to contrariety or contradiction (that is why he opposed duration to becoming); but he could do so only by attributing to quality a depth which is precisely that of intensive quantity. One cannot be against both the negative and intensity at once. (*DR* 239)

If Bergson is mistaken in attributing internal difference to quality, then this is because qualitative change can only proceed through a negation of that which it is said to differ from in kind (as a result of dividing the duration). As a result, Bergson is forced to return to all the problems of empiricism by having to treat qualities as self-identical and time and space as external to one another and already constituted, and to return to a dialectic of negation between qualities which are said to differ in kind. By contrast, intensity encounters none of these problems insofar as it posits a sort of identity in difference in the course of increase and decrease. Intensity is that which differs from itself without containing alterity, negation, or betweenness.

For Deleuze, the concept of intensity will be important insofar as it will allow him to show how extensities emerge from time, which, as we saw in the second chapter, is the domain of internal difference. It will be observed that intensity—the increase and diminution of a sensation that belongs to experience by right and is thus, in a strange way, as Kant himself noted, an a posteriori a priori—shares an intimate relationship to time. If I am able to conceive an increase or decrease of a sensation a priori, then this is because I can conceive it as unfolding in time as a becoming. We thus find here a reversal of the Kantian order of priorities. For Kant, it is not the intensive magnitude that renders extensive magnitudes possible, but rather extensity is a precondition of intensive perception.

> I call an extensive magnitude that in which the representation of the parts makes possible the representation of the whole (and therefore

necessarily precedes the latter). I cannot represent to myself any line, no matter how small it may be, without drawing it in thought, i.e., successively generating all its parts from one point, and thereby first sketching this intuition. It is exactly the same with even the smallest time. I think therein only the successive progress from one moment to another, where through all parts of time and their addition a determinate magnitude of time is fully generated. Since the mere intuition in all appearance is either space or time, every appearance as intuition is an extensive magnitude, as it can only be cognized through successive synthesis (from part to part) in apprehension. All appearances are accordingly already intuited as aggregates (multitudes of antecedently given parts), which is not the case with every kind of magnitude, but rather only with those that are represented and apprehended by us as *extensive*.[5]

In this respect, Kant subordinates all perceptions to extensity. As a result, the world of intuitions is subordinated to geometric intuition, in which only differences in degree and external relations can be found.

By contrast, Deleuze argues that extensity is an effect of intensity.

Kant defined all intuitions as extensive quantities—in other words, quantities such that the representation of the parts necessarily preceded and made possible the representation of the whole. However, space and time are not presented as they are represented. On the contrary, the presentation of the whole grounds the possibility of the parts, the latter being only virtual and actualized only by the determinate values of empirical intuition. It is empirical intuition which is extensive. While he refuses a logical extension to space and time, Kant's mistake is to maintain a geometrical extension for it, and to reserve intensive quantity for the matter which fills a given extensity to some degree or other. In the case of enantiomorphic bodies, Kant recognised precisely an *internal difference*. However, since it was not a conceptual difference, on his view it could refer only to an *external relation* with extensity as a whole in the form of extensive magnitude. In fact, the paradox of symmetrical objects, like everything concerning right and left, high and low, figure and ground, has an intensive source. (*DR* 231)

Under the Deleuzian model, it is not intensity that comes to fill in a preexisting extensity, but rather intensity that accounts for the genesis of space. If Kant was led to reverse this relation, this was because he already privileged the representational identity engendered and rendered possible on the basis of space. But these two points remain to be seen.

Depth and Extensity

If extensity is dependent upon intensity and not the reverse, this is because intensity entertains an essential relation to depth which renders the determinations of extensity possible. As Deleuze puts it,

> It is notable that extensity does not account for the individuations which occur within it. No doubt the high and the low, the right and the left, the figure and the ground are individuating factors which trace rises and falls, currents and descents in extensity. However, since they take place within an already developed extensity, their value is only relative. They therefore flow from a "deeper" instance—depth itself, which is not an extension but a pure *implex*. No doubt every depth is also a possible length and size, but this possibility is realised only insofar as an observer changes places and gathers into an abstract concept that which is length for itself and that which is length for others: in fact, it is always on the basis of depth that the old one becomes length or is explicated in length. (*DR* 229)

On the one hand, extensity fails to account for the individuations that occur within it because (1) extensity is an already actualized medium which functions as a field of homogeneity (hence this or that entity can occupy an extensity regardless of its own individuating factors), and because (2) determinations like height, handedness, and figure and ground will be relative determinations dependent upon an external relation to another object.

However, in both cases, what renders these relative determinations possible is a sort of absolute depth which Deleuze equates with intensity and the pure past.

> This synthesis of depth which endows the object with its shadow, but makes it emerge from that shadow, bears witness to the furthest past and to the coexistence of the past with the present. We should not be surprised that the pure spatial syntheses here repeat the temporal syntheses previously specified: the explication of extensity rests upon the first synthesis, that of habit or the present; but the implication of depth rests upon the second synthesis, that of Memory and the past. Furthermore, in depth the proximity and simmering of the third synthesis makes themselves felt, announcing the universal "ungrounding." (*DR* 230)

Why is it that Deleuze treats depth in terms of the pure past and equates it with intensity? Has he not fallen into metaphor by conceptualizing time in terms of a spatial determination and a spatial determination in terms of temporal determinations? Everything becomes clear once we recall that the defining feature of intensity is its property of increase and diminution. We can immediately see why there would be an intrinsic relationship between depth and intensity insofar as depth is the ever-receding field of increase and decrease in precisely the same sense that intensity increases and decreases. In both cases, neither intensity nor depth would manifest themselves if there were not a passage of time. If depth is to be equated with the pure past, this is because it is a determination which does not itself ever become present. It is the ever-receding field of that which can be presented but which does not present itself. It is not the future, because it manifests itself on the basis of that which has diminished, canceled itself, explicated itself, drawn itself out into extensity. If it accounts for extensity, then this is because it distributes the up and the down, the left and the right, the ground and the figure.

Depth and the Image of Thought

It is precisely within depth and the genesis of extensity it entails that we can locate the site of transcendental illusion or the Image of thought. As Deleuze puts it,

> Once depth is grasped as an extensive quantity, it belongs to engendered extensity and ceases to include in itself its own heterogeneity in relation to the other two. We see then that it is the ultimate dimension of extensity, but we see this only as a fact without understanding the reason, since we no longer know that it is original. We also then note the presence in extensity of individuating factors, but without understanding where their power comes from, since we no longer know that they express original depth. (*DR* 229)

In treating depth as an extensive quantity among others (rather than as the intensive dimension that it is), we privilege the actualized over the actualization, the product over the process. As a result, all of the postulates of the Image of thought become inevitable. It becomes inevitable that solutions shall be privileged over problems since the domain of the actual, the domain of extensities, is precisely that of solutions. It becomes inevitable that the form of the subject and the object (common sense) will be privileged insofar as these are actualized forms in space, the most general actualities pertaining to the extensity. Additionally, it becomes inevitable that a convergent use of the faculties shall be privileged insofar as the extensity re-presents an apparently identical medium upon which the faculties converge. If the distribution of the faculties in common sense is seen to proceed from the particular to the general, then this is because actualized extensity presents itself as a field of homogeneity wherein the differences belonging to the future can only differ in degree. However, all of this is undone when we recognize depth as intensity, as the pure past or duration. Where intensity reigns, depth can only bring difference and further individuations which undo those of the present actualizations. As Simondon pointed out, the pre-individual always contains the potential for further individuations. Depth can always give more.

The Genesis of Individuals and Persons

However, while the genesis of extensities accounts for the origin of the Image of thought—its tendency to homogenize and cover over the differential origins of individuations—it fails to explain the presupposition of the "everyone knows" and the moral character of the Image of thought. Extensity accounts for the medium of homogenization, its condition, its "purport," but does not yet account for the genesis of objects treated as identical or for the moral dimension involved in this "decision." The solution to this problem is to be found in the genesis or actualization of psychic systems or systems such as our own.

In Deleuze's account, the first stage of the individuation of psychic systems consists in the formation of a world. This stage can be said to properly constitute the individual.

> This surface topology, these impersonal and preindividual nomadic singularities constitute the real transcendental field. The way in which the individual is derived out of this field represents the first stage of genesis. The individual is inseparable from a world; but what is it that we call a "world"? In general, as we have seen, a singularity may be grasped in two ways: In its existence and distribution, but also in its nature, in conformity with which it extends and spreads itself out in a determined direction over a line of ordinary points. This second aspect already represents a certain stabilization and a beginning of the actualization of singularities. A singular point is extended analytically over a series of ordinary points up to the vicinity of another singularity, etc. A world therefore is constituted on the condition that series converge. ("Another" world would begin in the vicinity of those points at which the resulting series would diverge.) (*LS* 109)

Once again it must be emphasized that Deleuze is not asking what causes the individual, but rather is seeking the sufficient reason of the individual. At this first stage of actualization, we thus find a distribution of singular and ordinary points determined by the convergence of singular points. As we saw in the example of the square, this convergence is what constitutes the precipitation of ordinary points through the overlap of the convergent singularities. Here we find the genesis of extensities and the accompanying erasure of origins expressed in an alternative way. In other words, depth, the transcendental field, becomes the principle of its own erasure.

Deleuze's claim that the individual is inseparable from a world is extremely important for understanding the nature of his critique. By locating the principle of individuation in the convergence of singularities, Deleuze is simultaneously able to provide a principle of genesis (the synthesis of these singularities in a field of compossibility) that rescues the individual from being conceived as a particular of a general (since singularities are events and events pertain to existence), while also indicating the conditions under which the individual falls prey to transcendental illusion by universalizing the perspective upon which it is individuated. It is for this reason that Deleuze is quick to claim that

> to be actualized is also to be *expressed* . . . This thesis is poorly understood as long as we interpret it to mean the inherence of predicates in the expressive monad. It is indeed true that the expressed world does not exist outside the monad which expresses it, and thus that it does not exist within the monads as the series of predicates which inhere in them . . . The expressed world is made of differential relations and of contiguous singularities. It is formed as a world precisely to the extent that the series which depend upon each singularity converge with the series which depend on others. *This convergence defines "compossibility" as the rule of world synthesis.* Where the series diverge, another world begins, incompossible with the first . . . In each world the individual monads express all the singularities of this world—an infinity—as though in a murmur or a swoon; but each monad envelops or expresses "clearly" a certain number of singularities only, that is, *those in the vicinity of which it is constituted and which link up with its own body.* We see that the *continuum* of singularities is entirely distinct from the individuals which envelop it in variable and complementary degrees of clarity: singularities are pre-individual. (*LS* 110–11)

The importance of this passage is twofold. On the one hand, by asserting that the world does not exist outside of the monad that expresses it,

Deleuze collapses the fold of exteriority between world and subject which would otherwise ensure the homogenization of both. In order to see this, we need only consider that the claim that the world exists outside of the monad that expresses it is not only dogmatically metaphysical in character but also amounts to the claim that the world is self-identical to itself. But insofar as the world is considered self-identical to itself, and insofar as the world is a necessary condition of individuation, it would then follow that the conditions of individuation are the same for all individuals. But once we claim that the conditions of individuation are the same for all, we lose any ability to individuate insofar as all individuals, under this account, would in principle be the same. This, incidentally, is a key ideological mechanism insofar as it reduces the field of individuals to a single privileged field of individuation which then functions as an evaluative mechanism for all other individuals occupying the field. This is the peril of individualism. On the other hand, by demonstrating that the continuum is distinct from individuals, Deleuze avoids the second peril of subjectivism which renders the individual master of its own universe, free of any difference or alterity. The individual occupies the transcendental field, but is not identical to it. It is a result of a synthesis of singularities, but is not itself the origin of these singularities. A split subject is, by definition, incapable of being solipsistic.

The first synthesis accounts for the genesis of *individuals,* while the second, based on the first, accounts for the genesis of *persons.* Initially this might sound strange, since we are inclined to identify individuals with persons. However, if we pause to consider that the recognition of oneself as a person minimally implies that there are other persons, we can see why it is necessary to articulate this second stage of genesis. The identification of oneself as a person minimally requires the recognition of oneself as a member of a *class* (where class is understood in the set theoretic sense of the term, not in its Marxist sense). It is here, at this moment, that the moral dimension of the Image of thought begins to manifest itself. According to Deleuze,

> On the terrain of the first actualization, a second level is established and developed . . . Or more precisely, what is it that gives the monad the "sense-bestowal pertaining to the transcendency proper, to consti-tutionally secondary *Objective transcendency,*" as distinct from the "im-manent transcendence" of the first level? The solution here cannot be the phenomenological one since the Ego is no less constituted than the individual monad. This monad, this living individual, was defined within a world as a *continuum* or circle of convergences; but the Ego as a know-ing subject appears when something is *identified* inside worlds which are

nevertheless incompossible, and across series which are nevertheless divergent. In this case, the subject is vis-à-vis the world, in a new sense of the "world" (*Welt*), whereas the living individual was in the world and the world within him or her (*Umwelt*). (*LS* 113)

By locating this second level in terms of divergent series or incompossible worlds, Deleuze is in effect claiming that the second level pertains to cross-worldly relations or intersubjectivity. In this connection, it bears noting that the central problem of epistemology is not that of how a subject can know an object, but of how beings can be intersubjectively known. In other words, how is it possible for me to establish the intersubjectivity of my experience or that I belong to a shared world with other subjects? The second level pertains to relations between or among individuals. If such a relation is necessary for the actualization of persons, then this is because the Ego is essentially an Other. The Ego, as knowing subject, essentially encounters itself as Other. The individual, alone, is unable to encounter itself as an individual. It only finds itself enmeshed in an *Umwelt* or environment.

Yet what is it which allows the individual to identify something between worlds? Why is the world in which the individual is actualized subject to an illusionary closure so complete that it gives the appearance of allowing no opening onto any other world? Here Deleuze cites the genetic power of problems.

A problem . . . has conditions which necessarily include "ambiguous signs," or aleatory points, that is, diverse distributions of singularities to which instances of different solutions correspond. Thus, for example, the equation of conic sections expresses one and the same Event that its ambiguous sign subdivides into diverse events—circle, ellipse, hyperbola, parabola, straight line. These diverse events form so many instances corresponding to the problem and determining the genesis of solutions. We must therefore understand that incompossible worlds, despite their incompossibility, have something in common—something objectively in common—which represents the ambiguous sign of the genetic element in relation to which several worlds appear as instances of solution for one and the same problem (every throw, result of a single cast). (*LS* 114)

In other words, as I argued in chapter 2, the problem represents a sort of topological space of variation. However, it is not difficult to recognize the notion of intensity in this attribution of the ambiguous sign by virtue of its differential and heterogeneous power. It is on the basis of this ambiguous sign, which is common to many incompossible worlds without belonging to any of them, that the genesis of the person takes place. By virtue of this ambiguous sign, it becomes possible to generate predicates and categories defining worldliness as such. Thus,

> we are no longer faced with an individuated world constituted by means of already fixed singularities, organized into convergent series, nor are we faced with determined individuals which express this world. We are now faced with the aleatory point of singular points, with the ambiguous sign of singularities, or rather with that which represents this sign, and which holds good for many of these worlds, or, in the last analysis, for all worlds, despite their divergences and the individuals which inhabit them. There is thus a "vague Adam," that is, a vagabond, a nomad, an Adam = x common to several worlds, just as there is a Sextus = x or a Fang = x . . . All objects = x are "persons" and are defined by predicates. But these predicates are no longer the analytic predicates of individuals determined within a world which carry out a *description* of these individuals. On the contrary, they are predicates which *define* persons synthetically, and open different worlds and individualities to them as so many variables or possibilities . . . As for the variables which realize the possibilities of a person, we must treat them as concepts which necessarily signify classes and properties, and therefore as essentially affected by an increasing or decreasing generality in a continuous specification against a categorical background. (*LS* 114–15)

On the basis of this ambiguous sign, it becomes possible to envision worlds other than our own, for the ambiguous sign is what allows there to be multiple solutions to one and the same problem.

It is for this reason that Deleuze refers to the relationships among worlds as a disjunctive synthesis. The relationship between worlds is not one of reduction or assimilation. In being related to another world, the person does not reduce this world to their own individuated world, but instead encounters a field of individuation alterior to their own. If the ambiguous sign, object = x, or empty square, renders this possible, this is because it is not itself identical to itself. In a manner similar to Derrida's *différance*, the ambiguous sign both differs from itself and is deferred. As Deleuze puts it,

> Its peculiar property is not to be where one looks for it, and conversely, also to be found where it is not. One would say that it "is missing from its place" (and, in this, is not something real); and that it does not coincide with its own resemblance (and, in this, is not an image); and that it does

not coincide with its own identity (and, in this, is not a concept). "What is hidden is never what is *missing from its place,* as the call slip puts it when speaking of a volume lost in the library. And even if the book be on an adjacent shelf or in the next slot, it would be hidden there, however visibly that it may appear. For only something that can change its place can *literally* be said to be missing from it: that is, the symbolic. For the real, whatever upheaval we subject it to, is always in its place; it carries it glued to its heel, ignorant of what might exile it from it."[6] If the series that the object = x traverses necessarily present relative displacements in relation to each other, this is so because the *relative* places of their terms in the structure depend first on the *absolute* place of each, at each moment, in relation to the object = x that is always circulating, always displaced in relation to itself. It is in this sense that the displacement, and more generally all the forms of exchange, does not constitute a characteristic added from the outside, but the fundamental property that allows the structure to be defined as an order of places subject to the variation of relations. The whole structure is driven by this originary Third, but that also fails to coincide with its own origin. Distributing the differences through the entire structure, making the differential relations vary with its displacements, the object = x constitutes the differenciating element of difference itself. ("HRS" 275)

In Deleuze's account, the minimal conditions for structure consist of (1) a minimum of two heterogeneous series in which one is determined as signifying and the other as signified, (2) each series being constituted by terms which exist only in the relations they maintain with one another, and (3) these two series being linked together by the paradoxical instance of the object = x, or what Deleuze calls the "dark precursor" in *Difference and Repetition.* Now, if the empty square or object = x is what allows for the actualization of multiple worlds in the form of persons, this is because the empty square, traversing both series, distributes a set of empty and filled (structural) positions actualized in each of these worlds. Insofar as the empty and the full can only be determined on the basis of the "symbolic" structure (where position is to be interpreted as singularity), we simultaneously get an explanation of how two worlds can communicate and how they can diverge.

On the basis of this account of the genesis of persons, we are able to see how general classes begin to emerge. In an important formulation of this process, Deleuze remarks that

properties and classes are grounded in the order of the person. This is because persons themselves are primarily *classes with one single member,* and their predicates are *properties having one constant*. Each person is the sole member of his or her class, a class which is nevertheless constituted by the worlds, possibilities, and individuals which pertain to it. Classes as multiples, properties as variables, derive from these classes with one single member and these properties with one constant. We believe therefore that the entire deduction is as follows: 1) persons; 2) classes with one single member that they constitute and properties with one constant which belongs to them; 3) extensive classes and variable properties—that is, the general concepts which derive from them. It is in this sense that we interpret the fundamental link between the concept and the Ego. The universal Ego is, precisely, the person corresponding to something = x common to all worlds, just as the other egos are the persons corresponding to a particular thing = x common to several worlds. (*LS* 115)

Initially it may appear that Deleuze falls into a contradiction here. If there can properly be said to be a class with one single member such that its properties have one constant, this must belong to the order of the individual, rather than the person. However, a minuscule shift occurs between the first and second level of actualization. At the level of individuality or the constitution of a world, we had *analytic* predicates in the form of free and mobile singularity-events. Here there was difference, but it was difference without alterity. As such, we have here a transcendental field out of which the individual is eventually actualized. At the second level, the level of persons, we have *synthetic* predicates, which explains why we are now entitled to speak of classes with only one member and *properties* with only one constant. It is true that at the first level the individual body envelops singularities upon the transcendental field, but it does not necessarily synthesize them. At the second level, the predicates are synthesized forming a unity or identity. Consequently, classes must be thought as differing from singularity-events in that classes mark or name their membership. But this identity, in turn, is only rendered possible on the basis of an alterity, a difference, a divergence. Thus, I is an Other in at least two senses. First, I is Other insofar as it is split or fissured by the empty form of time. Second, I is Other insofar as it is only able to encounter itself as I through a disjunctive relation to other worlds which are not its own. I am not that! Such is the condition of being a person. Yet it is a paradoxical genesis insofar as something common must nonetheless be identified between these worlds for the differenciation to take place.

On the basis of this second level, it becomes possible to specify classes of increasing generality, thus effacing the disjunction of the many possible worlds which diverge from one another. This was already the significance of Deleuze's account of the genesis of extensities, and it applies equally well here. As Deleuze puts it,

> Just as the first stage of the genesis is the work of sense, the second is the work of nonsense, which is always co-present to sense (aleatory point or ambiguous sign); it is for this reason that the two stages, and their distinction, are necessarily found. In accordance with the first we find the principle of a "good sense" taking shape, the principle of an already fixed and sedentary organization of differences. In accordance with the second, we find the formation of the principle of a "common sense" as the function of identification. (*LS* 116)

In other words, there is a way in which the genesis of the Image of thought is already internal to the process of actualization. As a result, there can be no question of overcoming the Image of thought *as such* insofar as it is an inevitable result of the process of actualization. There can only be a resolution to strive to turn away from it, a choice which will always only be partially successful. With the genesis of extensities or persons, not only do the "origins" of individuation become hidden, obscured, canceled, but the divergences between worlds are covered over as well. It is this moment which Deleuze refers to when he indicates the formation of the universal Ego. It is also at this moment that we begin to catch sight of how the Image of thought is moral in character.

The Moral Ground of the Image of Thought

The morality Deleuze speaks of here is not that of moral rules and laws in the Kantian sense, though his account should ultimately be able to account for positions assuming the universality of the moral law as well. Rather, "morality" is being employed in the more etymological sense of *moralis,* which comes from *mos, moris,* which pertains to manners, customs, and conduct. It is in this respect that the moral dimension of the Image of thought pertains to the presupposition of "everybody knows," which is a matter of customs, conducts, and manners, and the genesis of extensities, which constitutes an ideal shared space which persons can in principle act within. The question to ask here is, what entitles Deleuze to claim that a genesis of this universal Ego takes place? What allows him to postulate this universal Ego as both the realization and the condition of the Image of thought? And second, how is this assumption moral in character?

The answer to this question is to be found in Deleuze's brilliant essay on Tournier entitled "Tournier and the World Without Others." It should be noted that this is not the only place where Deleuze refers to the Other as the condition under which the Image of thought is generated. For instance, there is a brief discussion of the Other toward the end of the "Asymmetrical Synthesis of the Sensible" in *Difference and Repetition* (*DR* 254–61). If "Tournier and the World Without Others" holds an exemplary place in Deleuze's discussion of the Image of thought, then this is because it provides us with an account of genesis that is able to account for the moral dimension of the Image of thought, the condition under which the convergence of the faculties is possible, the distribution into the *form* of subjects and objects, and finally the distribution of the faculties in the temporal order from the less to more general.

In "Tournier and the World Without Others" Deleuze presents a philosophical reading of Tournier's fascinating novel *Friday*, revolving around the question of what it would mean to live in a world without others. Continuing his project of a philosophical symptomatology first begun in "Coldness and Cruelty" and *Proust and Signs,* Deleuze gives a highly Lacanian reading of Tournier's text that revolves around the different structures of neurosis, psychosis, and perversion with respect to the Other.[7] In a somewhat fanciful and romantic twist, Deleuze strives to show that a world without Others represents a sort of perverse economy which opens the way to an elemental sexuality or manner of desiring no longer governed by the image of thought. Where neurosis and psychosis, according to Deleuze, are shackled to the Other and thus the Image of thought in such a way that they privilege a sort of universal ego, perversion, argues Deleuze, releases a double of the other, the other as difference, such that the artificial convergence of all worlds is no longer assumed. In the present context I leave this dimension of Deleuze's argument to the side, with the intention instead of determining the properties he attributes to the Other.

If, argues Deleuze, we are able to determine what a world without Others would entail, then it is first necessary that we be able to determine what the effects of Others are in our world. In other words, we must be able to determine what characterizes the Other *as such.* For this reason, the Other must no longer be conceived as this or that particular Other, but ought to instead be capitalized in order to indicate that which belongs to the Other by right, that which constitutes its condition of possibility. According to Deleuze, the first effect of Others consists in the organization of the world.

> The first effect of Others is that around each object that I perceive or each idea that I think there is the organization of a marginal world, a

mantle or a background, where other objects and other ideas may come forth in accordance with laws of transition which regulate the passage from one to another. I regard an object, then I divert my attention, letting it fall into the background. At the same time, there comes forth from the background a new object of my attention. If this new object does not injure me, if it does not collide with me with the violence of a projectile (as when one bumps up against something unseen), it is because the first object had already at its disposal a complete margin where I had already felt the preexistence of objects yet to come, and of an entire field of virtualities and potentialities which I already knew were capable of being actualized. Now, such a knowledge or sentiment of marginal existence is possible only through other people . . . The part of the object that I do not see I posit as visible to Others, so that when I will have walked around to reach this hidden part, I will have joined the Others behind the object, and I will have totalized it in the way that I had already anticipated. As for the objects behind my back, I sense them coming together and forming a world, precisely because they are visible to, and are seen by, Others. (*LS* 305)

Initially, we might be inclined to dismiss Deleuze's hypothesis on the grounds that the first synthesis of repetition or *habitus* ought to be more than adequate to account for the continuity of experience that Deleuze refers to here. However, a moment of reflection ought to be enough to see that *habitus*, while necessary, is only sufficient to establish random associations and not yet a fully fledged system of objects and subjects. If this is so, it is because the notion of an object entails a world independent of myself, independent of my random and free associations. In this respect, we can easily imagine a system of organized associations in which there were no objects.

If objects are to be possible as *phenomena*, then a certain convergence of perspectives, a continuity in time, an "aboutness" and "aroundness" is required. It is precisely this that the Other provides. "The other assures the margins and transitions of the world. He is the sweetness of contiguities and resemblances. He regulates the transformations of form and background and the variations of depth. He prevents assaults from behind" (*LS* 305). By contrast,

when one complains about the meanness of Others, one forgets this other and even more frightening meanness—namely, the meanness of things where there is no Other. The latter relativizes the not-known and the non-perceived, because Others, from my point of view, introduce the sign of the unseen in what I do see, making me grasp what I do not perceive as what is perceptible to an Other. In all these respects, my desire passes through Others, and through Others it receives an object. I desire nothing that cannot be seen, thought, or possessed by a possible Other. That is the basis of my desire. It is always Others who relate my desire to an object. (*LS* 306)

Already we can see just how profoundly the second level of actualization is dependent upon the Other. Although the first level of actualization is composed of analytic predicates, these predicates are not on the order of properties, but rather of events and verbs. As such, this first level of actualization is like the frightening world without Others, where all perspective is lost and continuity vanishes. It is a world of "discrete" events, not yet synthesized with one another . . . A pure transcendental field. Hence,

what happens when Others are missing from the structure of the world? Everywhere I am not total darkness reigns. A harsh and black world, without potentialities or virtualities: the category of the possible has collapsed. Instead of relatively harmonious forms surging forth from, and going back to a background in accordance with an order of space and time, only abstract lines now exist, luminous and harmful—only a groundless abyss, rebellious and devouring. Nothing but elements. (*LS* 306)

The world of the individual, in Deleuze's proper technical sense, is the terrifying world without continuity or order. By contrast, the second level of actualization brings about the synthesis of these devouring events, hammers their sparseness into continuities, and gives them an order in time and space. I borrow the eyes of the Other to see for me. It is for this reason that the second level of actualization consists in the person rather than the individual. I here recognize myself in the Other. But this is not simply a matter of seeing the Other as one who is like me. Rather, I see myself as being like the Other. I only recognize myself insofar as I first encounter an Other . . . as in Lacan's mirror stage.

However, insofar as (1) the Other is that which establishes continuities in my experience, and (2) is that which distributes subjects and objects, the Other cannot be another subject. If the Other were another subject, then it would be impossible for me to have any experience of continuity in my experience when the Other is absent. If the Other were another subject, then we would be at a loss to see how it serves to differentiate subjects and objects (since that which differentiates can never be identical to what it differentiates). Rather, the Other is neither an object in the field of my perception nor a subject who perceives me: the Other is initially a structure of the perceptual field, without which the entire field would not function as it does. That this structure may be actualized by real characters, by variable sub-jects—me for you and you for me—does not prevent its preexistence, as the condition of organization in general, to the terms which actualize it in each organized perceptual field—yours and mine. Thus the *a priori Other*, as the absolute structure, establishes the relativity of others as terms actualizing the structure within each field. But what is this struc-ture? It is the structure of the possible. A frightened countenance is the expression of a frightening possible world, or of something frightening in the world—something I do not yet see. Let it be understood that the possible is not here an abstract category designating something which does not exist: the expressed possible world certainly exists, but it does not exist (actually) outside of that which expresses it. The terrified coun-tenance bears no resemblance to the terrifying things. It implicates it, it envelops it as something else, in a kind of torsion which situates what is expressed in the expressing. When I, in turn and for my part, grasp the reality of what the Other was expressing, I do nothing but explicate the Other, as I develop and realize the corresponding possible world. (*LS* 307)

We must proceed with caution, for Deleuze's comments here are misleading. When Deleuze asks what the nature of this structure is, he does not answer by claiming that it is the face or the expression of an-other. If this were the case, then we would be returned to the position in which the Other is another subject. No, these expressions are *actualizations* of the Other-structure. The Other-structure is not the expression, but rather the sign-function which links expression to expressed in a field of continuity. Put in Peircian terms, we can say that the expression is the "representamen," the Other-structure is the "interpretant," and the possible world is the expressed semiotic object to which the expression is made to refer.

That Deleuze equates the Other-structure with the possible is ex-tremely important. The category of the possible is one of the primary targets of Deleuze's philosophy of difference insofar as the possible is a retroactive effect of the actual which functions, in turn, to limit what the future might bring. And indeed, we see how this functions in the case of the Other-structure insofar as the Other-structure functions to establish continuities, to ground what can reasonably be expected and what can-not be expected, thus limiting the potential of being, conventionalizing it. Thus, "the other is the existence of the encompassed possible. Language is the reality of the possible as such. The self is the development and the explication of what is possible, the process of its realization in the actual" (*LS* 307). The self becomes nothing but the morphogenesis of the possible, its definition, articulation, determination, and thereby comes to form a continuous world. We find here why Deleuze is inclined, following Bergson, to equate language with order-words. If language is composed of order-words, this is because it is defined by sign-functions for establishing continuities between an expressed and an expression.

Thus it can be seen that there is a profound ambiguity contained within the Other-structure. It will be recalled that Deleuze locates the origin of good sense in the first level of actualization. Alone this first level of actualization, consisting of the genesis of the individual, is not enough to constitute good sense. However, in relation to the Other-structure, good sense arises fully developed and determined. Good sense consists in the distribution of empirical selves and objects according to a linear arrow of time. If this is to be possible, then it is on the basis of the Other-structure that organizes the "matter" of the transcendental field out of which the subject is constituted into an organized structure of possibility generating a set of retentions and anticipations defining a field of continuity or consistency. It is here that the ambiguity lies. For on the one hand, the person (first level of actualization) ends up totalizing the world on the basis of the individual as "material purport." However, on the other hand, the person is dependent upon the Other for this to be possible. Now, since the other as actualization of the Other always represents a world that diverges from my own, it would seem that rather than establishing a field of continuity, the other instead marks the limits of my perception, the horizon of my world. If this is not, in fact, what takes place, then it is because the other as expression of a divergent world is turned back away from that divergence and captured in the semiotic web born out of my individuality. The other becomes both material and purport for the continuity the person seeks to establish.

Not only does the Other-structure serve as the condition under which perception of a world as continuity is possible, but it also presides over the distribution of subjects and objects. It is here that we encounter the genesis of common sense. The genesis of good sense consists in the distribution, formation, organization of a determinant system of possibility defining various paths of continuity. It is in this sense that it is based on a distribution of the faculties in each case with respect to empirical selves and objects. It establishes the role of memory, imagination, and perception in each case of a convergence of the faculties. By contrast, the fundamental effect [of the Other] is the distinction of my consciousness and its object. This distinction is in fact the result of the structure-Other. Filling the world with possibilities, backgrounds, fringes, and transitions; inscribing the possibility of a reassuring world when I am really frightened by the world; encompassing in different respects the world which presents itself before me developed otherwise; constituting inside the world so many blisters which contain so many possible worlds—this is the Other. Henceforth, the Other causes my consciousness to tip necessarily into an "I was," into a past which no longer coincides with the object. Before the appearance of the Other, there was, for example, a reassuring world from which my consciousness could not be distinguished. The Other then makes its appearance, expressing the possibility of a frightening world which cannot be developed without the one preceding it passing away . . . If the Other is a possible world, I am a past world. The mistake of theories of knowledge is that they postulate the contemporaneity of subject and object, whereas one is constituted only through the annihilation of the other. (*LS* 310)

It is here that we find Deleuze's greatest resemblance to Derrida. If the Other-structure is a necessary condition for the distribution of subjects and objects, then this is because it functions as the condition of the possibility of both continuity of self and continuity of object. Without the Other-structure, the "subject" and "object" would exist in a state of complete coincidence in a manner akin to Freud's undifferentiated world of the infant. There would be no distinction, gap, or difference between the subject and the object, but instead a flowing mass of undifferentiated impressions. To be continuous as self is to be accountable for what one has been, to be identical or the same with what one has been. Hence the manner in which the self is the "I was." By contrast, the continuity of the object is what will be. Hence, the Other-structure provides the perspective through which the subject can see its present self as continuous with its past self, while also providing the perspective in which the completeness of the object can be anticipated. If the subject does not encounter itself as a "might be," then this is because the subject, on the basis of the Other-structure, takes itself to be always already what it is. It is in this respect that Deleuze resembles Derrida. On the one hand, the Other-structure establishes the difference between subject and object. On the other hand, it establishes the deferral of both subject and object in terms of completeness. The completeness of the object is always deferred by the unfolding structure of possibility, while the fullness of the subject is always deferred by its status as an always already.

On the basis of the foregoing, we are able to see (1) how the Other-

structure works with the genesis of extensities to establish the ground
of the Image of thought, and (2) why this Image of thought is moral
in character. Extensities, as I argued in the last chapter, function as the
medium of the Image of thought by canceling difference and creating
the possibility of a smooth continuity among singularities through a distribution of ordinary points. Indeed, as Deleuze says, "the Other assures
the distinction of consciousness and its object as a temporal distinction.
The first effect of its presence concerned space and the distribution of
categories; but the second effect, which is perhaps more profound, concerns time and the distribution of its dimensions—what comes before
and what comes after in time" (*LS* 311). This first level pertains to the
individual and the genesis of good sense. Spatialization is also a movement from the more particular to the general insofar as I intend movement through space in terms of "more of the same." The second level,
pertaining to the genesis of the person, establishes the forms of the subject and object by establishing the possibility of a harmonious and convergent exercise of the faculties upon one and the same object in one
and the same subject. This takes place by virtue of a temporal difference
which distributes the object as a "will-be" and the subject as a "was." As
such, the second moment establishes the subject and object as *forms*. If
this is nonetheless *an* Image of thought, this is because events happen,
because there are always breaches within the Other-structure, because
there are catastrophes. The Apollonian world of individuation is where
man reigns supreme in his mastery, as *homo fabricans,* as he who molds
the world and pounds it into shape with his very words and thoughts.
But lurking behind this actualized order which might very well be called
the Image of thought lies the growling groundlessness of the terrifying
transcendental field. Between these two passages, power and the curse
become the complex ciphers of a dialectic unfolding between the aspirations for a totalizing individuation and mastery and the perpetual return
of the encounter which calls into question this smooth continuity and
sets it moving in another, unanticipatable direction.

By contrast, the Image of thought shows itself to be moral in a
threefold way. First, if the Image of thought is moral, this is because it is
predicated on a fundamental, even primordial, *decision* for the smooth
and reassuring world of continuity over the dark and ferocious world of
the event, of the encounter. The Image of thought establishes itself on
the repression and exile of the encounter, of difference, in a way that
can only be called evaluative. Despite the manner in which Deleuzians
often talk, this is not to claim that one *ought* to choose the encounter
over continuity. Encounters happen. Continuity is actualized. It is not
up to us to choose them. Rather, we are chosen by them. Both are pro-

cesses proper to be-ing. Rather, it is to claim that the Image of thought sets up a distribution, a choice, an evaluative system based on the binary between the monstrous and the collective, the anomalous and the ordinary. This distributive system is made possible on the basis of the Other-structure. Second, the Other-structure shows how the Image of thought is moral insofar as it establishes a set of manners, customs, and conducts on the basis of the Identification it effects in the subject and how it structures desire. This is the domain of language and order-words. Finally, the Other-structure establishes the morality of the Image of thought insofar as it grounds the possibility under which the presupposition of "everybody knows" is able to arise. Paradoxically, "everybody knows" becomes a distributive principle for selecting among those who do know and those who do not know insofar as this is a claim *in principle* which subjects *ought* to live up to. "If they were only authentic to themselves *as* subjects, as knowers, then they would know. They choose to live in their own ignorance."

Conclusion

Throughout this book I have sought to trace and resolve a particular puzzle, a knot, a paradox that runs throughout Deleuze's thought which revolves around empiricism and is of central importance in giving a clear articulation of what is meant by "transcendental empiricism." On the one hand, empiricism, argues Deleuze, is the source of illusion, it belongs to the domain of the Image of thought. This illusion arises in three interrelated forms: the recognition of only external differences rather than internal and determining differences; second, this illusion involves the activity of tracing the transcendental from the empirical; and third, this fallacy consists in privileging recognition as the model of what it means to think. In one way or another all of these fallacies are *effects* of the Image of thought, which in turn finds its ground in the process of actualization insofar as it generates extensities and the Other-structure. If these are fallacies, then they are such for the same reason that Whitehead calls the fallacy of misplaced concreteness a fallacy. As Whitehead puts it, "There is an error; but it is merely the accidental error of mistaking the abstract for the concrete. It is an example of what I will call the 'Fallacy of Misplaced Concreteness.' "[1] In an analogous way, if empiricism is a fallacy, then this is because it treats the abstract as what is truly concrete. This is a fallacy shared by rationalisms, empiricisms, and transcendental philosophies alike. In all of these cases, the form of the subject and the object, along with the distribution of empirical selves and objects in space, is treated as the concrete, and conditions are thereby traced, as it were, from the outline of these forms.

However, and this is where the paradox emerges, Deleuze nonetheless contends that only empiricism can protect us from the empiricist fallacy. As he remarks,

> I have always felt that I am an empiricist, that is, a pluralist. But what does this equivalence between empiricism and pluralism mean? It derives from the two characteristics by which Whitehead defined empiricism: the abstract does not explain, but must itself be explained; and the aim is not to rediscover the eternal or the universal, but to find the conditions under which something new is produced (*creativeness*). (*D* vii)

Thus, on the one hand we are told that empiricism is a fallacy, that it must be rejected, that it cannot deliver us true internal differences. Everywhere Deleuze rejects the adequacy of external differences, empirical differences, nominal or material definitions. Insofar as Deleuze equates empiricism with the external conception of difference, his critique of both empiricists and transcendental philosophies is identical. If Kant is to be rejected, this is not because he is a philosopher of the State—that is only a secondary reason for criticism, which can only be accepted after one understands how the State is linked to the Other-structure and the morality that goes with it. Rather, Kant is to be rejected because he leaves concepts and intuitions external to one another, because his thought, which is supposed to reach the transcendental, is nonetheless founded upon an empirical difference. Yet, on the other hand, we are told that only empiricism can save us, only empiricism can deliver us to the transcendental, to the real conditions under which experience is possible. How are we to resolve this paradox? What can Deleuze possibly have in mind?

It is clear that Deleuze is playing on two different registers of the empirical. On the one hand, the empirical signifies any position which treats subjects and objects as the two ultimate distributive categories within which all philosophical problematics must unfold. The question here inevitably becomes one of how to overcome or contend with the way in which the relationship between subject and object is mediated. In this case, we are given four rough options for dealing with this problem, as shown in table 3.

Now, in all four of these cases it is clear that the central assumption underlying these roughly defined positions lies in the presupposition of the primacy of presence. Whether it be a world absolutely immanent to the subject in the form of a pure immanence to consciousness producing being through its perception or differentiating itself through contradiction, or an absolute materialism where all is matter and configurations of atoms, or a naive realism where the subject somehow immediately knows the world, or a transcendental idealism where the subject imposes form on the world, all of these positions assume the primacy of some form of presence. They differ only in how they treat the intentional relation between subject and object. But insofar as it is always an intentional relation between subject and object, somewhere, someplace, an external difference will inevitably be posited and will parade itself in the guise of an internal difference. The conditions inevitably end up being traced from the conditioned.

If only empiricism can save us from the fallacy of misplaced concreteness, if empiricism is the only choice that can save us from empiri-

	Subject	Object
Subject	Absolute and empirical idealism: subject producing world/ variants of relativism	Transcendental idealism: subject imposing form on world
Object	Naive realism/empiricism/ objectivism: subject knowing world through sense impressions	Absolute materialism

Table 3: Schematic of possible philosophical positions based on the relationship between subject and object.

cism, then this is because *superior* empiricism radically calls into question the primacy of the subject and the object. This was already the claim of Deleuze's early work *Empiricism and Subjectivity,* and the nucleus of his interest in Hume.

> Hume constantly affirms the identity between the mind, the imagination, and ideas. The mind is not nature, nor does it have a nature. It is identical with the ideas in the mind. Ideas are given, as given they are experience. The mind, on the other hand, is given as a collection of ideas and not as a system. It follows that our earlier question can be expressed as follows: how does a collection become a system? The collection of ideas is called "imagination," insofar as the collection designates not a faculty but rather an assemblage of things, in the most vague sense of the term: things are as they appear—a collection without an album, a play without a stage, a flux of perceptions . . . The place is not different from what takes place in it; the representation does not take place in a subject. Then again the question may be: *how does the mind become a subject?*[2]

The empiricism of Hume, as Deleuze articulates it, begins not with the question of how a subject can know an object, nor with how subjects produce objects or objects produce subjects, but rather with the question of how both subjects and objects can be produced out of a field that does not assume them in advance. It is here that we can begin to see how "superior empiricism" avoids the fallacy of empiricism. Transcendental empiricism does not assume in advance what subjects and objects *ought* to be in the sense of formal essences, but instead sees them as productions out of a field of immanence where immanence is immanent to nothing save itself.

The second move consists in pushing Kant's revolutionary concept of time to its extreme conclusion, identifying it with the transcendental field (which can no longer even be identified with mind or consciousness), and treating subjects and objects as temporal determinations. With this critical reversal the assumption of presence is effectively undermined, and the subject and object must now be conceived in terms of both difference and deferral. A new option becomes possible which no longer falls within the options offered by the grid of metaphysics. Time becomes the dimension of the transcendental, its defining feature, and internal difference is to be equated with temporal difference. If this avoids the fallacy of tracing the transcendental from the empirical, then this is because the temporal, internal difference is no longer to be thought as resembling the empirical, but instead constitutes a domain all its own. The subject and the object are temporal determinations, not the reverse.

But if this must be called an empiricism, if we must nonetheless affirm empiricism, then this is because *we are subjects*. Since the transcendental is no longer to be traced from the outlines of the empirical, we can no longer rely on the being of a transcendental constituting subjectivity to bring us before the transcendental, but must instead seek out those gaps, events, traumas, shocks, and encounters which upset the smooth continuity of the subject, call its recognition into question, and introduce it to a domain that is neither that of the subject nor of the object. If these encounters, these curses, are signs of the transcendental, then this is because they announce a difference that is no longer that of the external or the material, but something unspeakable, ineffable, and indefinable in much the same sense that Derrida's *différance* is indefinable. But these encounters are nonetheless encounters, and for that reason the transcendental philosophy of difference must still be an empiricism. As Deleuze says, we cannot anticipate the outcome of research in advance.

Notes

Preface

1. This tendency, for instance, can be clearly discerned in Keith Ansell Pearson's brilliant text *Germinal Life: The Difference and Repetition of Deleuze,* which moves fluidly between Deleuze's works coauthored with Guattari, his historical works, and the works in which Deleuze explicated his own philosophy without even raising the question of whether these projects are all continuous with one another.

2. Alain Badiou, *Deleuze: The Clamor of Being* (Minneapolis: University of Minnesota Press, 2000), 15.

3. Gilles Deleuze, *Difference and Repetition* (New York: Columbia University Press, 1994), xv.

Introduction

1. Martin Heidegger, *Kant and the Problem of Metaphysics* (Bloomington: Indiana University Press, 1997), 15–16.

2. Ibid., 18.

3. Ibid., 19–20.

4. Ibid., 17.

Chapter 1

1. We might assume that Deleuze, in his choice to affirm internal difference over external difference, would side with Hegel. However, as Deleuze argues in his review of Hyppolite's *Logic and Existence,* Hegel still remains tied to the logic of external difference in that the difference between the *Phenomenology* and the *Science of Logic* is a non-dialectical difference. In this respect, Deleuze argues that Hegel remains tied to anthropomorphism and fails to truly reach determining difference. See Jean Hyppolite, *Logic and Existence* (Albany: State University of New York Press, 1997), 191–95.

2. Deleuze draws the term *multiplicity* from mathematics, where it is normally referred to as a manifold. The concept of a manifold refers to a certain sort of structure. No doubt the naming of the concept "manifold" as "multiplicity" has invited confusion on the part of readers of Deleuze who are inclined to conceive Deleuzian multiplicities as diversities rather than as structures. However, as De-

leuze consistently points out, a multiplicity is neither the one nor the *many*, nor the unity of the one and the many.

3. G. W. F. Hegel, *Hegel's Science of Logic* (Atlantic Highlands, N.J.: Humanities, 1969), 418.

4. Salomon Maïmon, *Versuch über die Transzendentalphilosophie* (Darmstadt: Wissenschaftliche Buchgesellschaft, 1963), 63–64.

5. Émile Bréhier, *La théorie des incorporels dans l'ancien stoïcisme* (Paris: Librairie Philosophique, 1928), 1.

6. Ibid., 19–20.

7. Mary Tiles, *The Historical Philosophy of Set Theory: An Introduction to Cantor's Paradise* (Oxford: Basil Blackwell, 1989), 69.

8. Ibid., 80.

Chapter 2

1. Henri Bergson, *Time and Free Will: An Essay on the Immediate Data of Consciousness* (Kila, Montana: Kessinger, 1910), 111–12.

2. Bréhier, *Théorie des incorporels*, 2–5.

3. For an excellent analysis of these sorts of natural styles of being, see Manuel De Landa, *Intensive Science and Virtual Philosophy* (London: Continuum, 2002).

4. Badiou, *Deleuze: The Clamor of Being*, 15.

Chapter 3

1. For Bergson's account of the method of intuition, see Henri Bergson, *The Creative Mind: An Introduction to Metaphysics* (New York: Carol, 1992), 30–90. Deleuze's discussion of Bergson's methodology follows Bergson's formulations so closely as to almost constitute a commentary. This is something that cannot be said of Deleuze's treatments of any other thinker.

2. See Bergson, *Creative Mind*, 30–37, for his discussion of intuition as method.

3. Ibid., 32.

4. Plato, *The Republic*, trans. Paul Shorey, in *Plato: The Corrected Dialogues*, ed. E. Hamilton and H. Cairns (Princeton: Princeton University Press, 1963), book VII, 523b.

Chapter 5

1. Pierre Lévy, *Becoming Virtual: Reality in the Digital Age* (New York: Plenum Trade Books, 1998), 23.

2. Paul Ricoeur, *The Conflict of Interpretations* (Evanston, Ill.: Northwestern University Press, 1974), 13.

3. Badiou, *Deleuze: The Clamor of Being*, 65.

4. Louis Hjelmslev, *Prolegomena to a Theory of Language*, trans. Francis J. Whitfield (Madison: University of Wisconsin Press, 1961), 9.

Chapter 6

1. René Descartes, *The Philosophical Writings of Descartes*, vol. 1 (New York: Cambridge University Press, 1985), 195.

2. René Descartes, *Discourse on Method and Meditations* (Upper Saddle River, N.J.: Prentice Hall, 1952), 3–4.

3. Hegel, *Hegel's Science of Logic*, 82–83.

4. Ibid., 105–6.

5. Ronald Bogue, *Deleuze and Guattari* (New York: Routledge, 1989), 57.

6. Immanuel Kant, *Critique of Pure Reason* (Cambridge: Cambridge University Press, 1998), A642/B670.

7. Ibid., A942–43/B670–71.

8. Ibid., A643/B671.

9. Ibid., A645–46/B673–74.

10. Ibid., A646/B674.

11. Ibid., A644/B672.

12. Gilles Deleuze, "Having an Idea in Cinema: On the Cinema of Straub-Huillet," in *Deleuze and Guattari: New Mappings in Politics, Philosophy, and Culture*, ed. Eleanor Kaufman and Kevin Heller (Minneapolis: University of Minnesota Press, 1998), 15.

13. See Bergson, *Time and Free Will*, 72–74.

14. Kant, *Critique of Pure Reason*, A651–52/B652–80.

Chapter 7

1. Immanuel Kant, *Critique of Judgment* (Indianapolis: Hackett, 1987), 275.

2. Kant, *Critique of Pure Reason*, B155–56.

3. For a discussion of the Kantian split subject in the context of psychoanalysis, see Slavoj Žižek, *Tarrying with the Negative: Kant, Hegel, and the Critique of Ideology* (Durham, N.C.: Duke University Press, 1993), 12–18.

4. Kant, *Critique of Pure Reason*, B406–7.

5. Todd May has made a similar argument in his essay "Difference and Unity in Gilles Deleuze" in *Gilles Deleuze and the Theater of Philosophy*, ed. Constantin Boundas and Dorthea Olkowski (London: Routledge, 1994), 33–50, but he dogmatically treats univocity as a metaphysical thesis rather than as a unity that is produced. This clearly cannot be the case insofar as univocity is a claim about the *sense* of being. Insofar as sense, for Deleuze, is an event, the claim that the sense of being is univocal cannot be treated as a metaphysical claim about the substance or essence of existence. As Deleuze remarks in *The Logic of Sense,*

> Philosophy merges with ontology, but ontology merges with the univocity of being (analogy has always been a theological vision, not a philosophical one, adapted from the forms of God, the world, and the self). The univocity of Being does not mean that there is one and the same Being; on the contrary, beings are multiple and different, they are always produced by a disjunctive synthesis, and they themselves are disjointed and divergent, *membra disjuncta.*

The univocity of Being signifies that Being is Voice that it is said, and that it is said in one and the same "sense" of everything about which it is said. That of which it is said is not at all the same, but Being is the same for everything about which it is said. It occurs, therefore, as a unique event for everything that happens to the most diverse things, *Eventum tantum* for all events, the ultimate form for all of the forms which remain disjointed in it, but which bring about the resonance and the ramification of their disjunction. (*LS* 179)

6. Gilbert Simondon, "The Genesis of the Individual," in *Incorporations*, ed. Jonathan Crary and Sanford Kwinter (New York: Zone Books, 1992), 301–2.

7. Ibid., 306.

Chapter 8

1. Bergson, *Creative Mind*, 27–28.

2. Ibid., 79–80.

3. Simondon, "Genesis of the Individual," 304.

4. Kant, *Critique of Pure Reason*, A165/B207–8.

5. Ibid., A162–63/B203–4.

6. Jacques Lacan, *Écrits: The First Complete Edition in English*, trans. Bruce Fink (New York: W. W. Norton and Company, 2006), 17. This note appears in the original publication.

7. For an excellent account of Deleuze's philosophical symptomatology, see Daniel W. Smith's introduction to Deleuze's *Essays: Critical and Clinical* (Minneapolis: University of Minnesota Press, 1997).

Conclusion

1. A. N. Whitehead, *Science and the Modern World* (New York: Free Press, 1967), 51.

2. Gilles Deleuze, *Empiricism and Subjectivity: An Essay on Hume's Theory of Human Nature* (New York: Columbia University Press, 1991), 22–23.

Bibliography

Badiou, Alain. *Deleuze: The Clamor of Being.* Translated by Louise Burchill. Minneapolis: University of Minnesota Press, 2000.

Baugh, Bruce. "Transcendental Empiricism: Deleuze's Response to Hegel." *Man and World* 25 (April 1992): 133–48.

Bergson, Henri. *The Creative Mind: An Introduction to Metaphysics.* New York: Carol, 1992.

———. *Matter and Memory.* Translated by N. M. Paul and W. S. Palmer. New York: Zone Books, 1988.

———. *Time and Free Will: An Essay on the Immediate Data of Consciousness.* Translated by F. L. Pogson. Kila, Montana: Kessinger, 1910.

Bogue, Ronald. *Deleuze and Guattari.* New York: Routledge, 1989.

Boundas, Constantin, and Dorothea Olkowski, eds. *Gilles Deleuze and the Theater of Philosophy.* New York: Routledge, 1994.

Bréhier, Émile. *La théorie des incorporels dans l'ancien stoïcisme.* Paris: Librairie Philosophique, 1928.

Brusseau, James. *Isolated Experiences: Gilles Deleuze and the Solitudes of Reversed Platonism.* Albany: State University of New York Press, 1998.

Crary, Jonathan, and Sanford Kwinter, eds. *Incorporations.* New York: Zone Books, 1992.

De Landa, Manuel. *Intensive Science and Virtual Philosophy.* New York: Continuum Press, 2002.

———. *A Thousand Years of Nonlinear History.* New York: Zone Books, 1997.

Deleuze, Gilles. *Bergsonism.* Translated by Hugh Tomlinson and Barbara Habberjam. New York: Zone Books, 1991.

———. "Bergson's Conception of Difference." In *The New Bergson,* by M. McMahon, 42–65. Manchester: Manchester University Press, 2000.

———. *Cinema I: The Movement-Image.* Translated by Hugh Tomlinson and Barbara Habberjam. Minneapolis: University of Minnesota Press, 1986.

———. *Cinema II: The Time-Image.* Translated by Hugh Tomlinson and Robert Galeta. Minneapolis: University of Minnesota Press, 1989.

———. "Coldness and Cruelty." In *Masochism: Coldness and Cruelty and Venus in Furs,* by Gilles Deleuze and Leopold von Sacher-Masoch; trans. Jean McNeil, 9–138. New York: Zone Books, 1991.

———. "Deleuze-Leibniz Seminar." Translated by Charles Stivale. http://www.imaginet.fr/deleuze/TXT/ENG/150480.html, 1980.

———. *Difference and Repetition.* Translated by Paul Patton. New York: Columbia University Press, 1994.

———. *Empiricism and Subjectivity: An Essay On Hume's Theory of Human Nature.* Translated by Constantin V. Boundas. New York: Columbia University Press, 1991.

———. *Essays Critical and Clinical.* Translated by Daniel W. Smith and Michael A. Greco. Minneapolis: University of Minnesota Press, 1997.

———. *Expressionism in Philosophy: Spinoza.* Translated by Martin Joughin. New York: Zone Books, 1992.

———. *The Fold: Leibniz and the Baroque.* Translated by Tom Conley. Minneapolis: University of Minnesota Press, 1993.

———. *Foucault.* Translated by Seán Hand. Minneapolis: University of Minnesota Press, 1988.

———. "How Do We Recognize Structuralism?" In *The Two-Fold Thought of Deleuze and Guattari,* by Charles Stivale, 251–82. New York: Guilford, 1998.

———. "Immanence: A Life . . ." *Theory, Culture and Society* (May 14, 1997): 3–7.

———. *Kant's Critical Philosophy.* Translated by Hugh Tomlinson and Barbara Habberjam. Minneapolis: University of Minnesota Press, 1984.

———. *The Logic of Sense.* Translated by Mark Lester and Charles Stivale. New York: Columbia University Press, 1990.

———. *Negotiations.* Translated by Martin Joughin. New York: Columbia University Press, 1995.

———. *Nietzsche and Philosophy.* Translated by Hugh Tomlinson. New York: Columbia University Press, 1983.

———. *Proust and Signs: The Complete Text.* Translated by Richard Howard. Minneapolis: University of Minnesota Press, 2000.

———. *Spinoza: A Practical Philosophy.* Translated by Robert Hurley. San Francisco: City Lights Books, 1988.

Deleuze, Gilles, and Félix Guattari. *Anti-Oedipus: Capitalism and Schizophrenia.* Translated by Robert Hurley, Mark Seem, and Helen R. Lane. Minneapolis: University of Minnesota Press, 1983.

———. *A Thousand Plateaus: Capitalism and Schizophrenia.* Translated by Brian Massumi. Minneapolis: University of Minnesota Press, 1987.

———. *What Is Philosophy?* Translated by Hugh Tomlinson and Graham Burchell III. New York: Columbia University Press, 1994.

Deleuze, Gilles, and Claire Parnet. *Dialogues.* Translated by Hugh Tomlinson and Barbara Habberjam. New York: Columbia University Press, 1987.

Derrida, Jacques. *Of Grammatology.* Translated by Gayatri Chakravorty Spivak. Baltimore: Johns Hopkins University Press, 1976.

———. *Limited Inc.* Translated by Jeffrey Mehlman and Samuel Weber. Evanston, Ill.: Northwestern University Press, 1988.

———. *Margins of Philosophy.* Translated by Alan Bass. Chicago: University of Chicago Press, 1982.

———. *Speech and Phenomena, and Other Essays on Husserl's Theory of Signs.* Translated by David B. Allison. Evanston, Ill.: Northwestern University Press, 1973.

————. *Writing and Difference.* Translated by Alan Bass. Chicago: University of Chicago Press, 1978.

Descartes, René. *Discourse on Method and Meditations.* Translated by Laurence J. Lafleur. Upper Saddle River, N.J.: Prentice Hall, 1952.

————. *The Philosophical Writings of Descartes,* vol. 1. Translated by John Cottingham, Robert Stoothoff, Dugald Murdoch. New York: Cambridge University Press, 1985.

Eco, Umberto. *A Theory of Semiotics.* Bloomington: Indiana University Press, 1979.

Foucault, Michel. *The Archaeology of Knowledge and the Discourse on Language.* New York: Pantheon Books, 1972.

————. *Death and the Labyrinth: The World of Raymond Roussel.* Translated by Charles Ruas. London: Athlone, 1986.

————. *Discipline and Punish: The Birth of the Prison.* Translated by Alan Sheridan. New York: Vintage Books, 1977.

————. *History of Sexuality: An Introduction.* New York: Vintage Books, 1978.

————. *The Order of Things: An Archaeology of the Human Sciences.* New York: Vintage Books, 1970.

Freud, Sigmund. *Beyond the Pleasure Principle.* Translated by James Strachey. New York: Bantam Books, 1959.

————. *The Ego and the Id.* Translated by James Strachey. New York: W.W. Norton, 1960.

————. *Group Psychology and the Analysis of the Ego.* Translated by James Strachey. New York: W.W. Norton, 1959.

Hardt, Michael. *Gilles Deleuze: An Apprenticeship in Philosophy.* Minneapolis: University of Minnesota Press, 1993.

Hayden, Patrick. *Multiplicity and Becoming: The Pluralist Empiricism of Gilles Deleuze.* New York: Peter Lang, 1998.

Hegel, G. W. F. *Hegel's Phenomenology of Spirit.* Translated by A. V. Miller. Oxford: Oxford University Press, 1977.

————. *Hegel's Science of Logic.* Translated by A. V. Miller. Atlantic Highlands, N.J.: Humanities, 1969.

Heidegger, Martin. *Being and Time.* Translated by John Macquarrie and Edward Robinson. New York: Harper, 1962.

————. *Kant and the Problem of Metaphysics.* Translated by Richard Taft. Bloomington: Indiana University Press, 1997.

Hjelmslev, Louis. *Prolegomena to a Theory of Language.* Translated Francis J. Whitfield. Madison: University of Wisconsin Press, 1961.

Holland, Eugene. *Deleuze and Guattari's Anti-Oedipus: Introduction to Schizoanalysis.* New York: Routledge, 1999.

Husserl, Edmund. *Ideas Pertaining to a Pure Phenomenology and to a Phenomenological Philosophy: First Book.* Translated by F. Kersten. Boston: Martinus Nijhoff, 1983.

Hyppolite, Jean. *Logic and Existence.* Translated by Leonard Lawlor and Amit Sen. Albany: State University of New York Press, 1997.

Kant, Immanuel. *Critique of Judgment.* Translated by Werner Pluhar. Indianapolis: Hackett, 1987.

————. *Critique of Pure Reason.* Translated by Paul Guyer and Allen W. Wood. Cambridge: Cambridge University Press, 1998.

Kaufman, Eleanor, and Kevin Heller. *Deleuze and Guattari: New Mappings in Politics, Philosophy, and Culture.* Minneapolis: University of Minnesota, 1998.

Lacan, Jacques. *Écrits: The First Complete Edition in English.* Translated by Bruce Fink. New York: W. W. Norton, 2006.

————. *The Four Fundamental Concepts of Psycho-Analysis.* Translated by Alan Sheridan. New York: W. W. Norton, 1977.

Levi-Strauss, Claude. *The Savage Mind.* Chicago: University of Chicago Press, 1966.

————. *Structural Anthropology.* New York: Basic Books, 1963.

Lévy, Pierre. *Becoming Virtual: Reality in the Digital Age.* New York: Plenum Trade Books, 1998.

Maïmon, Salomon. *Versuch über die Transzendentalphilosophie.* Darmstadt: Wissenschaftliche Buchgesellschaft, 1963.

Marks, John. *Gilles Deleuze: Vitalism and Multiplicity.* London: Pluto, 1998.

Massumi, Brian. *A User's Guide to Capitalism and Schizophrenia.* Cambridge, Mass.: MIT Press, 1992.

Mullarkey, John. *Bergson and Philosophy.* Notre Dame, Ind.: University of Notre Dame Press, 2000.

Olkowski, Dorothea. *Gilles Deleuze and the Ruin of Representation.* Berkeley: University of California Press, 1999.

Patton, Paul, ed. *Deleuze: A Critical Reader.* Oxford: Blackwell, 1996.

Pearson, Keith Ansell. *Germinal Life: The Difference and Repetition of Deleuze.* New York: Routledge, 1999.

Ricoeur, Paul. *The Conflict of Interpretations.* Evanston, Ill.: Northwestern University Press, 1974.

Rodowick, D. N. *Gilles Deleuze's Time Machine.* Durham, N.C.: Duke University Press, 1997.

Saussure, Ferdinand de. *Course in General Linguistics.* Translated by Roy Harris. Chicago: Open Court, 1983.

Stivale, Charles. *The Two-Fold Thought of Deleuze and Guattari.* New York: Guilford Press, 1998.

Tiles, Mary. *The Philosophy of Set Theory: An Introduction to Cantor's Paradise.* Oxford: Basil Blackwell, 1989.

Tournier, Michel. *Friday.* Baltimore: Johns Hopkins University Press, 1997.

Žižek, Slavoj. *Tarrying with the Negative: Kant, Hegel, and the Critique of Ideology.* Durham, N.C.: Duke University Press, 1993.

Index

About the Author

Levi R. Bryant is a professor of philosophy at Collin College in Frisco, Texas.